Sorcery and Shamanism

Sorcery and Shamanism

CURANDEROS AND CLIENTS IN NORTHERN PERU

Donald Joralemon and Douglas Sharon

University of Utah Press
Salt Lake City

Library of Congress Cataloging-in-Publication Data

Joralemon, Donald.
    Sorcery and shamanism : curanderos and clients in northern Peru /
Donald Joralemon and Douglas Sharon.
        p.   cm.
    Includes bibliographical references and index.
    ISBN 978-0-87480-640-3 (acid-free paper)
    1. Traditional medicine—Peru.   2. Shamanism—Peru.   3. Indians
of South America—Peru—Medicine.   I. Sharon, Douglas.   II. Title.
GR133.P4J67   1993
615.8'82'0985—dc20   93-25220

To our friend and teacher, Professor Johannes Wilbert

Contents

Acknowledgments

Our greatest debt of gratitude is to the many Peruvians who, as friends, collaborators, and interview subjects, gave us the opportunity to document a thriving ethnomedical tradition. The dozen *curanderos* whose life histories and ritual practices are documented in this text tolerated with great patience our seemingly endless questions and graciously permitted us to take part in their curing sessions. More than one hundred men and women who sought the help of these curers opened their private lives and personal pains to our anthropological documentation with absolutely nothing to gain for themselves.

We have depended heavily over the years on the support of faculty from the University of Trujillo, especially Dr. Hernán Miranda Cueto. We express our deepest appreciation to our good friends Carlos and Nancy Muñoz, not only for their logistical help with everything from housing to photographic work, but for their warmth and caring over many years.

We have been fortunate to have superbly qualified research assistants working with us in Peru. Rafael Vásquez Guerrero gave us so much more than his remarkable interviewing skills; he and his wife Eliana offered their friendship along with a complete commitment to our research project. Bonnie Glass-Coffin, nearly a native *trujillana* on account of the years she has spent in that city, was a capable and dedicated colleague. We are pleased to see the product of her own research on Peruvian curers coming to fruition. To Donald Skillman we express a special thanks for adding our patient-focused research to his own project and for his permission to include his own ethnography in this book.

The fieldwork on which the following account is based covers more than two decades and has been financially supported by a number of organizations. Sharon's work in the 1970s was funded

ix

ACKNOWLEDGMENTS

by a UCLA President's Undergraduate Fellowship, travel money from the UCLA Anthropology Department, a National Geographic Society grant, a National Defense Education/Title VI scholarship, the Tinker Foundation (NY), and the Social Science Research Council (NY). In addition, an ethnographic film, *Eduardo the Healer*, was underwritten by a grant from the National Institute on Drug Abuse.

Joralemon's original fieldwork (1980) was supported by a grant from the Organization of American States and by travel funds for doctoral research from the University of California, Los Angeles. The patient-focused research we carried out together (1987–1988) was funded by the National Institute of Mental Health, Behavioral Sciences Division. Joralemon received additional support for this project through a Jean Picker Fellowship at Smith College from 1990 to 1991.

Finally, some personal thanks. To Phoebe Porter, for encouragement, patience, and help with difficult translations. To Kaye Sharon for tolerating a lot of reverse culture shock over the years. Lyn Morgan provided extensive commentary and valuable suggestions for Part II of the manuscript, and Rosemary and Peter Joralemon contributed careful editorial work. Stephen Petegorsky worked miracles with our less than perfect photographic negatives. A special thanks is given to Professor Johannes Wilbert, who taught us both and whose work remains a source of inspiration; we dedicate this book to him.

An Orthographic Note

We have chosen to keep most Spanish words, even those which are used repeatedly, in italics to facilitate use of the Glossary and to avoid confusions when the original word employs diacritical marks. The only exceptions are the terms *curandero* (curer) and *mesa* (curing altar), which are italicized only on the first occurrence. The names given to the symbolic fields of the shamans' altars are treated as proper nouns in English (i.e., first letters are capitalized) after the first Spanish instance (e.g., *banco curandero* becomes Banco Curandero).

Introduction

BY DONALD JORALEMON AND DOUGLAS SHARON

Images of Peru

Cuzco and Machu Picchu. Andean peaks and Lake Titicaca. Arboreal oceans of verdant green, peopled by "stone age survivors." Tourist brochures dazzling the eye with scenic destinations and mysterious ruins. Postcards.

Desert and mud-brick ghettos. Elegance in Miraflores and squatter settlements in Chimbote. Mountain hamlets and forest valleys under military siege. Crowded buses and vibrant markets where people make their way through the daily routine.

The *curanderos* of the northern coast of Peru, traditional healing specialists who invoke Jesus Christ and the saints with a mescaline sacrament and a shamanic rattle, get trapped in anthropological representations somewhere between these visions of Peru. Analyses of pre-Hispanic precedents for their ritual symbols trumpet the traditional, the pristine cultural form; other accounts link sorcerers and curanderos to class tensions and economic oppression. Peruvians themselves offer ambivalent constructions and opinions about curanderos, who are honored as specialists in "folkloric medicine" for the purposes of international congresses and sensationalistic media stories, but whose practices are technically illegal. Asking questions about personal experiences with curanderos can occasion disingenuous denials or embarrassed disclaimers: "I would never go, but my neighbor . . . "

Any effort to write about curanderos must come to terms with these types of selective readings of Peru and the ritual healers of its northern coast. Curanderos are certainly not ethnohistoric oddities, remnants of earlier epochs about to be swept away by the progress of modern culture. They traffic in the intrigues, suspicions, and

1

apprehensions of contemporary urban life, and they find no short-
age of clients, from the wealthy to the poor. Still, their symbolism
and practices do draw heavily from colonial and indigenous roots
(see Gillin 1945:115; Dobkin de Rios 1969a; Sharon 1978) and, in
many ways, they do practice at the margins of society (see Joralemon 1983). The problem we as authors faced was how to capture
these distinct dimensions.

The strategy we have adopted in this book is to look at curanderos from two distinct vantage points. In Part I, we document the
lives and ritual practices of twelve curanderos to take a look at and
then gain perspective on the individuals who pursue this curing
role and to endeavor to discern the underlying "cultural ideology"
or set of values and knowledge they share. The symbolism of the
altars, or *mesas*, employed by curanderos and the organization of
their ritual sessions express an opposition between good and evil
forces; the curandero must exercise mastery over both forces in order to heal. Sharon concludes that the cultural source of this "dialectic" is deeper than the folk Catholicism of the colonial era, that
it represents the basic principles of an indigenous cosmology (see
Chapter 14).

In Part II, our attention shifts to the actual application of the
curandero's dialectical philosophy in the pragmatic work of healing. Here, we are interested in the testimony of individuals whose
personal crises led them to seek the help of a curandero. The actual accounts of suffering given by the patients of four curanderos
help us to find a context for the curer's practice in lived experience
and to see something of the dynamic of ritual therapy. With this
grounding, we are able to offer a broader analysis of the role
curanderos play in Peruvian society, especially in connection with
gender-based conflicts; for example, curanderos can be seen as acting simultaneously as apologists for, and avengers of social injustices (Chapter 20).

Curanderos of the Northern Coast

The trip north from Lima along Peru's coastal highway provides
a study in contrasts. Long sweeps of completely barren desert
are interrupted by agriculturally productive river valleys and
large urban centers, such as Chimbote, Trujillo, and Chiclayo (see
map).While this coastal region constitutes only 11% of Peru's

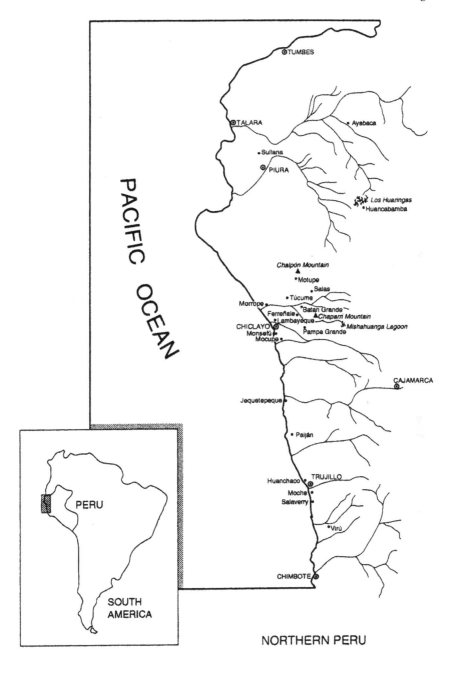

NORTHERN PERU

total territory, it is home to half its population (Reid 1985:4). Large portions of that population are migrants from the mountains who live in impoverished squatter settlements on the peripheries of metropolitan Lima and the other major cities of the coast.

The northern coast is known in Peru as the center of *curander-ismo*, a folk healing tradition which blends elements of popular Christianity with indigenous shamanism. While the highland lakes near Huancabamba, close to Peru's border with Ecuador, are famous as pilgrimage sites for curanderos, the cities of Trujillo and Chiclayo and their surrounding towns are widely recognized as the locus of curandero activity. Many of the curanderos included in this study live and work either in Trujillo or in one of its satellite communities. The remainder are from Chiclayo and the small towns nearby.

Peruvian curanderos are noted for their ritual use of a psychoactive substance, a liquid distilled from the mescaline-bearing San Pedro cactus (*Trichocereus pachanoi*), and for their complex curing altars, known in Spanish as mesas (from the Latin *mensa*, table or altar, Giese [1989:61]). The visions produced by the San Pedro cactus and the symbolic artifacts of the mesa are essential to the curandero's diagnosis and treatment of illnesses. Primary among the conditions they treat is *daño*, a sorcery-induced sickness that manifests itself in both physical symptoms and a variety of other personal misfortunes (see Chapter 15).

It is now accepted usage to refer to Peru's curanderos as shamans, because their vocation fits well with classical definitions of shamanic healers as religious specialists who undergo controlled trances in a community context (Peters and Price-Williams 1980:399). The manner in which curanderos learn their art, as well as the specific therapeutic procedures they employ, also match Eliade's (1964) comparative generalizations about shamans (see Joralemon 1983:8–9). For the purposes of this text, we use "curandero" and "shaman" interchangeably, although we recognize that this may not necessarily be appropriate for curanderos in other parts of Latin America.

Curanderos were described in the classic medical histories of Peru (Lastres 1951; Valdizán and Maldonado 1922) and in studies of colonial heresy trials (MacLean y Estenós 1942; for northern Peru see Dammert Bellido 1974, 1984 and Glass-Coffin 1992; see also Millones 1981, 1982 for early colonial sources on coastal and highland pre-Hispanic religion), but John Gillin's (1945:115–29) ethnography of Moche included the first anthropological account of their practices.[1] Soon after the appearance of that work, a number of ethnobotanical and pharmacological studies of San Pedro were published (Gutiérrez-Noriega and Cruz Sánchez 1947; Cruz Sánchez 1948a,b, 1951; Gutiérrez-Noriega 1950; Friedberg 1959, 1959–60, 1960a,b, 1963, 1979; Poisson 1960; González Huerta 1960; see Sharon 1982).

A major impulse was given to the study of curanderos by the Peruvian social psychiatrist Carlos A. Seguín, who directed a collaborative research project in the town of Salas in 1967 (see Seguín 1979). Team members, among them the American anthropologist Marlene Dobkin de Rios, wrote on themes and subjects as diverse as the sociostructural sources of sorcery (Chiappe 1969; Chiappe, Lemlíj and Millones 1985; Dragunsky 1968) and the pre-Hispanic roots of curandero practices (Dobkin de Rios 1969a; see also, Dobkin de Rios 1968, 1968–69, 1969b, 1976, 1989).

Studies focusing on the work of individual curanderos began to appear in the early 1970s (Yarrow 1971; Rodriguez Suy Suy 1973). The most complete of these was Douglas Sharon's detailed account of the life, beliefs, and rituals of Eduardo Calderón, captured in a variety of publications (Sharon 1972, 1976a,b, 1978, Calderón and Sharon 1978; Calderón, Cowan, Sharon and Sharon 1982), as well as in a documentary film (Cowan and Sharon 1978). Calderón is also featured in books by González Viaña (1979) and José Gushiken (1977). The notoriety Calderón gained both in Peru and in other countries as a result of these works and his articulate explanations of his work have led to some controversy about his reliability as an anthropological informant (see Joralemon 1990).

Sharon's work helped to set the agenda for Joralemon's research with a curandero, José Paz, whose personal history and approach to healing contrasted in significant ways with those of the more cosmopolitan Calderón (see Joralemon 1984a,b, 1985, 1986; Joralemon's work with Paz is summarized in Chapter 11). Joralemon was able to show that the dialectical symbolism of Calderón's mesa was similar to the interpretations Paz offered for his altar. In both cases, the mesas symbolically expressed the opposition between good and evil, curing and sorcery. Artifacts associated with the forces of evil and death (e.g., pre-Hispanic ceramics, poisonous herbs, books of black magic) were placed on the left side of the mesa, termed the *banco ganadero* ("bank or bench of the one who dominates"),[2] while objects linked to curative, positive forces (e.g., images of Catholic saints, curing herbs) were positioned on the right side, the *banco curandero* (curing bank). Furthermore, both informants identified a central field of mesa artifacts that symbolized a balance or mediation between these opposites.

For both Calderón and Paz, curing rituals (including orally spraying perfumes, saluting the four cardinal directions, reciting Catholic prayers, singing songs and whistling accompanied by a rattle, nasal imbibing of tobacco juice in rites called "raisings," ingesting San Pedro, and "cleansing" by rubbing with a staff) activate a dialectical process by which the forces of good and evil in both man and in nature are brought into meaningful interaction through the mediation of the middle field. The balance of forces or "complementarity of opposites" achieved through ritual is then symbolically transmitted to the patient.

At first sight the ideology behind the therapeutic practices of these two curers appeared to be derived mainly from Christian moralism and Catholic-influenced folk religion. This seemed logical for the Spanish-speaking middle-class *mestizo* population of the north, the great majority of whom are followers of Roman Catholicism. However, a review of the literature on highland Quechua and Aymara peoples revealed that—although coca is their ritual catalyst instead of San Pedro—they also use in curing rituals mesas which incorporate the dialectical ideology of balanced dualism or complementary opposites. Ethnohistorical analysis revealed this principle to be an integral part of an Andean cosmology which is traceable back to Inca culture (see Sharon and Donnan 1977; Sharon 1978:39–44, 93–99).

In the chapters that follow, Sharon's continuing work with curanderos is reported upon. Since 1978 he has expanded his network of shaman informants to a total of ten, including Calderón. He has cataloged their mesas, detailed their rituals through participant observation, and recorded their life histories. In addition to Sharon's informants, we also present chapters on José Paz and on a curandero with whom our colleague Donald Skillman has been working for the past several years. With this large sample, combined with comparative information from the literature summarized below, we believe that we can now confirm that the dualistic ideology that Sharon originally found to operate in Calderón's rituals represents the philosophical foundation or cultural ideology underlying the Peruvian north coast's healing tradition.

In recent years a number of other scholars have contributed to the growing literature on curanderismo in northern Peru.[3] In particular, two research projects studying curanderismo to the north of Trujillo have contributed important comparative evidence. First, an impressive documentation of northern mesas and rituals is presented in a recent doctoral dissertation by the German ethnographer Claudius Cristobal Giese (1989). Based on five field seasons (1981–1985), it focuses on the shamanism of a Chiclayo area curandero, adding comparative data from other healers, including seven sons and one brother of Giese's main informant and one Huancabamba area curer who practices in the vicinity of the Laguna Negra of the Huaringas group of highland lakes.

Giese provides verbatim transcriptions of his main informant's articulate descriptions of his work. Discussions of the healer's psychic sight (*vista*) and the different types of curing techniques he applies in therapy yield perceptive insights into healer-client transactions. Giese also gives a comprehensive ethnohistorical interpretation of the curandero concept of *encantos* ("charms"), powers animating the mythical universe of Andean shamanism. He also documents highland healing traditions and shamanic initiation. A comprehensive glossary of curandero terminology, an exhaustive catalog of healing herbs, and a list of visionary animal imagery associated with the use of hallucinogens are found in appendices.

For the purposes of the present study, it is noteworthy that Giese documents a tripartite division of mesa artifacts: *izquierda* (left), *centro* (center), and *derecha* (right), with an extension of the left (front and left) designated as *ganadera*. He correlates these three divisions of the mesa with the three levels of the aboriginal Andean cosmos. (A more detailed discussion of Giese's valuable cosmological analysis can be found in Chapter 14.)

The second recent research project deserving extended attention is that of the Italian archaeologist Mario Polia, who has published a comprehensive ethnography (1988a) and detailed glossary (1988b) of the shamanism of the northern highlands (Department of Piura, provinces of Ayabaca and Huancabamba[4]) based on fieldwork conducted with ten healers from 1971 to 1974 as well as ongoing research since 1985. He describes the power objects on a mesa in the following terms:

Each object present on the mesa is the visible support of a power that is invisible in the "normal" state of consciousness, but that becomes visible in the altered state produced by the hallucinogen; this is the dream or *vista en virtud* [literally "sight in virtue," i.e., second sight or psychic sight]: a magically "significant" object is not [significant] by itself but by the *power*, *virtue*, or *charm* that it possesses; it is the power latent in the object that converts it into a magically efficient [object], and it is the capacity to use this power that distinguishes the *curandero* from the non-expert or from the profane [Polia 1988a:27].

The mesa itself, which holds objects that are "active symbols of a universe of forces," is:

the symbolic and real compendium of the universe conceived of as a harmonious and constant play of powers. Acting on the object-symbols one can analogically act on the universal forces that are condensed in them and [in which] they find correspondence [Polia 1988a:27–28].

Polia (1988a:149) provides a chart documenting the three divisions of the most complete mesa in his sample, from left to right: *mesa negra* (black), *mesa mora* (Moor, i.e., pagan), and *mesa blanca* (white). He notes that this informant's exposition of the three fields is more explicit than explanations offered by other curers. In another publication Polia further clarifies the status of the tripartite structure:

It is a central idea of *curanderismo* that a good *mesa* should be able to: 1—attack and defend, 2—cure, 3—"flower" [i.e., promote good luck]. As a result the *mesa* is ideally divided into three sections in each one of which objects are located according to the function of that part. However, this is an ideal division in that . . . not all *curanderos* follow a rigid distribution of the artifacts [Polia 1988b:212, translations ours].[5]

Polia (1988a:127–28) acknowledges variation among curers in the organization of curing sessions, but he also contends that curanderos' rituals follow a general outline (paraphrased and slightly modified):

Opening invocations (often including the four cardinal points)
Spraying of the mesa (perfumes)
Offering to lagoons and mountains
"Raising," or nasal imbibing, of tobacco (defense)
"Throwing away" of negative influences
Drinking of San Pedro

Lights out/Silence
("Raising" of tobacco), "Cleansing" or "Sucking"
"Throwing away" of negative influences
Divination/Diagnosis
"Raising" of tobacco (luck)
Spraying of mesa (perfumes)
Spraying and/or drinking of powdered corn mixture

In summarizing the ritual sequence of the nine sessions observed by 1988, Polia (1988b:213–14) points out that six of the sessions begin with opening invocations addressed to positive forces associated with the right side of the mesa. Then all of the rituals progress from actual curing acts (cleansing and associated raisings) early in the night to good luck rituals (raisings referred to as *florecimientos*, or "flowerings") near the end of the session. Like Joralemon (1984:10) and Giese (1989:148), Polia shows how this sequence from curing to luck-enhancing is spatially expressed as a movement from the left to the right side of the mesa.

All of the research summarized thus far has been carried out with male curers. There are many curing roles for women in Peruvian society, especially as herbalists who diagnose and treat from market stalls or less formally in the household, but males appear to predominate as curanderos.[6] Recent research by Bonnie Glass-Coffin (1992) with five women who practice as *curanderas* in Chiclayo, Ferreñafe, Huancabamba, and Cajamarca indicates that the oppositional-focused curing ideology of males may not be as central to the practice of all women ritual healers. Two of Glass-Coffin's informants, who work as a team in healing sessions, preach acceptance and faith as keys to healing, rather than confrontation and retribution.[7]

Also notable in the research on curanderos is a relative lack of attention to the individuals these healers treat. An exception is a study by Chiappe and Campos (see Seguín 1979:55–59) carried out in the Salas area. Only patients suffering from alcoholism were included and the sample was small (fifty-seven cases). In other published accounts, broad assertions are made about the psychological and social-functional impact of curandero therapy without direct evidence or testimony from patients (e.g., Chiappe Costa, Lemlíj and Millones 1985; see also Chapter 15).

The project we report on in Part II, for which we carried out fieldwork over a period of two years (1987 and 1988), was designed to supply the heretofore missing coverage of patients' experiences.

Together with our research team (Americans Donald Skillman and Bonnie Glass-Coffin, and Peruvians Rafael Vásquez and Nancy Peña Pusma), we completed documentation of 129 patient cases, drawn from the clients of four curanderos. We interviewed each person before and after therapy, and recorded interactions between curandero and patient during rituals. We found that conflict between men and women was the most common source of the suffering described by our informants and that the view of health and sickness that emerged from patients' testimonies was consistent with the dualistic ideology of curanderos.

The "Ethnographic Present"

Scholars writing about curanderos, ourselves included, typically have failed to say anything about the temporal context of their research, i.e., what was happening in Peru as they interviewed curanderos and how might these events have influenced their informants' practices. Orin Starn (1991) chides Andean specialists for this lack of awareness of the here and now of ethnography and for their selective attention to evidence of cultural continuities at the expense of a sensitivity to the dynamics of change. Of course, it is not just Andean specialists, nor more specifically those who investigate curanderos, who freeze their ethnographies in a timeless present. The very conventions of traditional ethnography call for an undisciplined use of the present tense in writing.

To ground our account of curanderos in the experiences of their patients without also indicating something of the times in which those patients and their curers lived would be to repeat the mistake Starn identified. Therefore, we present here a sketch of some of the important national-level events in Peru during the 1980s, the period of our combined research. In addition, in Chapters 19 and 20 individual patients' stories are linked to the social and economic forces which influence their lives.

Our initial collaborative research began as Peru returned to a popularly elected government after twelve years of military rule (October 1968 to July 1980). The generals who had ruled the country left a somewhat contradictory legacy, at once reformist and conservative. On the one hand, the traditional concentration of wealth and power in the hands of the local oligarchy and foreign investors had been disrupted by large-scale expropriations under the government of General Juan Velasco Alvarado (1968–1975).

However, the subsequent rule of General Francisco Morales Bermudez (1975–1980) backtracked on many of the social and economic reform programs initiated by Velasco. Morales Bermudez's economic "stabilization" plan, largely modeled on International Monetary Fund (IMF) strategies, caused inflationary spirals, a decline in the Gross Domestic Product, increased unemployment and concomitant social upheaval. Nationwide strikes, followed by government repression, characterized the last years of military rule.

When Fernándo Belaunde Terry returned to the presidential palace in July 1980, Peru's economy was far more centralized than it had been when he was forced from office in 1968. The state controlled some thirty-six percent of national production and more than half of the financial infrastructure. However, foreign capital still exercised a powerful influence in the profitable oil and mining industries, and a growing "informal" economy (i.e., beyond legal controls) provided essential goods and services at discounted prices (Reid 1985:81). Belaunde, an architect by training, began a program of infrastructural development (e.g., roads, hydroelectric dams), while his free-market-oriented advisors promoted policies of privatization, elimination of governmental subsidies, and export expansion supported by foreign capital.

After an initial recovery early in Belaunde's term, by 1982–83 a combination of factors had led to what Finance Minister Manuel Ulloa called "the worst economic crisis of the century." Natural disasters of immense proportions, a debt crisis throughout Latin America, and declining export earnings contributed to Peru's inability to meet its debt obligations. The resulting IMF austerity measures that were imposed were increasingly difficult for the population to bear, especially under the conditions of a severe recession. In the southern highlands, a revolutionary organization known as the *Sendero Luminoso* (Shining Path: formally "The Communist Party of Peru — By the Shining Path of José Carlos Mariategui") found a fertile ground for growth and recruitment.

By the end of Belaunde's term in 1985, just before we began our patient-focused study, the crisis had deepened. The purchasing power of the average wage earner had dropped by over fifty percent in ten years (Reid 1985:97). There was a dramatic deterioration in all indices of health as well as an increase in criminality, including international trafficking in cocaine. The government retreated to some of the repressive measures of the earlier dictatorship, including press censorship and intimidation, suspension of civil rights under declarations of states of emergency, and a militarization of the campaign against opponents, especially the trade unions and Sendero Luminoso.

When thirty-six-year-old Alan García and his APRA party (*Alianza Popular Revolucionaria Americana*) won the presidential elections in 1985 there was a resurgence of hope for improved conditions. García's war of words with the United States and the International Monetary Fund may have won him few friends internationally, but it played well domestically. When his "heterodox" economic plan, "an odd mixture of supply-side and demand-side economics" (Bonner 1988:54; see also Paus 1991), resulted in a drop in the rate of inflation (from 158% to 68% by 1986) and a respectable 8.5% growth in the Gross Domestic Product, it looked as though the country might be on its way to recovery.

Appearances were deceptive. By early 1987, when our patient study began, Peru was on the way to exceeding even the "worst economic crisis" of 1982. Hyperinflation (2775% in 1989) and a massive contraction of the Gross Domestic Product (down 12.2% in 1989 alone) left one-third of the Peruvian population (some seven million out of twenty-one million) in extreme poverty (Paus 1991:427). By the 1990 election, the Peruvian currency, the *inti*, was nearly without value on world markets, production was at a standstill, and the war with Sendero Luminoso had moved from the remote highlands to urban centers throughout the country. One of the last sources of hard currency was the ever-expanding cocaine business and trade. García's own ministers began negotiations with international lenders to reopen lines of credit, which were effectively shut off when the president refused early in his term to honor the conditions of repayment while the country was in a state of economic crisis.

The progressive economic collapse and political chaos of the 1980s affected every Peruvian in some way. What we heard from the patients of curanderos is only intelligible if we keep this context in mind. Their personal suffering was framed by the uncertainties and misfortunes of a country in crisis; their stories convey a sense of vulnerability to the aggression of others, even lovers and friends, made more intense by the desperation of the times.

PART I

Peruvian Curanderos: Their Lives and Ritual Practices

BY DOUGLAS SHARON

With Chapters by Donald Joralemon and Donald Skillman

The following chapters record the life histories, altar symbolism, and rituals of twelve curanderos, ten of whom are documented by Sharon and one each by Joralemon and Skillman. The range of characters is impressive, from the unpredictable, young, and aggressive Roberto Rojas to the paternal, priest-like Jorge Merino. Some treat their curing work as a divine calling; others seem more like pragmatic businessmen. Yet, there are striking similarities in the paths that led these exceptional individuals to the occupation of curandero (see Chapter 13), and there is an underlying curing philosophy that unites them (Chapter 14).

Our primary objective is ethnographic, to record in detail the symbolic system which is the foundation of Peruvian north-coastal shamanism. The object-by-object account of curing altars, or mesas, follows the precedent of John Gillin's (1947) pioneering work, just as the precise description of ritual sequences emulates the model of Victor Turner (1969). Inevitably, there is more to this documentation than will be of interest to a nonspecialist reader. However, the alternative of burying mesa inventories and ritual descriptions in a series of appendices would imply that these are somehow peripheral to the story of curanderismo. Our informants consider it otherwise.

It is important to keep in mind that Peruvian curanderismo is a grassroots healing tradition that has at various times been subject to official condemnation and repression. This has inhibited the formulation of the kind of explicit theoretical basis that constitutes the shared therapeutic framework of other ethnomedical systems. Peruvian curanderos see their work in individualistic terms and would find questions posed at a general level (e.g., "What are the basic assumptions of curanderismo?") impossible to answer. They will tell you what they personally think and do, but they leave it to the researcher to piece together from their idiosyncratic accounts the components of the curing philosophy they share. This is the difficult task that Sharon undertook when he began interviewing his first curandero informant, Eduardo Calderón, and which we take a step further with the additional ethnographic information presented here.

I
Eduardo Calderón

First Meeting

I have written at length about Eduardo Calderón, including how I came to know him in 1965 (see Sharon 1978:1–22), and so will only briefly summarize here the details of his life. However, for those unfamiliar with Eduardo from my publications and/or the ethnographic film, *Eduardo, the Healer* (Cowan and Sharon 1978), I will begin with a few general characterizations.

Possessed of a warm, extroverted personality and a robust sense of humor, Eduardo Calderón immediately impressed me when we first met in July 1965 at the archaeological site of Chan Chan outside of Trujillo where he was the artist in charge of adobe frieze restoration. A formidable raconteur, he seemed capable of an infinite variety of facial expressions as he recounted story after story based on his unusually rich life experiences. Fisherman, artist, teacher, curandero, he had learned much about human nature, its strengths and frailties, and had emerged a confident and able spokesperson for the merits of traditional forms of healing. My apprenticeship with him over the course of seven years' was both an intellectual adventure and a close friendship.

Biography

Eduardo ("Chino") Calderón Palomino was born in 1930 in Trujillo, where his parents lived after migrating from the sierra near Cajabamba. Having to work from an early age, and being an adventuresome child, Eduardo made slow progress in school, finishing only first grade by the age of ten. His preference for wandering about the countryside eventually earned him the nickname "Tuno" (truant, cunning rogue), but it also led him to explore many of the archaeological ruins that surround Trujillo. He collected potsherds and artifacts, and he developed a lifelong interest in the art of pre-Hispanic cultures.

The cause of Eduardo's restlessness during those years, however, went deeper than mere childhood mischief. He remembers disturbing dreams and visions that he had during his early childhood and recalls fearing the ridicule of others if he were to share with them his experiences. As a result, he turned inward, keeping the frightening images to himself. It was only in later adolescence, when he began to develop a real intellectual curiosity, that he found some relief from his psychic tensions by dedicating himself to his studies.

To cover school expenses Eduardo worked in a Chinese dry goods store and as a porter in the local market. During summers he labored in the fishing industry out of the port city of Chimbote. He developed a stout, muscular frame which was well suited to the sport of weightlifting in which he also became interested during this time.

Feeling a "calling to serve humanity," Eduardo enrolled in Trujillo's seminary instead of in the public high school, but he rebelled against the discipline of orthodox religion and left the seminary in his final year. Financial constraints prohibited Eduardo from pursuing his next preference, a career in medicine; however, a long-time interest in art, with skills learned from his artisan father, provided a good outlet for his creative spirit. Eduardo showed a special talent for sculpture in clay, wood, and stone. After captaining his weightlifting team in the national championship competition in Lima, he remained in the capital and enrolled in the School of Fine Arts. He worked with his uncle as a bricklayer to pay for his night-school classes.

Life in Lima was traumatic for Eduardo, both personally and professionally. An academic approach to art conflicted with his less-disciplined, freedom-loving spirit, and he left art school before completing his first year. A marriage to a classmate was broken up by meddling in-laws, who disparaged Eduardo's humble origins and sent their daughter to live with relatives. After failing to locate his spouse, Eduardo returned to Trujillo in late 1951, took up life as a fisherman in a small seaside hamlet nearby, and occasionally exhibited his art in the city. In the meantime his wife gave birth to a child of his that Eduardo has never seen.

At the end of the period he spent in Lima Eduardo had suffered from a mysterious ailment that failed to yield to modern medical treatment. Since both of his grandfathers had been curanderos in the highlands, it was natural that Eduardo's family would decide to consult with a folk healer. Eduardo was treated and cured by a female curer, or *curandera*. Like the classic "sickness vocation" discussed by Eliade (1964:33–36), this experience inspired Eduardo to explore the world of curanderismo. He attended a few ritual sessions and then accompanied a friend suffering from the effects of a love spell to Chiclayo where they both participated in a séance conducted by an *enguayanchero*, or maker of love spells. Not only was his friend cured, but Eduardo experienced *"visión"* (psychic insight), which helped in the cure. Eduardo declined the sorcerer's offer of an apprenticeship, however, knowing intuitively that he was not inclined toward this darker side of curanderismo.

Once back in Trujillo, Eduardo began to learn more about curanderismo from the uncle of his second wife, Maria. He initially went to this relative in order to remove a spell intended to "pull" him into the service of the Chiclayo sorcerer. Gradually, however, while working as a stevedore on the docks of Trujillo's port (Salaverry), fishing in Chimbote, and exhibiting his art in Trujillo, Eduardo also became the uncle's main assistant, or *rastreror* ("tracker," one who helps the curandero "see" during curing sessions). His powers developed and, in one critical ritual, he felt called by the "Christ of the mesa" to effect part of the session. However, since he still did not feel competent enough to set up his own mesa, he pursued further apprenticeships with curanderos in Chiclayo, Mocupe, and Ferreñafe, where he learned the extensive lore relating to "power spots" invoked by curers (e.g., the mountains of Chaparrí and Yanahuanca and the sacred lagoons of Las Huaringas).

After four years of training, at the age of twenty-eight, Eduardo performed his first cure, for a cousin. Thus he began his career as a curandero, working with his own mesa and vowing to God never to abuse his powers and to work for good in the service of humanity.

Eduardo's growth as a curandero paralleled his development as an artist. In the early 1960s, after several years as a practicing curer, he had the opportunity to produce a great deal of wood sculpture for the appreciative staff of the American hospital ship *Hope.* His enhanced reputation as a local artist led him to be hired in the mid-1960s to direct restoration work at the archaeological site of Chan Chan, near Trujillo. During this time he also taught ceramics and was involved in the production of replicas of pre-Columbian ceramics for sale to tourists.

When the Chan Chan project ended in the early 1970s, Eduardo set up his own ceramic workshop and divided his time between ceramic production, teaching, and attending to the needs of the large number of patients who sought his services as a curandero. By the mid-1970s he had quit teaching and had set up a restaurant adjacent to his workshop. In the late 1980s he built a hostel near the expanded restaurant and contracted for the construction of three motorized launches to be used in a projected fishing business with his sons.

Through his exposure to archaeology and pre-Columbian ceramic motifs Eduardo learned much about the pre-Hispanic past of the north coast. Thus, in a very real sense, Eduardo's artistry has led him to a rediscovery of his cultural heritage. This has also been true of his shamanism. Together, art and shamanism have complemented his personal search for meaning.

Today, after three and a half decades as a full-fledged curandero, Eduardo is still learning and growing. He feels his knowledge and power increase with practice and experience. His active mind is constantly probing and seeking new challenges; this is evidenced by his extensive reading in theology, philosophy, psychology, art, the occult (through correspondence with Rosicrucians in the United States), and medicine. He obtained a nursing diploma by correspondence study and now applies this knowledge in his curandero diagnosis and therapy. Also, beginning in 1981 with a visit to the San Diego Museum of Man, Eduardo has traveled widely in Europe and the U.S. These foreign trips have been an outgrowth of organized tour groups which began visiting him in Peru in the late 1970s.[2]

But his erudition and travels only supplement the keen insight into human nature which Eduardo has gained from his wide experience in the workaday world. This experience has been obtained in a variety of jobs—fisherman, stevedore, artist, teacher, lay archaeologist. And it has been greatly refined by Eduardo's numerous consultations and sessions with his patients. He is open, direct, and candid in his dealings with his fellows. He does not believe in keeping his knowledge a secret and freely shares his ideas with any sincere person who inquires about curanderismo:

Figure 1 Calderón Mesa

> It is necessary to teach all so that they know what it is all about. One
> must never keep secrets—secrets that are not secrets. Rather, one
> must bring all out into the light (Calderón, in Sharon 1978:xiv).

Calderón's Mesa

A full discussion of the symbolism of Eduardo's mesa can be found
elsewhere (Sharon 1978:62–72, 159–70); for the purposes of comparison with the mesas of the other curanderos discussed in the
following chapters, a review of the major features will suffice. Figure 1 shows the mesa as it appeared in October 1989. The few
changes made since I first recorded the mesa (see Sharon 1978:
Figure 6–1) are indicated in Table 1 by the use of asterisks.

TABLE 1
EDUARDO CALDERON'S *MESA*

I. RIGHT-HAND FIELD: *CAMPO JUSTICIERO* (Field of the Divine
Judge or Divine Justice)
Artifacts: Crystals**; shells; a dagger; a rattle; three perfumes; holy
water; black tobacco; sugar; sweet limes; San Pedro; crucifix*;
eleven named staffs (left to right starting with fifth from left:
Swordfish Beak Staff, Mulatto Staff*, Eagle Staff, Greyhound
Staff, Maximón Staff*, San Pedro Staff*, Hummingbird Staff,
Staff of the Virgin of Mercy, Sword of Saint Paul, Saber of Saint
Michael the Archangel, and Dagger of Saint James the Elder*).[a]
Symbolic Associations: Forces of "good," "light," and positive magic;
governed by Christ, the "center" or "axis" of the mesa; magical
numbers seven (associated with the crucifix) and twelve
(governing the whole field).

II. LEFT-HAND FIELD: *CAMPO GANADERO* (Field of the Sly Dealer,
Satan)
Artifacts: Ceramic shards (including clay whistles**) and stones
from archaeological ruins and power spots; cane alcohol; a deer
hoof; a triton shell; a sling*; three named staffs (left to right:
Satan's Bayonet, Owl Staff, and Staff of the Maiden).
Symbolic Associations: Forces of "evil," "darkness," and negative
magic; governed by Satan; magic number thirteen.

III. MIDDLE FIELD: *CAMPO MEDIO* (Middle Field)
Artifacts: Statue of Saint Cyprian (a black magician who converted
to Christianity) on a deck of Spanish divining cards with a bag of
divinatory runes at his feet; bronze sunburst; bronze disc; "sea"
and "winds" stone; a glass jar or *seguro* of magic herbs (Eduardo's
"alter ego"); a "fortune" stone; a quartz crystal "mirror"; a stone
from the Shimbe Lagoon; one named staff (Serpent Staff*).[b]
Symbolic Associations: Balancing and governing forces; governed by
Saint Cyprian; the sacred number twenty-five (twelve from the
"right" plus thirteen from the "left") associated with the crystal
"mirror."

[a] The saints' images that were present in the 1970s were stolen in the 1980s and
have not been replaced.
[b] This is less sinewy and has a larger head than the one found on the mesa in the
1970s.
* = new
** = augmented

Eduardo's mesa is spatially divided into two major (though unequal) zones called *campos* (fields) or *bancos* (banks or benches),
which are separated by a narrow third sector between them. He
conceptualizes these divisions as a projection of his own inner curing power. Symbolically, they express a moralistic dualism of good

versus evil (see Table 1). However, due to the symbolic role of the third or middle field, it could be termed a "balanced dualism," probably best described as a dialectic of good and evil.

During a séance, which typically lasts from about 9:00 P.M. to 6:00 A.M., the passage of time is measured by Eduardo through the performance of his ritual acts. These include: the reciting of Catholic prayers and an imitation of the Mass; the spraying of perfumes; tunes (tarjos)[3] whistled and sung to the beat of a gourd rattle; invocations (spoken and sung) of cuentas (power "accounts" or stories stored in mesa objects [artes] and made manifest in tarjos), as well as invocations of supernatural forces (encantos) located in mountains, lagoons, and pre-Columbian ruins (huacas); ingestion of San Pedro; limpias or "cleansings," (i.e., rubbings with a selected staff); and periodic nasal imbibition of a mixture called tabaco[4] in a ritual "raising" (levantada or parada). Each act has its own specific time and order in the overall ceremony.

Through the medium of rituals performed until midnight, Eduardo treats time in a linear fashion. This is done by what he conceptualizes as a power buildup. The session opens with Catholic prayers and invocations to the four cardinal points, interspersed by Eduardo spraying the mesa with perfumes. In the 1980s Eduardo added an exhalation or blowing of tobacco smoke in the four directions, as well as an invocation to the four associated power animals (i.e., north—buffalo/horse/dragon, west—jaguar, south—eagle, east—serpent/sun).[5] Next is a series of songs and "raisings" to activate the crucifix and the three symbolic zones of the mesa along with their associated magical numbers. The sequence of activating or "charging" mesa sectors is as follows: crucifix and its associated number seven, Campo Justiciero (right) and its associated number twelve, Campo Medio (middle) and its associated number twenty-five. In the process of raising or activating the Middle Field, the Campo Ganadero (left) and its associated number thirteen are also brought to life.

After the mesa is fully activated, the two assistants and then the patients perform a ritual raising of the San Pedro brew. This is done by imbibing the tobacco mixture through the nostrils after actually raising it along the side of the container holding the cactus infusion. Next, the assistants proceed to raise the curandero by nasally ingesting the tobacco liquid after raising it along the healer's front and back. According to Eduardo, this helps him to realize his alter ego. Then he raises the San Pedro and inaugurates its consumption by drinking a glass at midnight. All participants must drink the brew after the shaman finishes the first cup. According to Eduardo, the rituals performed up to this point serve to "charge" the mesa, the San Pedro infusion, and his own alter ego.

Midnight marks a period of transition in the night session. With the consumption of the San Pedro brew by all participants, the linear ritual acts which activated the dualistic ideological areas of good (right side) versus evil (left side) come to an end. This occurs at the same time that one twenty-four-hour day is ending and another beginning. As the curandero, the San Pedro brew, and the symbolic zones of the mesa are activated in both space (ritual artifacts and zones) and time (ritual acts and numbers) the stage is prepared for the second part of the curing session.

After midnight, Eduardo begins the actual curing portion of the séance. During this therapeutic division of the ritual the space occupied by the mesa artifacts is conceptualized as the realm of the "four winds" and the "four roads," a veritable microcosmos replicating the interplay of forces in the universe. According to Eduardo, the "four roads" radiate out from the crucifix to the four corners of the mesa, dividing it into four triangles. Each triangle correlates with one of the four cardinal points, or "four winds." This quaternary structure (four triangles) of the mesa during the second stage of the session contrasts markedly with the ternary structure (three fields) of the mesa during the first stage. However, despite that contrast, the second stage is an extension and refinement of the dualism expressed by the first stage. Although this is not as clearly verbalized by Eduardo as is the first phase of the ritual, it is implicit in his descriptions and strategic groupings of power objects (see Sharon 1978:62–72, 101–11, 159–74 for a detailed analysis of Eduardo's mesa artifacts and associated rituals).

According to Eduardo, once the first stage of the séance produces a balanced power buildup, manifest in a "charged" mesa (including the San Pedro and the healer), this power is then ritually "discharged," that is, applied in therapy. This occurs during the second part of the session, which lasts from midnight until 6:00 A.M. and consists of curing acts. Throughout the therapeutic portion of the séance, Eduardo treats time in a cyclical manner by repeating a standard series of curing rituals for each person participating in the session.

As each participant takes his/her turn before the mesa, the curandero chants a song in his/her name, after which everyone present concentrates on the staffs and swords placed upright in the ground at the head of the mesa. One of these artifacts should vibrate, since it is the focal point of the forces affecting the patient. The indicated staff is given to the patient to hold in his/her left hand over the chest, while the healer chants the song of the staff to cause its powers to manifest.

Next, as everyone concentrates on the patient, Eduardo gives a long divinatory discourse. Once this ends and while Eduardo chants a final song, the two assistants (one behind the patient and one in front) "raise" the patient from foot to waist, from waist to neck, and from neck to crown, imbibing a liquid provided by the curandero (usually the San Pedro and tobacco mixture, but other liquids—often a perfume—may be chosen). This is exactly the same ritual that the assistants performed for the shaman just before midnight. Then the patient must nasally imbibe a liquid provided by the curandero while holding the staff by one end over his/her head. This is called "raising the staff." It marks a critical moment in therapy during which Eduardo may have to drive off evil spirits with a sword battle. Finally, an assistant or the healer himself rubs the patient with the staff (from head to feet on all four sides), orally sprays the staff with whichever liquid is indicated by the healer, and returns it to the head of the mesa.

The curandero closes the session, after all patients have been treated, in the same manner in which it was begun: with an invocation to the "four winds" and "four roads," combined with a ritual purification of the mesa. Before departing, everyone must be orally sprayed by the assistants with *refresco*, a mixture of holy water, white flowers, and white cornmeal. Meanwhile, after dismantling the mesa, Eduardo carves a cross in the ground where the mesa stood, and afterwards sprinkles the four corners of the area and the outline of the cross with the white cornmeal mixture.

At first sight, Eduardo's ritual seems to deviate from the left-to-right/cure-to-luck sequence noted by Joralemon, Polia, and Giese in the rites of other healers since he activates the right side of the mesa, then the middle, and finally the left before performing his curing acts. However, on closer inspection, parallels begin to appear. First, although Eduardo does not routinely cure and then raise the luck of all his patients, nonetheless, whenever he performs good-luck rituals, they always come after the curing rites and near the end of the session. Also, a careful reading of Polia (1988b:213–14) and Giese (1989:211–14) indicates that opening ceremonies activate positive forces associated with the right sides of their informants' mesas (Giese calls the process *juego de gloria*, "game or playing of heaven"). Then comes the activation of left-side ritual associations, followed by curing acts and finally by rites to promote good fortune. In effect, the sequence appears to be from right to left to right, as depicted below:

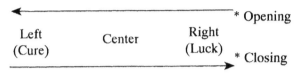

Left   Center   Right   * Opening
(Cure)   (Luck)   * Closing

The goal of curandero therapy is to cure sorcery or soul loss. According to Eduardo, this goal is achieved through the therapeutic application of the ritual "power" accumulated and "balanced" by the symbolic transformation of space and time that is delineated by a mesa during a curing session.

2

Víctor Neyra

First Meeting

When I first met Víctor Neyra my level of frustration was at an all-time high. For more than a month I had been attempting to meet Chiclayo-area healers who would be willing to share their lore with me. My search had begun by bringing Eduardo Calderón with me to try to contact the healers with whom he had worked more than twenty-five years earlier when he first began to learn to cure. To facilitate our search we had hired a taxi on a daily basis for the journey from Trujillo and for the many trips we had to take in and around Chiclayo.

In spite of this convenience, our efforts were totally fruitless. As the days passed, we discovered that all of the people with whom Eduardo had worked in his youth had died. For a while our hopes were rekindled when our driver introduced us to one of his aged relatives who was a practicing curandero. However, after weeks of patient cultivation and rapport-building, the old man met the request to learn about his practices with a simple, "No. That's sacred."

Additional efforts to meet new healers failed. My project was going nowhere. Time was passing, money was being spent, and nothing was happening.

That was the situation in early May 1978 when I made my way to the Brüning Museum to meet a relocated Trujillo scholar, Walter Alva, the new director. During my visit I mentioned the problem of finding informants. Walter responded by saying that he had an employee whose brother-in-law was a curandero. He called the man in and asked if I could be introduced to the healer. A meeting was arranged for that same evening.

At the appointed time I met the museum employee at the healer's house on the outskirts of a town near Chiclayo, where we drank beer and chatted for about an hour. Víctor Neyra was a

short, energetic individual in his early fifties. He had a quiet, almost shy manner; conversation was not one of his strengths. After
a month of setbacks I was overly cautious. Thus, although we both
knew the purpose of my visit, we avoided the topic of folk healing,
making small talk instead. Finally, losing patience with such pointless tact, Víctor announced that he had a session that night and
asked if I wanted to attend.

After a quick trip to Chiclayo to get my tape recorder and camera, I at last found myself back at work documenting folk healing
practices. For the next month I spent most of my time working
with Víctor. He had little patience for taped interviews but was extremely helpful during sessions, insisting that participation was the
only way for me to learn his lore. In addition, I discovered that
once a session had begun he became outgoing and charismatic.
This not only made him very effective with his patients, but also
taught me a great deal about his therapy.

I eventually was able to sit Víctor down with a tape recorder to
document his mesa, ritual, and biography. He found talking about
himself the hardest thing to do, a reluctance I was to find as well
with other traditionalists whose backgrounds were less cosmopolitan and urbane than was Eduardo Calderón's. Included here are
some of the fragments of Víctor's life that he was willing to reveal
to me in his unembellished and direct manner.

Biography

A distant cousin of a famous curer who was guardian of the
Shimbe Lagoon, Víctor Neyra Adriansén was born in 1927 near
the highland town of Huancabamba, considered to be the mecca
for northern curers and their patients. The oldest of three children, he was raised by parents steeped in the curing tradition. His
father was a curandero, his mother an herbalist; both had inherited their vocations from their parents. From earliest childhood
Víctor observed his mother and father work together as curers in
order to supplement the family income derived from subsistence
farming and a small bakery.

Informal exposure to curanderismo was reinforced by instruction from both parents. Speaking of this instruction from his father, Víctor told me:

> He taught me. From childhood he taught; he as well as my mother.
> In other words, this is an inheritance from my father, from my
> mother, and from my grandparents.

Víctor's father passed on to his son his power objects along with
the rituals associated with their use, while his mother taught him
the healing properties of the magical herbs. Their influence on his
practice was strong; he directly associated the lore and many of the
objects on the left side of his mesa with his father, while the right
side he associated with his mother. During difficult cures, with the
aid of San Pedro, he always called upon their departed spirits as
well as that of a paternal uncle to help him: "With 'the herb' [i.e.,
San Pedro], when there is something causing a blow, it calls the
spirit of my father or of my mother or of a deceased uncle."

When he was in his mid-teens, the young neophyte undertook his
first cure. This was a difficult case involving a mentally-disturbed
patient. Víctor's success in alleviating the man's suffering established
his credibility as a full-fledged healer with his family and friends.

In 1946, Víctor was drafted into the Peruvian army. At that time
he left behind his parents' way of life, since he had no desire to
involve himself in the constant quarreling and litigation over land
rights that went with the life of a small highland farmer. In the
army, he was forced to adjust to a life-style more exposed to the
dynamics of the twentieth century. Together with a woman from
Huancabamba he also started a family while in the service. Despite
these changes in his life, he found that he could occasionally keep
honed his emerging skills as a curandero by serving his comrades-
in-arms. This also taught him to adjust the more rustic version of
curing learned from his parents to the needs of Peruvians experi-
encing radical cultural change. He apparently adapted well to
army life, rising to the rank of sergeant.

When Víctor was discharged from the army in 1949 he went to
Talara, a coastal city built around the oil industry, where he continued his curing practices. Shortly thereafter he and his first mate
separated. By the mid-1950s he had moved to Chiclayo, the commercial hub of the north, and had developed contacts with an extensive network of herbal vendors to supply his curing needs. In
the late 1950s he moved to a community near Chiclayo, where he
divided his time between curing and farming lands he had acquired near town.

In the early 1960s Víctor met his second mate, Humildad. In 1970 they built the two-story house in which I first met them. Although she was initially skeptical, after a cure on her behalf performed by Víctor, Humildad eventually came to be an invaluable curing assistant. Most sessions I witnessed involved her aid as a *rastrera*, one who helps the curer in divining the causes of patients' ills. The continuing influence of Víctor's parents was apparent in his family-team approach to curing.

Víctor claimed that he was born with a natural gift (*un don natural*) for curing. Since curanderismo was an integral part of his family life and of his milieu, his gift was given abundant reinforcement. This natural inclination for healing received additional supernatural sanction in a fashion similar to that which many traditional northern healers experience as an initiatory turning point at sometime in their lives. When Víctor was just starting to practice, the devil—complete with horns and tail—appeared before him during a session in an effort to tempt the beginner with riches. But Satan did not even have a chance to verbalize his offer. Víctor quickly seized one of his swords, baptized in the service of God, and made the sign of the cross. The Tempter disappeared instantly and was only seen by Víctor again when he was involved in curses placed on unsuspecting patients.

The strongest single element in Víctor's work was the central role played by the magical herbs. He considered himself to be a *curandero yerbatero* (herbal curer). Whenever he could get away, he would make pilgrimages to the sacred lagoons above Huancabamba to bathe himself and collect herbs. Víctor described his commitment to heal others with the guidance of the magical herbs as follows:

> The pact is one's thought when one takes the herbs and enters into the charm. . . . One introduces one's thought into the very charm of the mountains or of the lagoon. That is the pact.

When working with his mesa, Víctor derived additional inspiration from Christ, Saint Anthony, Saint Cyprian, the Virgin of Mercy (patroness of the Peruvian army), and the Virgin of Perpetual Aid, all of whom "accompany the herbs and help to reflect the herbs, to reflect and clarify." Also, dreams provided a course of action for therapy: "Dreams guide one. They guide what one is going to do, how to cure the patient. All is revealed in dreams."

An integral part of Víctor's gift was *visión* or *vista* (psychic sight).

Here is how he described it and its relationship to the San Pedro remedy:

> The vision of the curandero is sight that is clarified by the remedy. It is clarified like seeing a movie. One sees people, symbols, everything. All is revealed; one sees it just like a movie. It indicates all, item by item. All. Point by point, there it is working.

Víctor's psychic sight extended to his own life. In mid-1988, he had a premonition that his death was imminent. One day, over a few beers, he tearfully confided his insight to a friend who promptly dismissed the notion as an effect of the alcohol. After all, Víctor was in perfect health, working as hard as ever on his land and holding curing sessions every Tuesday and Friday night as he had always done. However, later that same year he had a stroke and became partially paralyzed. He was treated by his colleague Masias, who was confident that Víctor would recover since Víctor had suffered partial paralysis on a number of occasions before and each time Masias had effected a cure. But this time it was different. Víctor's condition worsened. He talked with difficulty and would not eat.

One evening he asked his wife to set up his mesa and summon the family. With difficulty he performed the entire ritual, beckoning each relative for a turn in front of the mesa. Early the next morning he delivered his rattle to his wife, closed the ceremony, and was helped back to bed. While picking up the mesa, his loyal companion had a vision of Víctor seated upright in bed looking as young and vibrant as she had known him in his prime. She knew she was seeing his spirit.

Víctor Neyra never arose from his bed. He passed away on October 18, the Day of the Lord of Miracles.[1]

Neyra's Mesa

As was noted in his biographical notes, Víctor considered himself to be first and foremost an herbal curer (*curandero yerbatero*) in the tradition of his parents and forefathers. He maintained that in addition to extensive knowledge of the properties of medicinal plants, which anyone can acquire, a true shaman is distinguished by his psychic sight, or *vista*. This ability allows him to develop an intimate symbiotic relationship with the herbs. The shaman derives

Figure 2 Neyra Mesa

guidance and inspiration from them, as they actually "talk" to him during a curing session.

Since Víctor was a curandero, as opposed to a *brujo* or sorcerer, he was dedicated to the service of good and was aided in his work by Roman Catholic saints and virgins, who supplemented the positive direction and impulse provided by the herbs. However, like that of many other curanderos, Víctor's Catholic moralism was anything but passive in the face of evil, which was seen not as the mere absence of good but as an active force which finds concrete manifestation in the ailments of patients. There was no "turning the other cheek" in Víctor's approach; curing sessions were battles between the negative forces of evil, death, and destruction — sometimes, though not always, directed by the enemies of a patient with the help of a sorcerer — and the positive forces of goodness, life, and growth marshaled by the shaman.

This power struggle and the ideology behind it was not only acted out in ritual, but was also graphically expressed through the spatial arrangement of curing paraphernalia, or ritual power objects, on Víctor's mesa (Figure 2). A white linen cloth on the floor was divided into two symbolic zones of nearly equal size, referred to as bancos. On the right side were placed objects associated with positive or white magic; this was the *banco yerbatero* (herbal bank) or *banco gloria* (heavenly bank). Its function was to concentrate the therapeutic forces of good for the cure of the patient. The left side of the mesa, the *banco ganadero* ("winner" or "dominator," i.e., Satan, as the adversary of Christ in trying to win souls to his infernal legions), was linked to negative or black magic. It was the side of defense (*defensa*) against sorcerers' spells and dangerous supernatural forces. Its main function was to dominate the powers of evil in order to free the patient from their onslaught.

As its name implies, the Banco Yerbatero was the side of the mesa which facilitated the therapeutic action of the herbs. Together with San Pedro and tobacco, which were also classified by Víctor as "herbs," the magical plants were the most important power tools not only of this field but of the entire mesa. Collected at the sacred lagoons of Las Huaringas, near Huancabamba, they were kept in glass bottles (*seguros*). The two most important bottles were for the healer's personal protection. The curative properties of the herbs were given spiritual sanction by supernatural beings associated with *gloria* (heaven), the other name for this banco. These sacred personages included: Christ (a crucifix), the axis of the mesa; Saint Anthony (a wooden statue), guardian of children and curer of the folk illness *susto* (fright sickness or soul loss); the Virgin of Carmen (a bronze statue), the curer's protective guide and luminary; the Virgin of Mercy (a sword lying across the branches and shells to the right), patroness of the Peruvian army and defender of the faithful; the Virgin of Santa Rosa (another sword, the first on the right in the line of staffs at the head of the mesa), patroness of arms; and two glass Buddhas considered to be good-luck charms.

The two Christian swords (Virgin of Santa Rosa and Virgin of Mercy) at the head of the mesa were accompanied by five staffs (four *chontas* or palmwoods and one *ajojaspe*) and three pre-Columbian bronze chisels, called "bulls," the latter inherited from Víctor's father. The first staff (*ajojaspe*, second from the right) was hollow and was used by the curer to open the curing session by raising tobacco. The other staffs (third to sixth from right) and the chisels (seventh to ninth from right) were used to rub patients in cleansing rituals. There was an ambiguous quality to the chisels since all of the other pre-Columbian artifacts that Víctor inherited from his father were designated as *ganadero*, or as objects belonging to the left side of the mesa.

The remaining objects on the right side of the mesa reinforced the therapeutic actions of the herbs, supernaturals, and staffs. Included were the ingredients for the tobacco potion (San Pedro, limes, perfumes, and tobacco) and shells for serving and imbibing it; ingredients for *refresco*, a liquid (composed of sweet lime juice, sugar, flowers, white corn flour, and holy water) sprayed over patients at the end of the session; two shells used in a divination game of casting lots; a large shell (Tooth of the Sea Lion) rubbed over the body to remove pains; two rattles (one silver, one bronze—the latter from Víctor's father) for accompanying songs that brought the powers of the Banco Yerbatero to life; four stones (two dark crystals and two shiny blocks of iron pyrites) used to help clarify the curer's psychic sight for divination and to aid patients in perceiving solutions to their problems; branches of the *membrillo* (quince) tree for cleansing rituals; two magnets for removing sleepiness; a magnetic stone believed to attract good fortune; a bronze dog for sniffing out the causes of illness; a bronze deer for chasing off evil spirits; a section of fragrant *palo santo* wood for countering "evil winds"; and a wristwatch for keeping track of the hours of the session.

The rationale for a curandero to use the Banco Ganadero, which is dominated by the chthonic side of man and nature, is that it is necessary to fight fire with fire. This was most clearly evident in the use to which Víctor put the large number of stones which occupied much of the space on the sinistral side of his mesa. In contrast to the vital, more animate qualities of the herbs of the Banco Yerbatero, these stones were used for removing pain and/or anger and for "throwing away" evil associated with sorcerers' spells or malevolent forces of nature, such as "bad air" (*mal aire*) or whirlwinds (*remolinos*). Many of these stones were inherited from Víctor's father, following a sierra tradition dating to pre-Hispanic times of passing on from generation to generation sacred bundles of natural stones and carved figurines (*illas* or *incaychus*). Víctor's inherited stones included an Inca Sinchi Roca Stone; a buzzard stone for curing insanity; three black curing stones; and three flints along with two quartz crystals for making sparks to drive off sorcerers or evil spirits. Other items, such as two stone mace heads and a stone ball, were actual pre-Columbian antiquities. In fact, most of Víctor's inheritance from his father consisted of archaeological artifacts such as ceramics (pots and figurines) and bronzes (chisels and curved *tumi* knives). These supported the expulsive therapeutic action of the stones, but also added a human dimension by providing the ability to send evil back to the sender.

The defensive function of the Banco Ganadero was apparent in the numerous weapons found there. In addition to the bronze *tumi* knives and stone mace heads, there were three swords (third to fifth from the left at the head: the Dead Officer Sword from his father, the Las Huaringas Sword, and the Spanish Sword), a bayonet (second from the left at the head), and a pistol. Also reinforcing the idea of parrying the blows of an enemy were two animal fetishes, a bear's paw for mauling attacking sorcerers and a deer's hoof for driving them off; a pre-Columbian wooden statue (first on the left at the head); two wooden rods inherited from Víctor's father (one palmwood or *chonta*, one quince); and a hollow bronze tube called a "bull" (sixth from the left at the head) for raising tobacco to activate the Banco Ganadero against a sorcerer.

The remaining power objects of the left side of Víctor's mesa offered further aggressive/defensive capabilities. These were: a large number of shells (including one carved in wood), all inherited from Víctor's father and used to raise the tobacco potion against supernatural aggressors; ingredients added to the tobacco to make it stronger (e.g., sugar cane alcohol); two bottles of a red perfume (*cananga*) which symbolized fire to burn out evil; two bottles of vinegar used against evil winds; a *bejuco* or reed from the jungle for rubbing patients; gloves to keep the curer's hands warm during early morning hours; and Víctor's father's cacophonous bronze rattle to accompany the songs which activated the forces of this banco.

Víctor's sessions were conducted indoors with his mesa oriented either to the north (the direction of Las Huaringas), or to the east (the direction of the rising sun). His wife worked with him as a *rastrera* and her brother served as Víctor's other assistant, performing the duties of an *alzador* (i.e., he raised tobacco with the curer during rituals to activate the mesa and later aided in patient therapy).

Until about midnight the curer ritually activated the powers of his mesa and served the San Pedro infusion to everyone present. From midnight on he applied the earlier activated energies in the cures of his patients. Ritual activities prior to midnight were fairly standardized; however, the later curing activities were performed in a much more extemporaneous manner, according to the circumstances of each individual patient and the therapeutic actions divined to be necessary by the curer through his psychic sight. The main stages of Víctor's mesa ritual were as follows:

1 Opening ritual: Víctor grasped the Virgin of Mercy Sword from the right, brandished it, struck his chest, kissed the sword, and placed it in his belt on the left side of his body. Then he and his *alzador* "raised" or nasally imbibed the tobacco mixture five times each. The curer prayed before each raising, which he performed using his hollow Ajojaspe Staff. The assistant used a bivalve shell, which was filled by the curer for each raising. After completing the raisings, the healer and his assistant rubbed themselves from head to foot (sides, front, and rear) with their respective implements while the curer invoked the four cardinal points.

2 San Pedro: The liquified San Pedro was served to everyone present, using one glass passed around the room, starting with the curer and his assistants. Before drinking the brew, each patient placed an offering of money on the mesa, usually at the foot of the crucifix. When all had partaken, the room was darkened.

3 Defense: The curer picked up a long *chonta* staff, sprayed it three times with cane alcohol, swished it in the air, and then took it outside (to the left, behind the mesa) where he invoked a prayer of defense against sorcerers' attacks and planted it in the ground. When he returned, he sprayed the left side of the mesa three times with cane alcohol.

4 Silence: There followed a period of absolute silence, lasting from thirty to forty-five minutes.

5 Gloria song: The healer sang his first song (*tarjo*), which activated all of the powers of the right side of the mesa. One of the rattles from this side was used in the song.

6 Ganadero song: The healer sang his second song, activating all of the powers of the left side of the mesa with the help of the rattle from this side. He ended at about midnight.

7 Curing rituals: The order occasionally varied, but most of the following activities occurred:

    a The patient(s) (singly or in a group) raised the tobacco at the head of the mesa and to the right side (from the healer's perspective) or outside.

    b The healer divined for the patient(s).

    c The healer, assistant, and/or relatives raised tobacco on behalf of the patient(s), moving from foot to head, touching key points of the patient's body before each raising (how many times this was done was determined by divination). At times this occurred in conjunction with a *tumi* knife ritual.

d Song(s) were performed on behalf of the patient(s).

e The patient(s) was (were) rubbed with a power object (a staff or quince branch) by the curer or his assistant; or else he/she (they) was (were) instructed to rub himself/herself (themselves).

f Occasionally, the patient(s) was (were) instructed to perform a simple stamping dance together with family members or the whole group.

g In highly confidential cases, the curer or his *rastrera* took the patient(s) outside to consult and offer advice.

h In cures requiring a purge, Víctor administered a mixture of four purgative herbs which caused vomiting spells throughout the night.

8 Closing ritual: All present nasally imbibed a handful of Tabu perfume. The curer occasionally ended with an invocation of the Trinity, followed by a group prayer (usually "Our Father"). Afterward, the crucifix was passed around for all to kiss.

3
Ruperto Navarro

First Meeting

In late April 1978, after the first curer contact declined to participate in my study, the driver I had hired to go to Chiclayo provided another lead. Earlier in the 1970s he had been one of the people hired to work on an archaeological dig inland to the east of Chiclayo. During the project he had acquired what he and his fellow Peruvian workers recognized as *aire de huaca* (a sickness caused by the air from archaeological ruins).

My friend the driver learned that there was a retired driver living near the dig who was a healer adept at curing ailments related to ruins. He contacted the healer, whose name was Ruperto Navarro, participated in a session, and recovered. Before returning to Trujillo he gave me directions to the healer's home.

I was about to follow up on this lead when I met Víctor Neyra; but once I had the study with Víctor under way I headed inland to pursue my driver's lead. His directions were very good, and I found the healer's home without difficulty. Encouraged by my good luck with Víctor, I simply knocked on the door, presented myself as an anthropologist interested in his therapy—which I had heard about from a satisfied client—and hoped for the best.

I liked Ruperto immediately. Well preserved for his seventy-five years, he had a stentorian voice and a commanding, yet accessible, presence. He responded to my direct approach with equal openness and the easy manner of a professional driver accustomed to passing long hours on the road conversing with passengers or companions. He informed me that he had been engaged to perform a session the following weekend; its purpose was to eliminate the bad luck of a bus drivers' cooperative in Trujillo. I accepted his invitation to attend, glad that I had already planned to be in Trujillo at that time to work with Eduardo Calderón. Eduardo and I were finishing a collaborative book in Spanish, which I eventually used to teach a class on traditional healing at the University of Trujillo's School of Medicine.

On the appointed evening I found Ruperto at the home of a *compadre* in a small community outside of Trujillo. The session was held in the garage and parking area for the cooperative, amidst the buses. It was felt that both the group *and* their machines shared in the *mala suerte* (bad luck). It had to be removed from both.

Due to an involved schedule, I was not able to meet again with Ruperto until July. More intensive work occurred in September 1978, with follow-up visits in October 1979 and July 1980. Delays notwithstanding, the information flowed smoothly, at times even poetically, from this worldly and spellbinding storyteller. This is his tale.

Biography

Ruperto Navarro Solf is a man who has experienced much bitterness in his life. He was born in 1905 to a family of small landowners. His father, whom Ruperto greatly admired, was an outspoken, gruff individual. He ran his small *hacienda* with an iron fist; the pistol he wore at his side was used on more than one occasion in frontier-style shootouts with cattle rustlers and bandits who roamed the region during Ruperto's childhood.

It seems that the flamboyant rancher's manner gained him many enemies, and eventually led to his downfall, as well as to Ruperto's first experience with the dark side of northern shamanism. During Ruperto's early teens, his father was poisoned by a sorcerer hired by one of his enemies. Since the hardened rancher never put much stock in the stories told by his hired hands about *daño por boca* (sorcery poisoning by ingestion), it was too late for a curandero to cure him by the time it was realized that a physician's treatment was ineffective against his swelling stomach. His father's agonizing death left a lasting emotional scar on Ruperto's young psyche. Recounting the incident still brings tears to his eyes.

After his father's death, Ruperto had to help provide for the family. Two years of education he had received from a tutor came to an abrupt end as the teenager struggled to maintain the small herd of cattle inherited from his father. He managed well, until his sister sold the family ranch when Ruperto was in his late teens. He then sought full-time employment at a large sugar hacienda where he had worked sporadically since his father's death. At first he worked as a tractor operator and later as a chauffeur for the administrators.

Driving became Ruperto's main source of income for the rest of his life. As the road system of Peru expanded, he drove trucks for the hacienda and also eventually as an independent trucker between hacienda jobs. His driving took him to many parts of the country and brought him into contact with many people, which helped him develop a varied clientele when he began using a mesa.

Ruperto was strong and competitive. During his early twenties he discovered that boxing provided a legitimate means for him to channel his pent-up aggressions while also earning him some money. He was good enough to do a little prizefighting (a total of five bouts) in Chiclayo and Lima.

Unfortunately, Ruperto displayed his pugilistic talents outside the ring as well. His temper had a short fuse, and although he was good with words, when arguments during drinking bouts with other drivers got heated, he tended to settle things with his fists. This tendency, coupled with frequent absences from home while he was on the road, contributed to two divorces. He did not really settle down until he was in his fifties.

Ruperto was hardworking and resourceful. There was always plenty of money to be earned by drivers, not only at the expanding sugar haciendas but also at a nearby cement factory. As the years passed, he saved enough to buy a truck and later a tractor, which he rented out when he was not using them himself.

In the rigidly stratified world of the hacienda worker, Ruperto the progressive entrepreneur had to be careful not to stir the envy of those around him who as peons were trapped by the drudgery and peonage of daily life. Ruperto's *macho* braggadocio was not always the best way to win friends and influence people. On several occasions he was the target of sorcery, each time initiated by someone who had lost a promotion or contract to Ruperto. Once, when he was in his thirties, after he unknowingly incurred the wrath of a laborer on the hacienda where they worked Ruperto suddenly began to experience frequent vomiting and weakness. After a doctor failed to alleviate the symptoms, he took the advice of the hacienda's administrator and went to a reputable highland curandero who performed cures at the foot of a waterfall. The healer divined the cause of Ruperto's ailment and effected a cure.

Even in later life, when he was a practicing shaman himself,

Ruperto would still seek the help of a fellow practitioner when similar incidents occurred. For example, in the mid-1950s a colleague
who was unable to cure Ruperto took him to a famous healer who
practiced at one of the lagoons of Las Huaringas. The three men
got along well together, and Ruperto was able to purchase a mesa
from the lagoon shaman, many of the objects of which are part of
the mesa he uses today. These contacts with other shamans taught
Ruperto a great deal, and much of his shamanic art is directly derived from others.

Ruperto claims to have made a pact (*compacto*) with the devil. In
northern Peruvian folklore such pacts are instigated by the devil,
who appears to the neophyte when he is beginning to learn the use
of a mesa and demands the life of a loved one in exchange for
power and riches. A curandero resists this temptation while a sorcerer (*brujo*) is said to have accepted the offer by signing a pact in
his own blood, by which he agrees to be the devil's servant and to
deliver his soul to Satan at death. Ruperto's version of his pact,
however, has him seeking Satan and bending the devil to his will.

It all started in 1945 when Ruperto and his brother were among
the first truckers to drive the new road to Huancabamba. They
were invited to a celebration hosted by the town authorities. After
the festivities, one of the community leaders invited the Navarros
to a spiritist séance:

> At eleven o'clock in the evening it occurred to him to do the work.
> . . . After a few minutes there were three raps on the table. My fa-
> ther, Nestor Navarro, spoke, "I have two relatives here," he said.
> "My life was taken on the farm, on my hacienda."

Ruperto was fascinated by the man's ability to call up the spirits
of the dead and wanted to know how to do it. The man gave him
some materials to study and told him to come back in a year. Ruperto did both and reported:

> The year passed like a day. I told him, "This is the day." "Ah, that's
> true," he said. "O.K., don't wear a ring or a belt, none of those
> things, only the clothing on your body." Then we went outside Huan-
> cabamba to a nearby mountain. . . . There were three of us. Ocoña
> did the first ceremony; he shouted. He didn't like it or he was fright-
> ened. The other one called with the same result. I went. Once at the
> place, I began to say, "Adonay, Adonay, Adonay. Let the Prince of the
> Enemies present himself." A strong wind arose. I doubled up and
> turned sideways. At that point I saw the enemy, dressed in a black
> jacket with a red bandanna and red pants. He said to me, "What do

you want?" "What I want is that, wherever I put my hand, no one will take it away from there." He nodded in my direction, shaking his horns. . . . The others gave up. Not me. I held out, I held out and I doubled up when the wind came, damn it!

After this encounter with the devil, Ruperto sought to increase his ability to communicate with the dead. He spent many evenings chewing coca in the cemetery and invoking the help of the spirits of the plant which he refers to as "*Coca Maria.*" He had some interesting comments regarding these experiences:

> I went there to see if it was true that the dead could be seen, but there was nothing. The cemetery is the healthiest, most sacred field that there is. Not one dead person moves. On the other hand, where you can feel something is in church, where there are so many saints. In church you can hear or see somebody standing inside, but in the cemetery I have slept alone, I tell you, and it is something completely tranquil.

Ruperto's desire to master the supernatural realm was inadvertently facilitated by personal difficulties. He had a serious dispute with a hacienda engineer during which he struck his adversary. The man sought revenge by hiring four gunmen to ambush Ruperto. In the ensuing gunfight, Ruperto mortally wounded one of the assailants. For a year or so Ruperto became an outlaw, constantly running from the authorities. The solitude and privations he faced during those desperate months forced him to live off the land and to develop his own inner resources. Although he was eventually captured and jailed, he gained a full pardon by applying his growing powers of divination to solve a criminal case for the police.

Once Ruperto was released, he had to rebuild his life. His property had been confiscated by the police and his second wife had left him during his period on the run. Out of sheer economic necessity, he began to work with his mesa in earnest. Building upon his reputation from the successful police case and his network of friends and business associates on the haciendas and in trucking, he slowly began to develop a clientele. Throughout the 1950s he used both his driving skills and shamanism to restore his capital base and to purchase another truck, although, inevitably, there were some conflicts, including the case of sorcery mentioned.

Ruperto prospered during the 1960s, and he even counted some wealthy landowners among his clients. On several occasions he was invited to Chiclayo, Trujillo, and even to Lima to perform his rituals in the homes of the rich. He bought another tractor and a second home in Chiclayo.

In the 1970s Ruperto's fortunes took a downturn, paralleling the more general disruptions in the Peruvian economy resulting from agrarian reforms. The large sugar haciendas of the north were expropriated and turned over to government-controlled co-operatives. Despite his many years of service to the hacienda, Ruperto was denied a pension. He also lost clients, first from the families and retainers of the dispossessed hacienda owners and then, as an international economic crisis further worsened the local economy, among the administrators and workers. When I met Ruperto in 1978, all he had left was an old pickup truck, badly in need of repair, and his home on the hacienda.

Economics was not the only factor affecting Ruperto's practice. Old age and bad health had also taken a toll. A bad back, the result of a fall from a tractor, had plagued him for twenty years. This condition was exacerbated by prostate problems, which finally led to an operation in 1987. On several occasions during our conversations Ruperto exclaimed, "I never thought I'd get old."

Navarro's Mesa

Ruperto's pact with the devil prohibits the use of saints or other Christian icons on his mesa, with the exception of Saint Cyprian, a sorcerer who was converted to Christianity. The majority of his power objects are stones, which dominate his entire mesa. Thus, in spite of the influence of Christian folklore, Ruperto's paraphernalia are very much in line with the highland tradition of sacred stones, which is what one would expect given that he learned much of his lore from highland curers.

Ruperto divides his mesa (Figure 3) into two almost equal zones. His pact with the devil leads him to reverse the customary left/right associations by placing the Ganadero side of his mesa on the right, the Gloria on the left. There is a certain paradox of opposition involved here, perhaps best understood by those who, like Ruperto, have been relegated to the margins by their society. For, as American anthropologist Barbara Myerhoff (1978:64) shows, the symbolic logic underlying reversals, wherever they occur around the world, is that "things which appear to be the very opposite of each other are shown to be identical." In effect, left/right, evil/good,

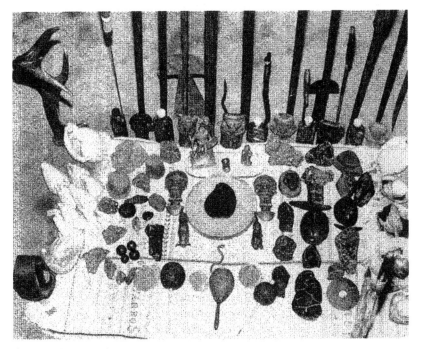

Figure 3 Navarro Mesa

sorcerer/healer—"all these are definable only in terms of each other. Paradoxes are resolved in this experience; formulations that tax the rational mind to its limits are managed comfortably and lucidly" (ibid.).

Ruperto found it difficult to explain the referents of his artifacts outside the framework of a session, saying that he needed the inspiration of San Pedro to guide him. To some degree, most curers show a similar hesitation; after all, an interview is an artificial situation. However, Ruperto's difficulty seemed to extend beyond the interview context. He simply did not know as much about his power objects as others I interviewed knew about theirs. One of Ruperto's peers, a *compadre*, attributed this to Ruperto's pact. He said that those who actively seek the shamanic role are not as "evolved" or effective as those who are selected by the supernatural because of an inborn "gift." They may appear more successful by their wealth and status but they are not as powerful as those with a mission, who may or may not profit through prestige and financial rewards.

The defensive nature of Ruperto's right-hand Ganadero zone is apparent from the large number of weapons on this side: two machetes, one spear, one sword, one dagger, one pre-Columbian *tumi* knife at the head of the mesa and another three on the ground (one a modern tourist curio), as well as a second sword in the lower right corner. Six curing staffs, a statue of a knight, and the Saint Cyprian image with a sorcerer's rattle in hand also contribute to this militant tone. In addition, there are two rattles (one made by "pagan" Indians of the jungle) and a deer's hoof on the right. By invoking unseen forces for aid, the rattles have both protective and offensive functions, while the deer's hoof is used to drive off enemies. Two thick glass windowpanes from a shipwreck, used for divination, support the protective role of the rattles: the elliptical-shaped pane, in consort with a special cup for serving San Pedro, helps the knight and Saint Cyprian, while the circular pane assists a curved black Siren Stone used in divination in cases involving the sea.

The chthonic element is definitely pronounced on the right; it contains more and larger stones, most of which were gifts from *huaqueros* (robbers of pre-Columbian grave sites), who found them in archaeological ruins near powerful mountains. For example, a cluster of five stones (one for sexual problems, one for rashes, one for eye problems, another for kidney pains or backaches, and a marriage stone for marital difficulties) were found at the foot of famous Chaparrí Mountain; one stone came from archaeological sites near Cock's Crow Mountain; another came from pre-Columbian burial sites near Eagle Mountain; and a whirlpool stone, used either to cure insanity or for attacking enemies, was found in a *huaca* (pre-Columbian shrine) near Gallows Mountain. Other stones from pre-Hispanic sites include two paganesses (*gentilas*) employed in cleansing rituals and a star stone which helps in divination. Four pieces of iron pyrites are used for hypnotizing patients during therapy.

The earthy underworldlike quality of the Ganadero is further manifested in three fortune stones, two representing gold mines, one a silver mine. Two cleansing stones from the sierra refer to animals—a turtle and a scorpion—the latter being one of the artifacts purchased from the lagoon shaman who cured Ruperto. Another animal referent on this side, also purchased from the lagoon shaman, is a ferocious bronze guardian lion. The feminine principle is expressed not only by the paganess stones, but also by two pre-Columbian female ceramic figurines at the head of the mesa. An additional pair of figurines, one male and one female, are classified by Ruperto as "*cholo*," a term for lower-class contemporary Indians or mestizos.

Three jars of herbs on the right are located among the staffs and figurines. One is used to alleviate pain, one for legal entanglements, and one for bringing back a rebellious fiancée or wife. Shells are for rubbing patients, as well as for divination (together with a small bronze snake), and for the personal use of the curer and patients to ingest San Pedro. All substances used in the tobacco potion as well as those with which the mesa is sprayed are placed in the lower right corner, next to the shaman's shell. San Pedro is placed in front of the mesa, on the line between the two zones.

The left side of Ruperto's mesa, besides being slightly smaller, contains fewer and smaller artifacts; those found on this side also have a less pronounced chthonic character than do the objects of the Ganadero. Stone predominates even in this zone, however: a star stone for divination, mine stones for luck, a black stone from a *huaca* to cure fright sickness, a medicinal altar stone to be placed in herbal mixtures, a moon stone for divination, a shell stone for clearing the sight, five lightning stones for protection against lightning, a Chalpón Mountain stone for invoking that powerful site, a blemish stone for removing facial skin problems, and five pieces of iron pyrites used for hypnotizing patients (supplementing those on the right).

In sharp contrast to the defensive nature of the artifacts at the head of the right side of the mesa, objects at the head of the left side are all used in cleansing rituals for patients; that is, patients are rubbed with them at critical moments in therapy. This is especially true for the four *chontas* in this section, but it also holds for the pre-Columbian *tumi* knife (and the tourist *tumi* on the ground balancing its counterpart on the right), the machete, the deer antlers, and a six-foot *chonta* embedded in the ground beyond the machete. The theme of curative cleansing is maintained by the three herb jars (one for legal cases, one for finding lost people, and one for sinuses), the two pre-Columbian female figurines among the staffs, as well as by the eight white-pointed shells (symbols of procreation), the strombus (complementing the one on the right) and the large bivalve which together dominate the whole left border of this side of the mesa.

Four black steel balls on the left are used to heal problems with male testes. Other curing tools on the left include: four divining shells complementing the two on the right; two black ceramic faces from archaeological sites used in divination; a magnet used to "ground" the negative charge sent by attacking sorcerers or to remove pathogens from patients; a bronze bull purchased from the lagoon shaman who cured Ruperto, used to cleanse and defend; a magnet stone, also from the lagoon shaman, for star divination; and a gourd rattle for activating the "accounts" or powers of the left side of the mesa.

An interesting aspect of Ruperto's mesa is the fact that it contains an incipient or potential middle field, manifesting itself in the area occupied by the two windowpanes from the shipwreck. The panes themselves are symbolically appropriate since a window has a dual dimension, providing either an inside or an outside view, depending on the position of the observer. Ruperto thinks of the panes as "crystals" used for "seeing" either the cause of sorcery on the Ganadero right side, or the elements of a cure on the healing left side. Other artifacts support the balancing function of this middle zone: Saint Cyprian as the mediator between Christian and pagan worlds (sorcerer turned saint); the San Pedro cup, by which both sides are activated; a central rattle situated between the rattle on the left and the one on the right (not shown in photograph); and a bronze snake and two shells used for impartial judgment in divination. It is apparent from Ruperto's delineation of only two zones that he is not consciously aware of any middle field. Nevertheless, his mesa seems to provide a balance otherwise lost in the bitter "one-sided" orientation metaphorically expressed in the pact with the devil. In his twilight years, he appears to be finding resolution for his internal conflicts wrought by life's trials.

Ruperto's ritual is very simple and relatively unstructured. If the session is held at his house, he sits in the dining room with his patients, chewing *coca*, drinking cane alcohol, and chatting, from about 10:00 P.M. until midnight. The mesa would have already been set up in his backyard, oriented to the south. During the conversation, he discusses the patients' ills and promotes his own therapeutic abilities by recounting past successes. He often brings out books on herbs and the occult sciences to demonstrate his knowledge of curing lore. When Ruperto is traveling, he usually stays at the home of a local *compadre*, who organizes a group of patients at a central meeting place. This does not allow for the same degree of intimacy prior to a session since much time is taken up with transportation to the ritual site and the setting up of the mesa (which is frequently oriented to the east).

At about midnight the session begins. The ritual area is kept lit the entire night by a lantern or by a battery-run lamp. The initial rituals roughly follow this order:

1 Ruperto sprays the mesa with perfume.
2 The assistant (there is only one) raises the tobacco on behalf of the patients, sometimes accompanied by a short *tarjo* sung by Ruperto.
3 San Pedro is served to all present. Often a token offering of money (about the equivalent of fifty cents) must be deposited on the mesa by each patient while Ruperto sings another very short *tarjo*.
4 All patients raise the San Pedro with tobacco, while Ruperto talks with patients or sings.

The foregoing acts set the tone for the curing rituals. Ruperto's primary method consists of informal conversation—including anecdotes, popular sayings, and jokes. As he did earlier before the session proper, he converses about his personal life and past cases, chews *coca*, and drinks *yonque* (cane alcohol). Sometimes he drinks to excess and becomes quite abrasive. Often, he cannot remember details of his divinations when a session is over, claiming that the San Pedro took over, using him merely as a medium.

Ruperto's monologue is interspersed with questions for specific patients and descriptions of people and events, clairvoyantly "seen" by the healer. Since there is no fixed order in which individuals are selected, there is little structure to the curing acts and a variety of techniques are employed. Patients may be called before the mesa so that the assistant can raise them with the tobacco, rub them with a staff or mesa artifact, and then have them raise the tobacco or a perfume. Or the shaman might converse with the patient while casting divinatory shells to determine whether or not a past or future action is favorable. Other procedures include directing all participants to raise a staff with the tobacco on behalf of a single patient, instructing selected patients to discern symbolic patterns in the reflections cast by the iron pyrites on the mesa, exchanging aphorisms and puns with individual patients or groups of patients, preparing jars or herbals for certain patients, administering additional San Pedro or mixed herbal remedies, and so forth. Patients are often singled out several times in an evening, and they may be treated either with a variety of techniques or with one at a time.

One very dramatic intervention which Ruperto always performs once the session is under way involves hypnotizing skeptics or patients who resist therapy. After placing his arm behind the person's back, Ruperto holds one of the pieces of iron pyrites (the "stone for hypnosis") over his/her forehead. The patient often is rendered unconscious and usually goes stiff. Then, with the help of his assistant, Ruperto lays the person on the ground. On one occasion, the patient was so stiff that she was placed with her feet on one chair and her head and shoulders on another, with no support between. In this position, during questioning, she confessed some incriminating information and was not aware of what she had said when she was brought back to consciousness. However, many patients successfully resist hypnosis and simply go along with the operation since stiffening the body is the only way to be laid out comfortably, given that the person is bent over backwards with the assistant only supporting the shoulders. When the hypnosis has been successful, Ruperto awakens the patient by having him/her raised by the shoulders while he says, "Rise, Lazarus." Upon reaching the standing position, the patient loosens up and has no recollection of what transpired while hypnotized.

The overall mood of a session with Ruperto is that of an evening of humor and drama—one in which a personable pitchman promotes his therapeutic abilities to his audience while getting increasingly inebriated. Bargaining and witty repartée go on all night. Ruperto skillfully narrates an endless variety of personal anecdotes, spiced with poetry, puns, popular sayings, jokes, and folktales about buried pre-Hispanic treasures protected by supernatural guardians (*carbuncos*). In difficult cases, a strategy frequently used by Ruperto is to tell the patient that the cure cannot be guaranteed, but a careful diagnostic session should be performed (for a moderate fee); a successful session will be expensive, but there will be no charge if the therapy fails. The old cowboy/truck driver travels the road of life with a tale to tell and a service to sell.

4
Masias Guerrero

In July 1978, after a month in the United States premiering the documentary film on Eduardo, I was back in Chiclayo working with Víctor Neyra. When I returned to Víctor's house, he told me that he felt in need of a "cleansing" (*limpia*) to relieve himself of the heavy burdens he had taken on in healing his patients. He confided that whenever he felt overburdened and in need of a respite he would visit a *compadre*, Masias Guerrero, a curandero who lived in the countryside near the town of Motupe.[1] His friend Masias would perform a night session on his behalf. Seeing an opportunity to meet another curer, I asked Víctor if I could accompany him on his visit to Masias. Víctor liked the idea, so we began planning the trip.

A week later I accompanied Víctor, his wife, her brother, and a compadre to the *chacra* (farm) of Masias. This stout and relatively old farmer had a deliberate manner and spoke in a grainy voice. While Víctor introduced us, Masias sized me up through squinting eyelids. He accepted my offer to work as an assistant on behalf of Víctor and his party, but said that he detected something about me, possibly a light case of fright sickness or soul loss (*susto*), that also needed to be treated. This was fine with me since I felt it would help build rapport and enhance my understanding of the healer's therapy.

The session went well. The next morning, after a brief nap, I began documenting the mesa and reviewing the taped ritual. Some sketchy biographical information had been obtained, but we were all tired and felt that this could be pursued in greater depth later on. Besides, I noted the same difficulty that I had encountered with Víctor—Masias was a pragmatist who learned by doing and did not relish lengthy interviews about his life and work. Nonetheless, over the next two months and in follow-up work in the fall of

1979 and the summer of 1980, I managed to get Masias to tell me some of his life experiences.

Biography

Born in 1910 near the town of Ferreñafe, Masias Guerrero Valladolid was the second son of a peasant family. Wage labor was the family's livelihood and Masias was expected to contribute his share of hard work. However, he was able to attend school long enough to gain a rudimentary education, including the ability to read and write.

Masias's father worked at a variety of agricultural jobs, but it was in the rice paddies of the region that he worked most of the time. When Masias was eight the family moved about eighty kilometers away to Motupe, where fruit picking provided another source of income, with children and parents working in the orchards together. Before long Masias began to work with his father in the rice paddies. Hardship and adversity, including the death of his mother when he was sixteen, were facts of life which Masias soon learned to accept.

In 1933, Peru was involved in a border dispute with Colombia and Masias was drafted into the Peruvian army. He had reported for duty several years earlier, but had been excused from service due to a bad arm, injured by a fall from a burro. However, as a result of the state of emergency declared to deal with the Colombian conflict, Masias found himself serving in the artillery in Piura for two years. After his discharge, he went back to work as an agricultural laborer on the estates of the Chiclayo region.

In the late 1930s Masias became involved in curanderismo, starting out as an *alzador* or curer's assistant. His maternal grandfather had been a curandero, which predisposed Masias to the curing art. As Masias puts it, he had an *afición* (inclination) for healing. He prides himself on the fact that no one taught him to cure—except the spirit of his dead grandfather. He learned by performing the numerous chores of an assistant and by observing the methods of several curanderos. Practical experience, not a teacher's lessons, taught him the mechanics of curing.

As Masias gained confidence in his curing abilities, he attempted to aid family members—primarily his brothers, sisters, and their children. His first cure, a case of soul loss suffered by one of his nephews as a result of the shock of seeing a dead person, occurred about 1945.

Over the years, Masias experienced two confrontations with the devil. The first happened when he began treating his relatives. He was living with his father, and his first son had just been born. One evening, during a session, Masias heard a strange, heavy voice coming from under the ground. The temptation the voice offered was contingent upon his delivering his father and firstborn son:

> But I didn't permit him, because when one wants, one wants. I prefer to live in poverty and not like that. He said to me, "Do you want to be the first, or with a glance at a person know who he is?" I heard the voice, but didn't see him.

On the second occasion, one night when he was holding a session in Chiclayo, Satan appeared riding a horse and clenching a victim. He had a light complexion and was wearing the elegant white clothing of a country landlord. This time Masias drove the intruder off by waving a sword at him. According to Masias, the San Pedro brew had taught him that the rider in white is the Enemy of Man. He must not be permitted to enter the area of the mesa since he will confuse the curer in his efforts to heal and perhaps even kill the shaman or his patients.

Another danger from which Masias had to learn to protect himself was the blow (*golpe*) of an attacking sorcerer. On several occasions during his years of practice he has been caught off guard. He described the worst mishap as follows:

> It happened to me one time when I was working just before dawn, and they "turned me around." I was pursuing the lost cows of some friends from Huancabamba for which they didn't even pay me. I was divining, divining, going where the remedy was telling me to go, when I lost consciousness. You see, I lost consciousness and didn't know what to do. Fortunately, my mate woke up and saw me there. She made me re-set the mesa. I was completely demoralized.
>
> Fortunately, that evening a friend arrived with a patient for me to cure, and my companion, my *señora*, said, "Listen, Santos, namesake [her name is also Santos], I charge you with Masias who was *golpeado* [hit by a blow] last night and is not himself." Well, he was the one who cleansed me because he knows the technique. Right there at my mesa he worked as an assistant. I cured myself with his help.

Masias says that with the help of the San Pedro cactus he learned to work with the spirits of the dead, especially the spirit of his deceased grandfather. The spirits guide him in therapy and protect him from the attacks of sorcerers. As a result, Masias specializes in illnesses caused by the spirits of the dead, such as *susto* (soul loss), *aire de muerto* (air of the dead; especially common near cemeteries), and *aire de huaca* (air of dead pagans, *gentiles*; found especially near archaeological ruins). Masias emphasizes that the cactus remedy is the medium through which he is aided by his grandfather:

> In my case, for example, at the beginning with the remedy, when it gets to me, this inclination comes out and the spirit of my grandfather congregates in my brain, and an idea comes to me, an idea from the herbs.

Masias was quite popular with women as a youth; he once spent twenty-seven days in jail because he got into a fight over a woman. By middle age he had children from two unsuccessful unions; but by the early 1950s he had finally settled down as a tenant farmer with his present companion. Together they have raised seven children.

In 1970, due to agrarian reform legislation favoring small farmers, Masias was able to set up his own farm. His main subsistence activity became goat-herding, the best adaptation to the marginal, mostly arid land available to independent farmers. But he still had to engage in wage labor in order to maintain his small parcel of land.

Life is a constant struggle for this tough old farmer and herder. His herd has to be shepherded, wells must be maintained, briar fences kept up, and corn planted and harvested on what land can occasionally be irrigated. But Masias is proud of his little homestead and his independence. They are the well-earned fruits of a life of perseverance and hard work.

An interesting development in the Guerrero household involves the transmission of the curing tradition from one generation to another. In 1979 I observed that one of the healer's sons was a fine curing assistant, a fact not surprising since he had been working with his father from the age of twelve. When I visited Guerrero's home again in December 1988 I found that Masias was in Lima working with another curer, but his eldest son, Alberto ("Beto"), was living at the farm after having worked for several years in Lima. Following in his father's footsteps, he had become a full-fledged curandero three years earlier.

In September 1989, nine years after our last visit, I finally had a chance to see Masias again. His sight had been bad before, but had gotten worse. In addition, he had developed a hearing problem. He was still working the land and tending his goats, but it soon became apparent that he had come to rely heavily on his son. When asked about curing, Masias deferred to this mild-mannered young man, indicating that he was now in charge.

The two healers, father and son, had worked together the night before I arrived and were still recovering from the effects of an all-night ritual. I left so that they could rest and returned the next morning, only to find that Masias had already left for the grazing area. His son had stayed behind to bring me up to date on his father's life and curing practice. My new informant clarified some details of the healing rituals and delineated a few of the changes in the mesa. In February 1991, although Masias was in Lima for prostate surgery, I was able to redocument the mesa and participate in a session with Alberto. During these meetings I learned how he had become a curandero.

In 1985, during a curing session, Masias suffered a blow from a sorcerer which left him weak and debilitated. He read the Tarot cards (*naipes*) to see if there was a mesa that could cure him. The divination showed that not even the lagoon shamans could heal him; the only mesa that could restore his power was his own.

Masias arranged for a session with his two most faithful assistants, his son and another relative. But when the time came to begin the ritual, the older assistant said that he did not feel capable of handling the Guerrero mesa. By default, the task fell to Masias's son. Not wanting to fail his father in his hour of need, the novice accepted the responsibility—and succeeded.

After three years of practice, the young curandero felt the need for a visit to the lagoons. Journeying with a friend, he went to Shimbe Lagoon and there, during a ritual bath, he saw the lagoon give off a ray of light. Later, while performing the raising ritual after the bath, the hollow bull's horn in which the *tabaco* was served slipped from the lagoon shaman's hand as he was handing it to Alberto. It landed open-side up, which was interpreted as a good omen by the officiating shaman, who shook hands with the novice, embraced him, and offered hearty congratulations on a bright future. In the Guerrero family, the cup had been passed from father to son.

Guerrero's Mesa

Masias recognizes two major segments of his mesa (Figure 4): Curandero (right) and Ganadero (left). A third sector, *gentil* (pagan ancestor) or *moriscano* (pagan Moor),[2] is located in the upper center left of his mesa, and appears to function as a subdivision of the

Figure 4 Guerrero Mesa, 1979

Ganadero; however, during the original documentation of the mesa, Masias did not clearly distinguish between Gentil and Ganadero. The *mesa moriscana* is sometimes called *el medio* (the middle) or *el centro* (the center). The right is the side of curing, associated mainly with magical herbs (including *mishas* or daturas) and perfumes. The left, the Ganadero side, with its "minerals" and archaeological artifacts, is for "delivering a blow" (*golpeando*) or "turning around" (*volteando*).

The San Pedro brew and the tobacco mixture, the major catalysts for the entire session, are on the right side, along with a large number of bottled magical herbs (*seguros*), perfumes, and the ingredients for *refresco* ("refreshment," a mixture of perfumes, white corn flour, sugar, and holy water which is sprayed on patients after a session to reduce the effects of the San Pedro).

The activities of the healing side of the mesa are concentrated in four staffs (from right to left): *Chiri Chiri*, a palmwood "guide" in therapy which protects the San Pedro "like a watchdog"; the Saint Cyprian Rod (reinforced by a *tumi* on the Ganadero side and a bronze statue on the Curandero side) to assure the aid of the

patron saint of curers; the Sword of Saint Gabriel, commander of
the celestial armies, used to dominate the devil; and the Longinus
Lance[3] for raising luck and curing sorcery caused by evil spirits
and air of the dead. Saint Gabriel and Saint Cyprian are assisted by
Saint Anthony (a bronze statue), who is considered to be a protector of pregnant women. A great variety of both bivalve and spiral
shells are used for serving the tobacco. Two manufactured magnets
and a natural one kept in a round jar are used to extract pain.

Although stones are considered to belong mostly to the Ganadero side of the mesa, some very special ones are reserved for the
right: three quartz crystals associated with light and purity and
used to drive off sorcerers; the Chaparrí Mountain Stone, which
symbolizes this powerful local peak that is invoked for protection
by many northern healers; and the Las Huaringas Stone, symbolizing the curative powers of these highland lagoons. Cigarettes and
incense are occasionally used to produce purifying smoke. Finally,
a bronze rattle with a golden bell attached to it is used to activate
the healing powers of the right side.

The central Gentil sector of the mesa is composed almost entirely of archaeological ceramics. They include the following: two
female figurines used to cure illnesses caused by the bad air around
archaeological sites; a llama head and two dog figurines for curing
soul loss brought about by a shocking confrontation with animals; a
feline ceramic for ailments caused by poisons placed in food; a "de-
mon" figurine used to extract stomach pains in women; two small jars
for curing the bad air of archaeological sites and swollen stomachs; a
monkey figure to retrieve souls captured by pre-Columbian ruins; a
human couple used to overcome love magic; a buzzard to cure sick
cattle; and an animal's paw to heal face burns caused by a sorcerer's
spell or potion. Three "staffs" are at the head of the Gentil sector:
Chonta Jívaro, fifth from the right, used against bad air; the Maiden
Staff, sixth from the right, for invoking the sacred lagoons with the
aid of associated magical plants as well as for curing love magic; and a
small bronze llama, between the other two, which aids the shaman
in spirit journeys to the highlands.

The left side, the Ganadero, contains archaeological bronzes
and stones. The latter, some of which come from archaeological
sites, are collectively called "minerals," or *illas*, an Aymara name for
animal figurines used in highland fertility rituals. Pre-Columbian
bronzes on the left include a *tumi* knife dedicated to the patron of
shamans (Saint Cyprian), used to induce vomiting for sicknesses

caused by sorcerers' potions; a small rod for putting patients to sleep when required; two chisels for rubbing and raising patients; a defensive *tumi* found in an archaeological site at the foot of Chalpón Mountain; a palmwood stick banded with bronze strips, used to defend against sorcerers by rendering them stiff; and an ancient rattle used for activating the powers of the Ganadero zone and for calling the spirits of the pagan ancestors.

Among the minerals which dominate the left side of the mesa are stones symbolizing body parts (brain, chest, stomach, kidney, penis, and knee); three flint stones for making sparks to drive off sorcerers; three black "diamond" stones (one for countering sorcerers, one for blinding sorcerers, and one for curing sick cattle); two stones representing the sun and stars; two rocks from powerful mountains (Putay and Caracol); two "water" stones to cure fright sickness caused by water; a wasp stone and a rash stone for eliminating head sores; a stone of the dead for curing air of the dead and spirit attacks; a "refreshment" stone for rubbing away drowsiness caused by San Pedro; a shell stone for curing insanity; a fish egg stone for guiding cures; a potato stone used against highland sorcerer attacks; a puma claw stone to remove pain and induce vomiting; an eagle claw stone for defense, shamanic flight, and to protect cattle; and a butterfly stone for divination in life-or-death cases.

Staffs utilized for the activities of the left side of the mesa are (seventh to eleventh from right to left): Inca Drill, or *indio moro*, for protecting the San Pedro brew, extracting spells involving potions or the spirits of the dead, and recalling captured souls; Bronze Lightning Rod for removing air of archaeological ruins; Swordfish Sword for driving aggressive spirits into the sea; Volcano Sword for defense; and Rajado Mountain Bronze for defense. In addition, a five-foot *chonta* is placed behind the healer to the left in order to protect his back; two quince branches are used for switching the air to drive off attacking sorcerers; and a powerful Tiger Sword (lying in the Ganadero section) is used for spirit battles. A deer's hoof is used for fending off troublesome people, including a spouse in a case of divorce. Besides two small bivalves for serving the tobacco in counterattacks against sorcerers and spirits, the Ganadero has three large conch shells used to rub patients for their defense as well as a cluster of bivalves stacked on their sides in the lower left-hand corner.

There is one final artifact from Masias's mesa (at the foot of the Sword of Saint Gabriel) which deserves a separate discussion. This is a smooth oval stone which he calls *doga*, the popular name for a huge jungle snake, probably the anaconda. This is definitely the most powerful object of the mesa in Masias's eyes; he calls it the "queen of the mesa" and claims that in visions he sees it coiled around the sacred space delineated by his power objects, protecting the entire area from danger. This artifact, originally found in the Marañon River, was given to Masias by his grandfather, who had used it on his own mesa. It also is used to calm patients who may become agitated from the effects of San Pedro, or to induce vomiting in victims of a sorcerer's potion placed in food or drink.

Participation in sessions in the late 1970s indicated that Masias follows a simple format in his curing rituals, which are conducted behind his house, located near the foot of powerful Chalpón Mountain. After spraying the mesa with perfume, he usually opens a session between 9:00 and 10:00 P.M. with a song, and occasionally with an invocation to the four cardinal points. He then requires all present to raise perfume. After another song, everyone drinks the San Pedro brew. There follows a series of songs which are used to "call" (*llamar*) forces associated with the three sectors of the mesa, that is, *yerbas*, *gentiles*, and *minerales*. During this time the San Pedro brew is taking effect on the participants. The remainder of the session consists of a series of songs interspersed with dialogue, divination, the casting of shell lots, rubbing or cleansing (*limpia*) with a staff and/or mesa artifact, the periodic imbibing or raising of tobacco, and battles with a sword or staff against spirits. After the mesa is sprayed again with perfume, the session ends with a purification ritual in which all participants are orally sprayed with *refresco*, a white corn flour mixture.

A patient is often attended to several times during the night and early morning hours. For example, the first time the curer addresses the patient he/she might be required to raise an artifact from the mesa, rub his/her body with it, and then hand it to the curer to be sprayed with a perfume. During the raising and/or rubbing, Masias might sing a song or cast shell lots to interpret an aspect of the patient's problem. The second time, some hours later, the patient's luck would probably be raised by the curer or by one of his assistants in an operation called *parada de suerte*. This often consists of one assistant serving the tobacco liquid either to the other assistant or to Masias, who imbibes it through each nostril at the feet, waist, and head of the patient. On a third occasion, which occurs near the end of the session for all serious cases, the healer

Figure 5 Guerrero Mesa, 1991

performs *chupas* (suckings). This involves holding a sword against a
sore part of the patient's body, taking a mouthful of perfume, and
sucking the area. The idea is to suck out the spiritual essence or
"humor" related to the patient's malady.

The two unvaried end points of a Masias session seem to be
the ingestion of San Pedro at the beginning of the evening and
the sucking cures near the end. His songs provide the thread of
continuity linking the many tasks of a session. The order and performance of these ritual acts vary from patient to patient and are
determined by the healer as he intuitively apprehends the individual's personal situation.

Fieldwork with Alberto in 1989 and 1991 allowed me to document the current mesa and ritual. Since Masias was not present
during our meetings, it was possible to gain some sense of the perceptions of a new generation. However, since Alberto has only
worked as an assistant to his father, this information probably reflects the familial tradition fairly well.

The most evident modification of the mesa (see Figure 5) is a
clearer delineation of the Gentil or Moriscano sector governed by
the Maiden Staff (fifth from the right), a carved Saint Cyprian

Staff (sixth from the right) which has replaced the Jívaro Staff, and the iron Inca Drill (seventh from the right) which has been moved out of the Ganadero sector. The pre-Columbian pottery which dominates this zone has been augmented by two ceramic effigies, one male and one female, found below the male figurine at the foot of the Inca Drill. A large new ceramic vessel dominates the lower left corner of the Moriscano sector. On the right border of the Moriscano zone six pairs of natural magnets have been added, lining up between the Maiden Staff and the tip of the Tiger Sword lying in the Ganadero sector. They are used for "pulling" and "throwing out" evil winds from pre-Columbian ruins.

Replacing the Chiri Chiri Staff in the Curandero section is a new sword, Justine (second from the right), companion of Saint Cyprian. A "diamond" stone of iron pyrites has been added between the Saint Gabriel Sword (third from the right) and the Longinus Lance (fourth from the right). It "illuminates" the healer and promotes good luck. On the upper left border the young healer has his own magnetic stones—baptized at the Shimbe Lagoon—in a circular container next to his father's. Between them is a shepherdess effigy, a guide for therapy and patroness of livestock. To the right of the healer's two personal shells for imbibing or raising *tabaco* (tobacco juice, perfumes, and cane alcohol) is a spatula from the cathedral at Motupe. Farther to the right and slightly below the spatula is a box containing two bull-calf horns to supplement the shells.

At the head of Ganadero there is a new bronze chisel (third from the left) and a *chonta* staff as yet unnamed (fifth from the left). The Swordfish Staff has been lost.

Within the Ganadero section, Saint Anthony (now in wood) has been moved from Curandero and is used to "pull in" and punish souls. The shells along the left edge of this zone are most prominent. The lower shells are pairs of *tabaco* containers which were all enclosed within one another and placed on their sides in the mesa photograph from the late 1970s. However, above them are two pairs of spondylous shells, as well as a complete bivalve and a small conch which were added in the late 1980s. In the lower left corner is a large bivalve, the Siren, for deflecting curses into the sea. This activity is reinforced by two large stones representing the mountains Huanacauri (near Cuzco) and Guitarra (on the north coast). In general, bivalves are used for raising *tabaco* to "throw away" sickness and evil while spiral conches are for blowing them away. Supporting their functions are deer antlers, which have replaced the deer hoof.

Alberto is much more clear about the phases of a mesa ritual than his father. He starts at about 10:00 P.M. by spraying the mesa with florid water (*florida*) and red *cananga* perfume. Three successive songs or *tarjos* address and activate the three divisions of the mesa in the following order: Curandero, Moriscano, and Ganadero. After the songs, first the healer and then his assistants raise *florida* four times in the name of San Pedro and the mesa in general. Patients follow but only raise twice. Then all drink San Pedro in the same order. Three more *tarjos* are sung by the curer, addressing the sectors of the mesa in the same order as before.

At about midnight, the principal assistant raises *tabaco* on behalf of each patient, rubbing or cleansing himself with a staff afterwards. At this juncture, the healer tosses shells to divine the course of the evening's therapy and then follows with a seventh song.

The actual treatment of each patient follows a standard format. First the healer sings in the name of the patient in order to "pull" his spirit. Then the assistant raises the patient from feet to head and cleanses him from head to feet. The healer usually converses with the patient and may divine with shells before the raising. Curing rituals continue until about 3:00 A.M.; from then until 4:00 A.M. good-luck raisings are performed. In serious cases, sucking (*chupas*) occur from about 4:00 to 5:00 A.M.

Before dawn the shaman "flowers" (*florece*) the patients and mesa. This phase begins with the healer raising the patients' hands with *florida*. Then he sprays *florida* over the mesa and in the direction of the four cardinal points. Next he rubs the patients, from head to foot and on all sides, with two crossed swords. After the rubbing, the patients step forward once and then backward once over the crossed swords. The healer serves them *refresco*, which they use to wash their hands, faces, and necks. Finally, he sprays all sectors of the mesa with *florida*. When the artifacts have been put away, the curer cuts a cross in the ground and sprays it with *refresco*.

5
Porfirio Vidarte

First Meeting

It was late July 1978 and my project was progressing very well. The work with three healers was almost more than I had time for and so I was in no hurry to meet other curanderos. Unfortunately, the search for informants is sometimes one of feast or famine — either I could find no one willing to work with me, as in April, or there were more leads than I could manage. So it was when an opportunity came my way to meet another curer during this busy time.

At my first session with Víctor Neyra in early May I had met and later became friends with a couple who were Víctor's compadres. The husband was among those who accompanied Víctor to the ritual session with Masias Guerrero. On the return trip from that session he took me aside and asked if I was interested in meeting another healer, one of his compadres, who lived in a neighborhood on the outskirts of Chiclayo. This old man held sessions whenever there was enough demand for his services, but he was most likely to be working Saturday nights. Since the next Saturday was only a few days away, we felt it would be a good idea to meet with him immediately.

Porfirio Vidarte lived on a dusty, unpaved street on the north side of Chiclayo. He was a lean, leathery-faced gentleman with a small, square moustache. Initially, he was very formal and reserved, obviously caught off guard by an unexpected visit from a foreign anthropologist. However, the fact that I was accompanied by a trusted *compadre* soon put him at ease. Once I had explained the nature of my work and the purpose of my visit, he appeared intrigued with the idea of participating in the study. As my friend had predicted, a session was scheduled for Saturday and we were invited to attend.

When I started to interview Porfirio after the Saturday session I found that he was uncomfortable with the tape recorder and that his memory was weak on details of his life. We tried two techniques to resolve these difficulties. Since Porfirio emphasized that his memory was sharper when he was *enyerbado* (under the influence of San Pedro) and, since part of his ritual therapy involved sermonizing with personal anecdotes, we agreed that he would try to cover his life history during his "sermons" whenever I was present at a session. Also, we enlisted the aid of Porfirio's second son, a radio announcer and his father's best ritual assistant, to administer some of my follow-up biographical questionnaires. Although the results were mixed, I thus was able to supplement information gathered at my original interviews. The following is what I was able to learn in the late summer of 1978 and in subsequent follow-up work (fall 1979, early summer 1980, and late summer 1987).

Biography

Porfirio Vidarte Díaz was born in 1906 in the highland province of Santa Cruz, Department of Cajamarca, the first of five children in a family of well-to-do farmers. Prior to his birth there had been indications that something was different about the unborn child his pregnant mother was nurturing. As Porfirio tells it:

> Before I was born I had cried three times. My mother told my father one night in bed, "Ay, what a child I've got inside me." "Ah," she said, "we're going to have a wise child or he's going to possess some mystery." Between the two of them they decided not to talk to anyone about this. They kept it to themselves.

Later, during Porfirio's childhood, there were further signs, which he interprets as early evidence of shamanic propensities. When he was about seven he had a dream:

> I saw coming down from the sky what seemed like a weaving of four or five colors: green, yellow, white, red. Then I said, "Papa, I see this. Mama, I see this," right? "I've dreamed of it." "Ah," said my mama, conversing with my papa, "The boy is announcing. One of us is going to die, you or me first." This was the beginning of the virtue that I had announcing itself.

When Porfirio's father passed away shortly thereafter, his mother began to do what she could to discourage his development as a shaman. Despite her efforts, the normal boyhood passion to fill one's pockets with "pebbles and snails and puppy dogs' tails" soon evolved into a search for objects that would later be used as a part of a mesa.

There were a series of civil disturbances in the Santa Cruz area during this period. As arson, pillaging, and murder became commonplace, Porfirio's family's fortune had deteriorated, and he was denied formal education as a result of demands for him to help at home. At one point, when one of the factions in the civil strife took over the Vidarte residence as a temporary headquarters, the family was forced to camp at a nearby site called El Verde. While there, Porfirio's mother had no choice but to pay attention to her son's developing psychic abilities. As he recounted the story:

> I was sleeping in the open when somewhere between sleeping and waking I saw that fire was coming to the site right where we were. In my dreams, right? Then I remember saying, "Mama, send my uncle up to the ridge to order them to send us mules right now because they are going to burn us out tonight." "Son," she said, "you've got this nonsense in your head." "No, mama, they are going to burn us out tonight." Then and there she sent for the mules. We went to a site called El Calvario set up by the Franciscan fathers, and as we arrived we saw behind us that they put El Verde to the torch. "See, mama," I said, "if we hadn't been warned they would have burned us."

Porfirio's family, having lost most of their property, fled the violence and chaos in Santa Cruz, moving to Ferreñafe on the coast. Porfirio was in his early teens at the time. He became a sacristan at the local church, but was still not able to attend school since he was busy helping his mother with the family. He did, however, learn Bible stories and the Roman Catholic liturgy in the course of performing his religious duties.

At this time Porfirio had a near-fatal accident. He was swimming with his uncles when

> I was seized by a whirlpool. Once I was seized by the whirlpool, I was thrust into a hole made by it and everything was spinning around me: stones here, stones there, and the stream poured down on me. The whirlpool seized me and held me down with the stones beating me.

Porfirio was wearing a religious amulet, a splinter from the miraculous Cross of Chalpón (see Note 1, Chapter 4). He managed to invoke it with a simple, "You are witness to my life," before being knocked unconscious by a blow on the head.

Suddenly, he awoke. He had been thrown clear of the whirlpool, and emerged with only a slight bump on the head. That day Porfirio became a devotee of the Cross, and subsequently made a pilgrimage to Chalpón Mountain to give thanks for the miracle that saved his life. To this day he maintains a small chapel dedicated to the Cross in the courtyard of his home, the courtyard where he also performs his curing rituals.

When he was in his mid-teens, Porfirio experienced the key event in his life, an event which established his credentials as a legitimate curandero working for the good of his people. The devil came to tempt him one night, between midnight and 1:00 A.M., while he was practicing with his still-developing mesa in the company of a younger brother. A *gringo* dressed in white suddenly appeared:

> I thought that it might be some good celestial spirit or some other shadow or spirit of a friend. . . . Then I prayed. My brother was at my side. . . . I grabbed a little holy water just in case and asked him, I said, "Who are you? What's your name?" He didn't answer me, nothing. I said, "What do you want here? Tell me, who are you?" The only thing he did was signal in the direction of my brother. Then I got cautious, realizing it could be the devil. I sprayed some holy water and swished in his face with a staff. Then he blew up like dynamite. . . . He began to bellow . . . like a bull.

According to Porfirio, when a curer is just beginning to learn the curing art, he is tempted by the devil to make a pact. This often takes the form of delivering the life of some loved one to Satan in exchange for money and power. If the novice accepts the devil's offer, he is bound for life and can never become a true curandero. Porfirio contends that only inferior shamans, those who do not have a natural gift for the healing and divining art, succumb to such temptations. A legitimate curandero is born a shaman and knows it. He does not need worldly wealth and influence since he is already a rich man who possesses a special gift (*don*). He can learn from other practitioners but is not dependent upon their approval or sanction. In fact, Porfirio prides himself on the fact that he has never worked as a curing assistant for any curandero. He says that after he realized his calling in life it took him seven years of practicing alone with his growing mesa before he was sufficiently strong to dominate the devil, with the guidance of the celestial spirits, the stars, the herbs, the minerals, and the archaeological objects of his mesa.

At about the time of his confrontation with the devil, Porfirio's
family moved to Oyotún, where he began to work as a hired hand
on the local estates. He apparently was diligent and hardworking.
As he got older he was given greater responsibilities, first as a cattle
boss and later as a *mayordomo*.

Porfirio's curing abilities emerged as he matured, leading to his
first cure sometime in his late teens or early twenties. One of his
sisters pleaded with him to cure her daughter, who was so badly
afflicted that she drooled uncontrollably and exuded a disgusting,
putrid odor. During the session Porfirio administered an herbal
purgative which caused his niece to vomit the undigested pieces of
an apple which had been infected with a sorcerer's curse.

Throughout his twenties, Porfirio did not do much curing since
he was too busy working and saving his money. However, in his
mid-to-late twenties a significant event occurred:

> I was working when I found myself in space. It was confusing with
> blue here, blue there in space. I wasn't on the earth. Then I entered
> a kind of *traga luz* [a place where light is sucked in or "swallowed"].
> [Question: "Was it like a tunnel?"]
> Yes, like a tunnel. I passed inside and then saw a huge throne. . . .
> I saw one seated there who frightened me a bit because he had a
> beard to here [motioning to his waist]. Only his eyes could be seen
> through his hair that he had to here [again, motioning to the waist].
> . . . They couldn't be seen very well, but they had a unique force.
> [Question: "Did he have a crown?"]
> No, what I asked myself was, "Could this be Christ? Who is he?"
> He made a sign to me meaning the Ten Commandments. It was the
> Eternal Father . . .
> [Question: "Did he say anything to you?"]
> Yes.
> [Question: "What did he say to you?"]
> "I am the Eternal Father." And, as he spoke, one heard
> "rrruuum."
> [Question: "Like thunder?"]
> Like thunder and a sound like many other things from beyond.

Porfirio had saved enough money to set up his own household
by the time he was in his thirties. He married, began renting land
to raise cattle and grow fruit, and eventually opened a small store.
He also began to cure on a regular basis. As the years passed and
his family grew (eventually numbering nine children), he made the
transition from farmer to merchant and vendor of herbal remedies. The time came, in the 1950s, when a move to Chiclayo, with

its large markets, was in order. Porfirio prospered in this thriving commercial center; at one time he had as many as six stands operating in the Central Market.

Porfirio's healing practice seems to have grown right along with his commercial ventures. Besides regular Saturday night sessions in his home, he was also often called away to other parts of the Chiclayo region to serve his patients. In recent years, the ravages of old age have forced Porfirio to curtail many of his activities, but he still holds regular sessions in his home and has an extensive clientele. It is clear that he will continue to heal until his dying day.[1]

Vidarte's Mesa

Christian ideology is very strong in Porfirio's mesa (Figure 6) symbolism and in his ritual. He refers to his ritual paraphernalia as a *mesa de gloria* (table of heaven). It is propped up on sawhorses facing the chapel mentioned above, in the eastern end of his courtyard. He considers his mesa an altar.

Although Porfirio recognizes the term Ganadero and knows that many curanderos have two major divisions of power objects, the Ganadero/Gloria dichotomy is not operative in his practice. Time and time again, while we were documenting his mesa, he stressed that for him everything on his altar formed a single, indivisible unity which is consecrated to good in the service of humankind. This is borne out by the referents of his artifacts. There is no clear grouping of negative icons on the left and positive icons on the right. Rather, there appears to be a balanced blending of curing and defensive power objects. Also, artifacts with a clearly defensive designation serve a deflective function which is subordinated to Porfirio's main goal—the healing of his patients. The major defensive artifacts, a *chonta* and a sword, are placed behind him to the right.

Porfirio's concept of the power behind the mesa objects is particularly interesting:

> They are nothing more than adornments. . . . The artifacts are for nothing more than activating the "genies"; then the genies take over the artifacts. . . . The songs serve as much to animate the genies spiritually as the spirit of the person who is going to be cured.

Porfirio's mesa is unified by a symmetrical pairing of many artifacts. This is most obvious with the staffs at the head of the mesa,

Figure 6 Vidarte Mesa

which are paired on opposite sides of the centrally positioned can of San Pedro brew as follows (moving from the outside inward toward the San Pedro container): Spanish Sword (right)/Sword of White Steel (left), used for defense against sorcerers' attacks; dagger (right)/cruciform lance head (left), for defense; Entwining Steel Serpent (right)/serpents of steel and wood (left), to eat supernatural illnesses; Aguaruna Indian *chonta* staffs (two on the right, two on the left), for cleansing and curing patients; two plexiglass "crystal" rods (one on each side of the San Pedro), for illuminating the mesa and the curing rituals.

The pairing continues with the artifacts spread out on the white cotton tablecloth: two smooth granite "Inca" stones for cleansing rituals; two light bulbs to give light; two virgins (Mary—on the right in wood—to provide Christian aid in curing, and the Virgin of Nature—in stone on the left—for calling up nature spirits or genies); two carved crystal bottles symbolizing lightning, which are used to raise the personal herb jars of patients; two spiral shells from archaeological sites, which absorb patients' maladies; two bivalve shells used by assistants and patients for raising the tobacco liquid, together with a silver-colored steel pinball accompanying the right-hand shell and a black ball to accompany the left-hand shell, both for protection; two open bivalve shells (the one on the right containing eight stones, the left containing a quartz crystal), used for a flowering or refreshment ritual in the morning at the end of the session; two mounted crystal balls which Porfirio calls "X rays," used for seeing hidden things, especially ailments; two chimes (like those used in the Catholic Mass) for activating the accounts or powers of the mesa in support of the healer's *tarjos*; four shells (two on each side) for divination; and four rattles (two on each side; one in bronze from an archaeological site, representing the past; and one made by Porfirio from a gourd, representing the present), which are used to activate the accounts of the mesa.

In addition to this pairing, a further indication of the unity principle governing Porfirio's mesa is the fact that, for the most part, power objects of different categories are not restricted to the left or right sides of the altar. For example, the tobacco and liquids for purification rituals are found on both sides; holy water and two types of perfume (in three bottles) are on the right, while on the left is a third perfume, an herb flower bottle (for purifications), sugar, and the white corn flour mixture (*refresco*). Holy personages from the Roman Catholic religion are located on each side of the mesa: a bronze statue of Saint James the Apostle helps the Virgin Mary (in wood) on the right; bronze statues of Saint Anthony (for finding lost or stolen objects), the Child of Prague (for sustaining both good and evil), and Saint Cyprian (governing the mesa along with Christ) are all placed on the left.

Herbal jars (*seguros*) also are not restricted to one side of the mesa. Three for promoting good luck are found on the left side, while one used in a purification ceremony, one for curing, and another prepared for a patient are on the right.

Animal figurines are more numerous on the right, including a bronze elephant to promote luck, a polar bear symbolizing the freezing qualities that Porfirio focuses against curses activated through fire, and a bronze bull for defense. However, a stone carving of monkeys, representing the trickery necessary to overcome the intrigues of sorcerers, is found among the staffs on the left; it is paired with the elephant among the right-hand staffs.

Supporting the defensive role of the staffs are a carved Soldier Stone and two small aerolitic Thunder Stones on the right, along with a large aerolitic stone dubbed "King" on the left. Symbols for light and illumination are found on both sides—there is a flashlight on the left and three quartz crystals on the right (which also symbolize San Pedro cacti and the divinatory clarity they provide).

Only a few artifacts lack counterparts on the opposite side of the mesa. Four stones on the left (two "maize," one "banana," and one "bean") from archaeological sites symbolize crop fertility. A Magnet Stone on the right symbolizes the attraction of good luck as does also a bottle of quicksilver (related to the discovery of mines and wealth). Finally, a Blood Ray Stone from an archaeological site is located on the left and is used to counter hemorrhages.

The central axis of Porfirio's mesa, running from the San Pedro can to the tobacco container in front of the curer's seat, contains all of the icons that encapsulate the ideology governing his ritual manipulation of power objects. The themes they share are those of light and regeneration, or transubstantiation. First comes the San Pedro, the catalytic agent for patient metamorphosis; it is followed by a huge block of quartz from a powerful mountain, symbolizing clarity and psychic insight. The theme of light and illumination is reinforced by the Crystal Star which guides the healer, and the Bronze Sunburst which helps him orient to the sun's movements.

Similarly related to light are the paired light bulbs, bottles, and crystals which parallel the central axis.

Christian rebirth symbolism is embodied in the wooden carving of Christ's face, the marble crucifix, and the combined *ara* (altar) stone and bottle associated with the Virgin Mary, all of which play key roles in Porfirio's performance of a Mass during a night session. The ideas of psychological completion and suspension (or undoing) of time involved in the notion of spiritual regeneration are expressed by the circular pre-Columbian Roll Stone, used to "disentangle" the patient from his personal problems, and by the pre-Columbian ceramic set (Roll-and-Square), which symbolizes the therapeutic dances performed around Porfirio's mesa. The three marble eggs at the foot of the ball and platform are graphic symbols of nurture, birth, and new life. At the base of the mesa's central axis, literally at the shaman's fingertips, is the tobacco potion, which reinforces the catalytic action of the San Pedro brew by "waking up" the patient and giving him "force."

In earlier years, besides using a traditional mesa, Porfirio was a practicing *espiritista* (spiritist medium). He used a round, three-legged wooden table, fitted together without nails, which is now kept in his chapel. The surface of the table has four concentric circles etched on it. The inner circle contains eight cabalistic symbols. The second circle holds three undeciphered inscriptions. The third and largest circle contains a six-pointed star and three "angels of light" (Jehovah, Elohim, Adonay), with three associated symbols. The fourth, outer circle is empty.

Porfirio officiates over his ritual like a priest performing the Mass. Donning a headband, a crucifix on a chain around his neck, and wearing a stole similar to that of a priest, he opens the session at about 10:00 P.M. by ringing the two bells on the mesa (left and right) and then sprays the artifacts four times with holy water. Then he crosses himself, mixes the tobacco liquid and serves his two assistants, who raise it four times in front of the mesa, facing the curer. One assistant performs the ritual on behalf of the mesa; the other does it for the San Pedro. During the raising, the curandero begins to pray softly. As the assistants finish the tobacco and retire to the chapel beyond the head of the mesa to the east, the praying becomes audible. Major invocations are made to the four cardinal points, the four winds, the four seasons, the three kingdoms of nature (animal, mineral, and vegetable), sacred springs, the eastern jungles, *chonta* staffs from the jungles, the seven winds of the lagoons of Las Huaringas, diamonds, crystals, pearls, churches, the seven virtues, and the seven "justices" of Christ (that is, the seven major deeds of his life).

After the opening prayers, Porfirio raises the tobacco two times, rings the two bells (the right first), and then performs his first song or *tarjo*, accompanied by a rattle from the right side of the mesa. This *tarjo* begins with a strange gurgling sound and ends with a prayer; no singing or whistling is involved. Once this is completed, the first assistant serves a cup of San Pedro to the healer, who prays over it, rings the two bells (right first), drinks, and then rubs the empty cup over his head. The assistant pours a second cup, hands it to Porfirio, who blesses it and returns it to this assistant to drink. Once the assistant has established his serving role, he acts as the mediator between Porfirio and his patients. By midnight, when all have been served the San Pedro, the healer rises, rubs his hands together, and flicks his arms in the direction of the four cardinal points.

After midnight the healer divines by throwing shells, rings the bell on the right side two times, and performs his first complete *tarjo* of the evening. This time the singing includes invocations addressed to Mary, Christ, and the Trinity, imploring them to use their white magic to protect the participants against a long list of hexes and curses. The closing statement, "With God and Holy Mary," is accompanied by one ring from the right-hand bell.

The Christian *tarjo* is reinforced by a long Christian prayer, lasting nearly one hour and performed by Porfirio standing up. When it is over, the healer raises the tobacco two times and chimes the right-hand bell two times while repeating the invocation, "With God and Holy Mary."

Again, Porfirio stands and delivers another long prayer, this time directed to "pagan" supernatural forces. He finishes, raises the tobacco two more times, and chimes the left-hand bell twice. San Pedro is served to everyone a second time, in the same order and with the same procedures as in the first serving.

At this point, Porfirio gives a long, two-part sermon. Included in the first part are the following "lessons": all men are brothers and equals; the world will return to the way it once was, with nation pitted against nation in bloodshed; those who see this approaching evil should speak up; to have the gift of psychic sight is a rare blessing; the ability to cure is a blessing, as is marriage; a thief must survive just as everyone else, robbing the rich is not a sin, but stealing from the poor is; the magical herbs will help farmers, herders, and merchants; the "occult sciences" can see into the future; demons come in the form of soldiers and animals; among others.

After a short break, the second part of the sermon warns against referring to Porfirio as a diviner; if he were, he could be rich with the treasures of the ancients. Peru is a country seated on a bench of gold; however, all her wealth goes outside the country. The mesa is the greatest thing in the world, with its staffs and *adornos* (adornments, i.e., artifacts). Many types of sickness are brought to the mesa, but all are curable. Porfirio is a representative of God, the Saints, and the Virgin, who actually carry out the cures.

The sermon ends and Porfirio serves a shell of the tobacco, prays over it for his first assistant, and ends by raising the assistant two times. The two assistants remove their overcoats, revealing white clothing underneath. Then the first assistant raises the healer two times, concentrating on the top of the head. Once this anointing is finished, Porfirio serves everyone in pairs so that they can raise each other in the same fashion.

There then follows a series of ritual dances. First, the principal patient is instructed to perform a shuffling two-step, counterclockwise around the mesa, while shaking his entire body as if he were discarding his malady. The curer provides the beat for the dance with the rattle from the left side of the mesa, held in his left hand. During the dance the principal assistant raises the tobacco, twice in front of the mesa and twice on the right side. At the end of the dance the curer raises the tobacco two times and rings each bell one time.

Standing up, Porfirio performs a fourth *tarjo* with only the rattle (no singing, no whistling). He then goes to the chapel, where an assistant serves him a third glass of San Pedro. Emerging, he sings a fifth *tarjo*, which refers to the four winds and pre-Columbian shrines (*huacas*).

When Porfirio is seated again, the main assistant stands facing him at the head of the mesa. Shaking his body and acting as though he were hyperventilating, the assistant dances counterclockwise around the mesa, followed by the curandero. As the dance party reaches each participant, the assistant looks into the patient's face and pronounces, "With God and the Holy Virgin"; the patient repeats the invocation.

Porfirio returns to his seat as his two assistants lead each person, supported at the elbows, in a dance around the mesa. Three counterclockwise circuits around the area are followed by three counterclockwise and three clockwise turns at the head of the mesa.

At about 3:00 A.M. the curer performs a sixth *tarjo* to summon the patients' *sombras* (shadows, spirits). Some patients are given the tobacco or a perfume to raise. There follows a lengthy series of spontaneous verbal interactions between the curer and his patients, involving a great deal of questioning, probing, and divination, interspersed with more dancing. This lasts until about 4:00 A.M. From then until nearly dawn Porfirio chats informally with the participants.

At dawn, Porfirio raises the patients and their herbal bottles or *seguros* with liquid from a *cristál* (crystal; a fancy, cut-glass perfume bottle containing special herbal potions or a special concoction from the healer's *seguro* for flowering). Then the patients raise their *seguros* with San Pedro, after which the curer drinks the last of the brew and sings a seventh and final *tarjo* consisting of prayers accompanied by rattling and ritual crying over the crucifixion of Christ.

Porfirio closes the session by spraying his mesa four times, each time with three perfumes. Between each spraying he whistles four times. Each patient then is sprayed four times with *refresco*. After this, the healer sprays the mesa and the four cardinal points with liquid from his *seguro*, crosses himself, and finishes with a simple "You are served."

6

Roberto Rojas

First Meeting

In 1979, I was back in Peru from late August to mid-November conducting a preliminary case study of the patients of Eduardo Calderón. By October, this project was progressing well and I was able to take time to follow up on the work done the previous year with the Chiclayo healers. By November, my colleague Donald Skillman had joined me to take over the research on Calderón's patients, which allowed me to concentrate on investigations with additional curers.

Time was short, but during the preceding months I had developed some new leads. During the filming of the documentary on Eduardo two years earlier, we were looking for a second curer's assistant to work with Eduardo and his brother Alberto. Eduardo's wife, Maria, who often served as the third member of the team, was nine months pregnant and could not be expected to do the job. A young man named Roberto Rojas, to whom we had been introduced by Alberto, initially indicated an interest, but subsequently declined. We learned from Alberto that Roberto's mentor was jealous of his assistants and had made it abundantly clear to the young apprentice that he was not to work for the competition.

Two years later, however, Roberto attended the first session that I documented with Eduardo in the new study. He was practicing on his own at the time and living in the Virú Valley about an hour to the south of Trujillo on the Pan-American Highway. We talked about getting together once I could get away from the project in Trujillo. That was in August; in November I was finally free to follow this lead. Fortunately, Eduardo's nephew was a good friend of Roberto and he was willing to take me to the shaman's home.

We were lucky to encounter Roberto in the town of Virú, saving the trip out to his house. In his early twenties, this pleasant, slightly unctuous youth was noticeably shorter than my guide, his peer. He was warm and hospitable, if a bit self-conscious about his developing career as a curer. It was not necessary to be subtle about the purpose of my visit, and within the hour we were out on the desert sands beyond the Virú oasis, on the chicken farm where Roberto held his sessions, documenting his mesa. Once this was finished, I asked about Roberto's next curing ritual. A session was scheduled for a few days later, and I was invited to attend.

The night of the session I made the rendezvous with Roberto, accompanied by my colleague Don Skillman. We arrived at about 9:00 P.M. and found Roberto chatting with a friend, Rodrigo López, while sharpening the glass point of one of his mesa lances over a fire. In the dimly lit hut he invited us to sit on a nearby bench. Don accepted the offer, and ended up sitting on the newly sharpened lance point!

Although the wound was clean, the point having been sterilized in the fire, we decided Don needed medical care and so excused ourselves from that night's session. We managed to stop the bleeding, but the trip back to the Pan-American Highway was difficult—two foreigners, one with bloody jeans, out on the desert in the middle of the night are not the sort of hitchhikers that passing trucks and buses are likely to pick up. We eventually straggled into the emergency ward of Trujillo's University Hospital at midnight.

Several days later, I finally attended a full session with Roberto, although Don Skillman declined the pleasure of our company! However, another colleague, Rafael Reichert, professor of art history at Fresno State University, joined us for the evening.

I returned to work with Roberto in July 1980 and again in February 1988. Roberto's story is troubling in a way those of my other informants are not, in that his development as a curandero was significantly shaped by an apprenticeship to a sorcerer. My first ritual experience with Roberto, documented below, revealed a hostile and paranoid side to curanderismo that I had not witnessed previously, and which I preferred not to explore in greater depth.

Biography

Roberto Rojas Tacía was born in 1956 in the northern highland city of Cajamarca. His first four years were spent in the countryside, where he was exposed to his mother's extensive knowledge of herbs. She died when Roberto was only six, but he continued to learn herbal lore from his father's brother, who assisted in the boy's upbringing.

In spite of the fact that his relatives were herbalists who did not cure with a mesa, Roberto found himself throughout his childhood accumulating objects that had a special attraction for him. Some of these later formed part of his first mesa. However, it was not until he was ten that he actually witnessed a curing ritual conducted with a mesa. During the divination he was able to "see" the people who had put the curse on the patient, Roberto's cousin.

Roberto was so intrigued by the curer's rituals that a few nights later he tried imitating the songs and invocations that he had heard. As a result, he claimed, "The spells and mountains began to open, and I found myself entering, and I began to enter a palace." It turned out that the healer he was imitating was a sorcerer who had made a pact with the devil. His spells were malignant and dangerous. The palace contained "a monster, a ghost bleeding from the face." Roberto was frightened out of his wits. He ran for his life, barely escaping before the mountain closed its passages and captured his soul.

Fascinated by the world that had been revealed to him, Roberto, then in his teens, sought to learn more by working as an assistant for local shamans. One of those shamans divined that the young novice would eventually become the apprentice of a renowned coastal practitioner.

In his early teens Roberto had a dream about a powerful black bull bearing a mysterious book. When he related his dream to one of the shamans he was assisting, he was told that this was a sign that he must make a pact with the devil. He was instructed to bathe in the blood of a black chicken and a black cat at midnight, while the sorcerer invoked "The Enemy," so that Roberto could then sign a pact in blood.

Although quite susceptible to the idea, Roberto was hesitant to follow the sorcerer's advice. Upon conferring with his herbalist uncle, he was told that such a pact was unnecessary—the assembling of the proper *seguro* of herbs was all the pact he needed. The herbs themselves would bond with his soul and provide the necessary guidance for him to be able to cure.

Thus, during his impressionable adolescence a major conflict began in Roberto's life: the tension between two approaches to therapy. On the one hand was the tradition of harmony and growth, represented by the natural herbalism practiced by his mother and other relatives. On the other was the legacy of power and mystery embraced by the local sorcerers in selling their souls to the Prince of Darkness. In essence, Roberto had begun to wrestle with the age-old human dilemma—choosing whether or not to sell his birthright.

Apparently, Roberto's father was busy with the burden of raising six children alone and had little time for his son's psychological turmoil. Occasional advice from his uncle was hardly enough to provide a consistent role model for the troubled teenager. In 1972, at the age of fifteen, Roberto left Cajamarca and moved to Trujillo in search of the coastal shaman who it was divined would be his teacher. He began working as a waiter in the temporary restaurants that accompanied regional fairs. He eventually became a cook's assistant and then a cook. He finally settled down in Trujillo with a steady job at a local restaurant. This allowed him to resume his schooling, but the constant demands of his fluctuating work schedule eventually led him to quit high school before finishing the third year.

At this frustrating point in his life, when he was seventeen, Roberto met a well-known Trujillo sorcerer, a charismatic, mercurial individual noted for his brash, outspoken manner with patients and his tyrannical treatment of assistants. Roberto's landlady had suffered a sudden fit of bizarre behavior and was taken by her family to the sorcerer. Roberto helped them get her to the session and offered to assist the shaman. During the session, much of his earlier learning came back to him and he was very helpful in effecting the cure. After the evening ritual, the healer invited him to work as an assistant.

Roberto worked for the sorcerer for the next three years. However, although he learned a great deal, they were stormy years, indeed! On several occasions he left his teacher, swearing that he would never return. One time, he left because he and the other assistants were disgruntled when the shaman did not pay them their fair share of clients' fees. On another occasion Roberto returned to Cajamarca where he held his first independent session for his aunt, uncle, cousins, brother, and sister-in-law. The cure was successful, but the sorcerer responsible for the curse countered with a *golpe* (blow) directed against Roberto. He became sick and had to return to the coast and humbly seek the services of his teacher. When he was cured, Roberto had to pay off the debt by working for his mentor. Eventually, they had a serious falling-out, exacerbated by a good deal of malicious gossip.

When I began working with Roberto in Virú in 1979, he was engaged to be married and was farming a small plot owned by his future father-in-law. He had been practicing as a curer on his own for two years. His clients were drawn from the rustic farmers of the area. In observing his rituals, it was apparent that he was strongly influenced by his teacher, who had met Roberto's need for a role model. This, despite the fact that, shortly before leaving his mentor, Roberto had located in Ferreñafe the famous coastal shaman whom he had sought in his teens.

Roberto related that, soon after beginning to work on his own, he had another encounter with the devil during a session at the foot of Napo Mountain:

> I called him because the case was going badly and I needed backup; all I wanted was for him to back me up. But the only thing he said to me was that he didn't have any reason to back me up because I hadn't made any contract, there was no pact with him. He told me that, if I wanted to have a pact with him, I should deliver one of my sick patients to him.
>
> I told him that he couldn't touch a single one of my patients, that the only payment I was going to give him, all I offered him was tobacco, so that he would take care of those who were against me. "My enemies who are trying to tempt me, they are the ones that I will cede to you, but in my work, if you ask me for X, no way."
>
> [Question: "And what happened?"]
>
> I gave him the payment of tobacco and he backed up my account in the morning, and I sent him back to his charm, to his mountain with the account that if he found any temptation or curse with which they had cursed me that he carry them away, make them retreat.

Roberto went on to describe the devil as appearing first in the form of a large goat and then, transformed, as a mulatto with horns and a tail, riding a vicious coffee-brown horse chafing at the bit. The reader may recall that Ruperto Navarro, like Roberto, told of bending Satan to his will.

In 1980, Roberto married his fiancée. He continued to work on his father-in-law's land until 1981, when he began practicing as a full-time shaman. It seems that Roberto had not totally mastered the curing art, however. When I revisited him in February 1988, he confided that he had been unsuccessful in defending against an

attacking sorcerer and, as a result, had been forced to stop using a
mesa for two years. During that time he was treated twice by the
famous Ferreñafe shaman whom Roberto had once sought as a
mentor. One session was held in the vicinity of the powerful Mulatto Mountain, the second at the foot of Chaparrí Mountain. He
also took advantage of this hiatus in his own curing to learn more
herbal lore, and he made several collecting trips to lagoons in the
highlands to the east of Cascas.

By about 1984, he had assembled a new mesa and resumed his
curing practices. He also began planning a trip to the Aguaruna
Indian country with his Ferreñafe benefactor, a trip which was
postponed because of an accident the old man had suffered.

In 1986, Roberto became acquainted with one of the famous
curers of Las Huaringas. He met the shaman at a second residence
the old man had built near Chiclayo. The relationship between the
two was just developing when the veteran healer died of diabetes
in 1987.

When I saw Roberto again in 1988, he had constructed a house
in Virú and was the proud father of four children. He was holding
regular sessions as a shaman, working not only in Virú, but also in
Trujillo, Cascas, Chiclayo, Chimbote, Huamachuco, and Lima. His
adolescence behind him, he had clearly chosen his path in life.

Rojas's Mesa

Prior to 1982, Roberto's first mesa (Figure 7) was very crowded;
even he thought it needed to be simplified. The numerous power
objects were systematically organized into two major sections: *mesa
negra* (or Ganadera) to the left, and *mesa blanca* to the right. The
latter division was alternately designated *mesa de gloria* (of heaven),
mesa yerbatera (herbal), *mesa del astro* (of the star—i.e., star lore related to one's destiny), and *mesa del imán* (of the magnet—i.e., of
luck or fortune attracted by the magnet). As will become apparent,
all the artifacts associated with fortune or fate clustered together
into a distinct subdivision of the Mesa Blanca that could reasonably
be interpreted as an incipient middle field. Roberto called this ill-
defined section of the mesa the *centro medio* (middle center) and
suggested that it "dominates" the left and "defends" the right.

After indicating the two containers at the head of the mesa (the
larger one for brewing San Pedro, the smaller for preparing herbal
potions) and the white cloth on which everything rests, Roberto

Figure 7 Rojas Mesa, 1979

described his power objects, starting with the right side and often clustering many of the artifacts together. First came eleven "staffs" at the head of the right section: three bows (one with an inset crystal); four arrows; two lances (one steel, one of wood); one small wooden serpent; and a smooth branch of a quince bush. The weapons were used to defend the right side of the mesa, while the serpent and the tree branch were used in cleansing rituals.

The staffs were followed by a grouping of "saints" and related religious paraphernalia: a framed print of the guardian angel who protects children; a wooden statue of Saint Anthony for finding lost objects; a plaster-of-paris statue of the Christ of Prague for curing children; a set of religious books; a crucifix; a wooden statue of Saint Cyprian in his role as Christian martyr, to balance Cyprian as sorcerer on the left side; a limestone statue of Christ on his throne as King of Heaven; and a lead portrait face of Christ which worked together with the crucifix in governing the powers of heaven on the right.

The cluster of objects on the right that best demonstrated why Roberto designated that as the side of the herbs consisted of herbal concoctions and related *materia medica*—found there were *seguros* for luck, health, love, and soul loss, as well as perfumes and powders for refreshing patients and the mesa.

The largest set of right-side artifacts included those objects relating to "minerals" and good fortune: a magnifying glass with a crystal globe and magnetized stone on top, symbolizing lagoons and associated "orchards" (*huertas*) of herbs with their power to attract good luck; seven crystal chandelier ornaments representing tears and fertilizing rain, as well as having the ability to invoke stars associated with the patient's soul and destiny; a rock crystal from White Mountain; a marble imitation pre-Columbian Chavín ceramic piece used to promote the curer's luck; a mineral stone; a bronze tourist *tumi*; two magnets (one of steel, one of stone) for attracting good fortune; an aluminum Venus figure and shell called a "queen" or governess of mineral charms; two Buddhas (one of aluminum, one of marble) to promote business; a marble egg used to enhance the fertility of chicken farmers' poultry; the tusk of a sea lion to bring success to fishermen; two lead hands to bring money to business ventures; two small silver shells to attract wealth; a skull stone to balance the human skull on the left side of the mesa; a wooden bull for fertility and to balance the bull stone on the left; and an Aguaruna Indian shell necklace to work in conjunction with the Aguaruna "staffs" at the head of the mesa.

The remaining objects on the right side of the mesa were mainly utilitarian in nature: two tin cups to serve San Pedro, two tin bowls to serve the tobacco, a bell for marking the stages of a cleansing ritual, and a gourd rattle made by Roberto for activating the powers or accounts of the right with the help of a harmonica.

"Staffs" at the head of the left-side Mesa Negra included (from right to left): a wooden statue of the "Inca King"; a curved Steel Serpent Rod and a straight Steel Bull Rod, both for Roberto's personal protection; two short serpent *chontas* for "tying" and "untying" spells; ten bamboo Aguaruna lances for launching attacks against sorcerers; a deer's hoof to drive off people bothering the patient; a pre-Columbian *chonta* which when sprayed with cane alcohol protected against attacks from ghosts of the past; and an iron rod and spur for making sparks, used in conjunction with the skull in order to dominate infernal forces.

Another group of objects consisted of pre-Columbian artifacts: a rattle for activating the charms of the left; clay whistles for calling the spirits; eight ceramic figurines for controlling the forces of the left or for rendering *golpes* (blows); two shells for serving tobacco; a *tumi* and two bronzes at the head of the mesa and to the left of the rod and spur for cleansings; two stone axe heads for *golpes*; and a skull for invoking the spirits of the dead. These objects from the past were supplemented by books on black magic, a lead statue of Cyprian as sorcerer, and a bottle of the tobacco liquid.

The remaining fifty-four objects were stones—mostly from ancient ruins—which dominated the entire left side. Many of the largest (at the far left) were from magical or powerful mountains (Napo, Calavera, Negro, Dos Puntas, Vinzos, Huandoy), all considered to be loci for the forces of darkness; these forces occasionally manifest themselves as animals (most frequently as a black bull, but also as an owl, greyhound, wolf, whale, serpent, and condor). These large fragments of powerful mountains were literally designated as *cerros* (mountains), not as stones. The same term is applied to mesa stones by Jorge Merino (see Chapter 12). A few stones used in curing represented blood and human body parts affected by sorcery (e.g., brain, foot, eyes, stomach, and kidneys). Two flints in this grouping were used to produce sparks to burn the forces causing the patient's malady.

Finally, as an extension of the Ganadero, Roberto also had a *contra mesa* (counter mesa) in front of the main altar. It was composed of three skulls and a *chonta* from a pre-Hispanic tomb. It was used to draw off the negative energies associated with a sorcerer's attack.

Roberto's new mesa (Figure 8) is evenly divided into two halves, Gloria and Ganadero. However, twenty of his staffs are on the right side, Gloria, and only two, Swordfish and Steel Serpent, pertain to Ganadero. Those at the head of Banco Gloria, from right to left, are: the Guayacán Staff; two steel Justice Staffs; a Dolphin Dagger; two hollow imbibing *chontas* for serving perfume; two Skull Staffs for cleansing those possessed by spirits; a Warrior Staff; a Bronze Condor Staff to guide the shaman; a Lance of Light to clarify the seer's vision; the King Staff, considered the herbal center; an Aguaruna Arrow; the Saint Cyprian Staff, classified as the "center of the mesa"; another King Staff for good luck; an Aguaruna Bow; an Aguaruna Arrow; a Dragon Staff; and two *chontas*. The weapons are for defense, while the staffs are for cleansing. At the foot of the right-hand staffs is a carved algarrobo head, a *Tucuricoc* ("chief" in Quechua), considered to be the "center" and "guardian" of the mesa.

Figure 8 Rojas Mesa, 1988

As one would expect, the herbs, in two huge *seguros madrigueros* ("of the burrow, den, lair"; see Chapter 12), are on the right. A gourd rattle, a harmonica, and a brass bell are used in the songs for Gloria. A metallic crowned head of Christ symbolizes His presence in association with the herbs. Roberto no longer uses a crucifix.

Unusual artifacts for the right include a Giant Snake Stone, the *guardián del yerbatero*, and a protective Owl Stone. A lead Daughter of Venus Shell holds the ingredients used to *refrescar* (refresh) or *florecer* (flower) patients at the end of the session. A piece of iron pyrites is used to promote good luck. A marble egg is used to help chicken farmers have fertile hens. Two spiral shells are used to "untie" spells.

The rest of the Gloria side is taken up by crystals, which occupy most of the space allotted to this banco. These crystals are mostly naturally occurring stones: a huge, clear quartz crystal in the upper right corner; a yellow quartz near the Snake Stone; a cluster of crystals above the head of Christ; and six clear crystals near the rattle used for making sparks. These are complemented by man-made glass objects which are also classified as *cristales* or *diamantes*: a bull, two goblets, a crystal ball, and an image of Christ. A large number of perfume essences (not shown) also can be found on the right side.

The largest cluster of objects on the left side of the new mesa consists of eighteen pre-Columbian "Warrior" Ceramics that form Roberto's "army" of spirits, helping him to cure curses and ailments associated with pre-Hispanic ruins. The next largest group includes stones from pre-Columbian sites used to "counter-arrest" the attacks of sorcerers: a Skull Stone; a Mace-Head Stone (paired with a Bronze Mace-Head); two Sea Stones; two Seashell Stones; a Yellow Ray; a White Ray Stone; a Black Ray Stone; a Mule-Hoof Stone; and two *golpe* stones. Instrumental artifacts include a gourd rattle for Ganadero songs, two pre-Columbian bronze chisels for cleansings, and a variety of implements used for raising the tobacco (these include two hollow bull horns, two shells from pre-Hispanic ruins, and three hollow sea lion teeth). A deer's hoof is for driving off "The Enemy." Two bronze snakes are used for defense, for cleansings, and for undoing spells. The skull and shark jaw are used for curing cases of spiritism.

Roberto's ritual consists of a cumulative power build-up, symbolized by the progressive activation of the divisions of the mesa. Once the entire mesa is "charged," the accumulated power is "discharged" or ritually transmitted to the patient. Prior to 1982, the phases of Roberto's session were as follows:

1 After the mesa was assembled, Roberto invoked the four cardinal points and "opened" the right side representing Gloria (heaven) and the *yerbas* (herbs) through a series of songs. Although the order seemed to vary, ideally subsections of the right side were activated in turn, beginning with the saints and ending with the herbs, especially the San Pedro. The latter was also raised with tobacco by the healer and his assistants. Activating the herbs was referred to as "opening the orchards."

2 Roberto then opened the charms on the left or Ganadero side, which represented the forces associated with sorcery. The song used to activate this side invoked the Aguaruna Indians, a subtribe of the Jívaro/Shuar, who formerly were headhunters.

3 Roberto activated the mesa in general by serving the San Pedro. As each patient was served, the healer prayed, sang, and played the harmonica, ending the series of acts by spraying the mesa with perfume. The ritual was punctuated by the ringing of a bell.

4 Roberto served the tobacco and performed *limpias* (cleansings). While each patient raised tobacco, the healer prayed, sang, and divined. After the divination, the patient was sprayed with perfume. The bell again marked the stages of the ritual.

5 After a closing song addressed to the two fields of the mesa, and a ritual dance performed by the patients, Roberto sprayed the mesa and the patients with perfume.

One aspect of Roberto's pre-1982 ritual showed the influence of the sorcerers he has known in his life, particularly the man who tutored him in the use of a mesa. During the cleansing of patients in the early morning hours, Roberto frequently performed the delivering of a *golpe* (blow) against the sorcerer responsible for a particularly strong curse. Grabbing his iron serpent from the head of his mesa and the skull from the Ganadero, Roberto would charge into the open and engage in an aggressive spirit battle with his adversary. He would curse, yell, and throw the skull and serpent staff at the enemy, unseen except by him.

This dramatic battle, performed for difficult cases, also is found among other shamans, although the specific techniques employed vary according to the personality and style of the healer. Roberto's battle was distinguished by its long duration and paranoid quality—something I learned during my first session with him.

Early that night Roberto chewed on a cud of herbs which he informed his clients was very potent. As the evening progressed his manner became progressively more domineering. At about 3:00 A.M., while Roberto was treating a patient, a gunshot rang out far away across the plain. This sparked Roberto to release an angry, venomous monologue that lasted until the end of the session. He interpreted the shot as an effort by a neighboring shaman to disrupt his session; this caused Roberto to fly into a rage and to perform a *golpe* with his serpent and skull. When he returned to his place at the mesa, rather than resuming the cleansing ritual as other shamans might, Roberto began to brood over the "attack." From that point on he simply lost control over the proceedings. He ranted and raved about his "opponent," and boasted of his own superiority; he belittled his assistants, bullied his patients, and engaged in long diatribes about the unconquerable power of darkness and destruction.

Roberto never got that session back on track. Dawn, by which time mesas should be deactivated, came and went. The young practitioner became totally absorbed in cursing his enemies. After sunrise these curses became more formal and ritualized. Finally, at about 8:00 A.M., after a polite reminder that some of us had to catch a bus to Trujillo, Roberto closed the account. However, he was still huddled over his mesa, dark circles under his eyes, muttering curses, when we left. The sorcerer's apprentice truly let the spells get out of hand!

When I later worked with Roberto again I noticed that his ritual had changed considerably. A major difference is that he no longer raises tobacco during a session. Instead, he and his patients imbibe *agua florida* when circumstances require. Roberto believes that the negative influence of a sorcerer's attack is countered with the "*pura dulzura*" (pure sweetness) of the perfumed water. The use of *agua florida* is reinforced by adding expensive perfume essences for the morning *florecimiento* (flowering), performed by Roberto for all his patients at the close of his ritual.

The last session I observed with Roberto turned out to be "*una noche muy pesada*" (a very "heavy" evening). It was held inside (although outdoors is preferred) with the mesa against the east wall of the room. At a certain point, Roberto asked me to turn off the tape recorder and not use my flashlight for note-taking because the last half of the session was not progressing normally (the flashlight had a very disruptive effect as the strong San Pedro served by Roberto took effect). With these fieldwork limitations in mind, what follows is a rough approximation of Roberto's ritual:

1 After midnight Roberto begins with a long prayer (accompanied by the rattle) which first opens the "orchard" of San Pedro and the magical herbs; and it then activates the Ganadero.
2 About twenty minutes later Roberto sings his first *tarjo*, invoking the names of his patients.
3 At about 1:00 A.M. Roberto serves the San Pedro. First, everyone is instructed to breathe out heavily in unison. Then, one by one, each drinks a glass of the brew after a prayer by the shaman. Roberto drinks last.
4 Staffs are distributed to patients. Each comes forward, pays the healer a token fee (the prescribed fees are paid in the morning), receives a staff, and begins to cleanse him/herself to the rhythm of the healer's rattle.
5 There follows a long silence, punctuated occasionally by the sound of the shaman's rattle.
6 For about another half an hour Roberto sporadically rattles, whistles, chants, blows, and addresses the devil, during which

he queries and taunts Satan while forming his Ganadero "battalions."

7 By about 2:00 A.M. Roberto sings a beautiful *tarjo* that he learned from Eduardo Calderón relating the life of Jesus Christ. A type of Christian sermon follows.

8 The next *tarjo* is like a war chant in which Roberto prepares to take on his adversary.

9 By about 2:30 A.M. Roberto has everyone raise *agua florida* from the palms of their hands.

10 Roberto acknowledges the entrance of the spirit of his current mentor, the Ferreñafe shaman. By this time his voice has taken on a distinctly older-sounding tonal quality. As the San Pedro and the two herbal mixtures that he uses take effect, he quivers and hyperventilates.

11 The "magnetism" and power of Saturn are now invoked.

12 By about 2:45 A.M. Roberto invokes the warlike qualities of the planet Mars and begins "forming" his own spirit.

13 At about 3:00 A.M. Roberto raises his Aguaruna Bow with *agua florida*.

14 Shortly after activating the bow, Roberto plays his harmonica to accentuate the effects of the herbs.

15 At about 3:15 A.M. everyone again raises *agua florida*.

16 At about 3:30 A.M. Roberto acknowledges the arrival of the spirit of an Aguaruna shaman who works with his Ferreñafe teacher.

17 At about 3:45 A.M. Roberto makes sparks with his crystals to counter the effects of attacking sorcerers.

18 The remainder of the morning is taken up with occasional self-cleansings by patients, vomiting, sporadic divination by Roberto, and occasional raisings and sprayings of perfume.

19 By about 6:30 A.M. Roberto performs cleansings for the patients and sprays them with perfume.

20 At about 10:00 A.M. Roberto closes the account.

One of Roberto's colleagues described the transformation that occurred whenever their sorcerer-teacher activated his pact with the devil. It correlates well with the behavioral changes I observed in Roberto during his session:

> The voice is transformed; it gets increasingly hoarse. His attitude changes, his manner of conversing, of expressing himself is changed.
>
> [On some occasions] the smallest thing sets him off ranting and raving and he becomes fierce and ill-tempered. That is the "current" that is felt when the pact is invoked.
>
> The whole mesa acquires that current which comes with the spirit. The whole mesa is "pacted," all the artifacts begin to oscillate as if they were expanding and contracting like sponges.

One feels different. It's like a current that one feels here in one's whole body. Even the assistants feel it because, when the spirit enters into the Ganadero, one feels as if a person passes and a current enters the body. And one feels like a superman, even though one is only an assistant.

Roberto's colleague then related why he has no desire to use the power associated with a pact:

The business of the pact is very fierce. It is a very strong spirit and the *maestro* who dominates it has to dominate it totally because there comes a time when the devil himself dominates the *maestro* and knocks him down right there at his very mesa. He punishes him, betrays him or induces him to do evil things. The devil wins.

7
Rodrigo López

First Meeting

When I began working with Roberto Rojas in November 1979, Eduardo's brother, Alberto, told me about another healer, Rodrigo López, who was a friend of Roberto. Alberto said that they had both worked as assistants for the same practitioner and had begun working on their own at about the same time. In his practice, Rodrigo commuted between Trujillo and the town of Túcume, near Chiclayo. Alberto commented that Rodrigo was *"muy caballero,"* very gentlemanly.

The night of my abortive first session with Roberto, Rodrigo López had been the friend who was visiting with the young shaman (see Chapter 6). Rodrigo had a quiet confidence about him, and was, as Alberto had said, very much a gentleman. Before Skillman and I began our long hike back to Virú that night, I obtained Rodrigo's address and made an appointment to meet with him on the evening of his next session, a few nights later.

Rodrigo was staying at the home of another curer, Helmer Aguilar (see Chapter 8), a fisherman who lived near Trujillo. On the appointed evening I found Rodrigo at the Aguilar home. He introduced me to Helmer, who struck me as bright, articulate, and energetic. Helmer offered to accompany me and explain Rodrigo's rituals.

The site of the session was a small farm in the countryside near the town of Moche. We shared a taxi to the nearest point on the Pan-American Highway, and then walked across the fields to the farm. Once we arrived, while Rodrigo removed his mesa from a storage shed, Helmer showed me objects from his own mesa, which was stored alongside Rodrigo's. He told me that Rodrigo, Roberto, and one of Rodrigo's assistants for the night, Nilo Plasencia (see Chapter 10), had all been tutored by the same shaman and had recently begun practicing on their own. Helmer had also worked with this teacher, but had learned from a number of other healers as well.

The session went very well for me. As I taped and took notes, I had Helmer right at my elbow explaining everything. My job had never been easier! This ease continued for the next few days as I worked at Helmer's house, documenting Rodrigo's mesa, clarifying notes and recordings of the ritual, and taping his biography.

The following June 1980 we met again at Helmer's house for a couple of days of follow-up. What I found particularly interesting was that, in spite of the fact that these two shamans and Roberto had all had the same teacher, their mesas and rituals were all different. Helmer's story is told in the next chapter. The story below is what I learned from Rodrigo.

Biography

Rodrigo López Inoñan was born in 1946 in the town of Motupe, where he attended school until the end of his third year of high school. When he was seventeen, an illness in the family forced his parents to return to their hometown of Túcume where they could count on the support of relatives and friends. Rodrigo was forced to leave school at that time and go to work in the fields to help with the family finances.

After about a year, Rodrigo began commuting to the departmental capital, Lambayeque, where he worked for seven years in a cotton factory. There he developed skills as a machine repairman, a welder, and an electrician. Along the way he also learned the work of a tailor.

Several uncles on his mother's side of the family were healers. As a result, during his childhood Rodrigo was often taken to sessions and shown the basics of curing by his uncles. Also, on a number of occasions his mother was cured, and he also was treated for soul loss.

In his late teens Rodrigo was exposed to curing when his aunts and uncles from Chiclayo would come to Túcume for sessions with local healers, one of whom had a national reputation. When Rodrigo was twenty he was cured for a twisted face, the result of a curse placed on him after an argument with a woman.

For a brief time Rodrigo worked as a curer's assistant for the famous Túcume shaman, but he did not become serious about this work until he was in his mid-twenties. At that time he met a shaman who had moved to Túcume from Olmos in order to work with the healer whom Rodrigo was assisting. This man from Olmos was the same one who eventually trained Roberto Rojas. Although he settled in Túcume, the newcomer was an itinerant practitioner with a large clientele in Trujillo. He and Rodrigo got along well and as a result of their friendship Rodrigo decided to work with him, commuting regularly to Trujillo with his new teacher.

Other journeys became a regular part of Rodrigo's life in the 1970s—initiatory pilgrimages to sacred lagoons in the highlands to bathe, to collect herbs, and to hold night sessions. These trips were organized by the famous Túcume shaman for a select group of practitioners, among them Rodrigo's mentor, and their assistants. Participation was by invitation only. Before their departure, invited shamans were required to present lists of participants at a special ritual session, during which the host shaman "presented" the future pilgrims to the charms that were to be encountered.

The first trip, in 1972, was to Páramo Blanco. The actual lagoon dried up many years ago, but there is still a spring-fed stream in the area which forms a waterfall into a depression in the highland plain, resulting in a small semitropical oasis.

The group arrived at noon and the host shaman saluted the charms of the area with an offering of perfume. He then bathed under the waterfall. The same procedure was followed by each of the shamans, and then by their assistants. As each person emerged, he was sprayed with perfume by the one who had preceded him. The rest of the day was spent gathering herbs to fill *seguros* and collecting water from the sacred stream. That night, a mesa was held by the presiding shaman, who raised the luck of each person present, beginning with the shamans and ending with their assistants. He also introduced the group to the charms of the stream. The trip left a deep impression on Rodrigo:

> The stream impressed me a great deal, looking at the waterfall and seeing the reflection of the sun's rays, at times brief glimpses of sun in the waterfall and shining on the water. I had heard that the *maestro* said that a rainbow forms in Páramo Blanco where the light of the sun . . . shines, and I saw the rainbow that was formed, that was drawn by the solar rays in the water. One could see the rainbow reflected and it was beautiful, a beautiful impression. At that time I was influenced with regard to the life I was going to live later on. I held onto these impressions for myself.

A year later, the group traveled to Mishahuanga Lagoon. The

same ritual format was followed. This time, however, during the night session, when the presiding shaman introduced the group to the charms of the lagoon, Rodrigo's impressions were even stronger—resulting in a vision:

> At that point it was seen that the lagoon was transformed, that is, one was looking at the water, and one didn't see water anymore. Instead, one could see houses—because the lagoon is immense, it's big—one could see houses and people inside.
> [Question: "Modern houses?"]
> Colonial-style houses, and there were people inside, good friends, and one could see that they called us, they invited us inside, but we had the idea that we were seeing a charm and we could not enter. We were afraid, since the *maestro* had said that one can remain in the charm and can become "enchanted." Being afraid, we were less impressed.
> But one man was overcome, and went into the water. The *maestro* realized what was happening and yelled, "Grab him! Because he's up to his knees, and if he gets in any deeper no one should get in because they can remain there as well." Then, as quickly as he could, another guy jumped in and pulled the man out by his sweater. The lagoon had overcome him, since he had been concentrating on it, and he went straight in. He could have drowned, and the *maestro* said that the serpent was lurking out there. It was a huge serpent.

After introducing everyone to the lagoon, the shaman sat quietly on the shore for a while. The lagoon became transformed and animals began to take shape.

> They were like monsters. Whatever he said took shape. When he said a goat would appear, a goat would appear, or a chicken. Near the shore of the lagoon there was a rock, and that rock transformed into animals. We heard the water, and the *maestro* said that it was the snake swimming around. He said that the snake was a *maestro* who came to the lagoon to bathe since he was a *maestro*. What happened? The lagoon overcame him. He became enchanted, and remained there.

Offerings of wine were made to the serpent and the "kings" and "queens" of the lagoon. The water began to bubble, and the shaman exclaimed that the lords of the lagoon were drinking the offerings.

Beyond the main lagoon there is a string of smaller tarns and these "began to shine, like light bulbs." The *maestro* said, "These are my lagoons. My Saint Anthony is also coming from there, and one could see a great light coming."

These trips had a profound effect on Rodrigo. To this day, his

ritual is built around the concept of "bringing the queens" from
Páramo Blanco and Mishahuanga to his mesa to effect his cures
(see Giese [1989:98, 141, 159, 160, 177] for more on queens and
Mishahuanga).

In 1975, 1976, and 1977 Rodrigo made three more pilgrimages
with his teacher to the highlands, each time to visit the healer of
the Shimbe Lagoon. Although these trips were more for specific
curing sessions than for training, one of them did involve a dem-
onstration of the charms of Shimbe:

> As a result of the effects of the remedy, I began to see the charms, to
> see the mesa artifacts transformed in the air. You could see the fig-
> ures of the artifacts. You could see dragons and snakes that were
> formed, and you could see lights that emerged from the mountains.
> Whatever the *maestro* mentioned took shape. At times a cluster of
> stars formed which the *maestro* called a park, and we saw the heart of
> Jesus take shape.

In 1978, after seven years of apprenticeship, Rodrigo felt he had
learned his herbal lore and so he assembled an adequate mesa to
begin practicing on his own. His first cure involved a girl brought
to him by her mother for what the family thought were heart problems. During the session, Rodrigo divined that the girl had fallen
from a horse at the foot of a pre-Columbian ruin. The fright
caused by the fall had brought on soul loss, and the girl's spirit had
become imprisoned in the ruin. After the divination, Rodrigo
raised the girl with tobacco and called back her soul. By the next
evening, as Rodrigo tells it, the patient was perfectly normal and
suffered no further attacks.

After setting up his own practice, Rodrigo continued to com-
mute between Túcume, where he had a wife, son, and three
daughters, and Trujillo. He also began to make trips to Lima,
where he slowly started to build up a clientele.

Unlike most of the shamans encountered thus far, Rodrigo has
never experienced any unusual psychological crisis related to his
shamanism. As we have seen, a common way such a crisis manifests
itself is in the form of a temptation by the devil. With regard to
such an experience, Rodrigo says, "I am a son of God, and I work
with the blessing of God. Before working I invoke God the Divine
and perhaps for this reason I have never had a confrontation with
the devil to make a pact." He attributes his ability to operate a mesa
to a strong desire to learn, and an "aspiration to cure." Unusual

events only occurred on pilgrimages or during sessions with his tutor when, due to the action of San Pedro, Rodrigo experienced, "apparitions of spirits, or the mountains burned or there were noises of animals growling or of horses . . . or voices of people." Regarding the effect of San Pedro, he pointed out that during a session it is, "guiding the curer and indicating what he ought to do, what he should not do, or if he can cure a patient, or if he can't cure him, or predict the future. . . . Therefore, we herbalists in general work with San Pedro, which is the principal base of all curing."

It is interesting to note the contrast between the character and philosophy of Rodrigo and that of his colleague, Roberto Rojas. Both of them served long apprenticeships under the same man, with Rodrigo's training even lasting longer. Despite this, Rodrigo is every bit his own man. What he learned has been critically evaluated and applied according to Rodrigo's individual psychological inclination. Unlike Roberto, whose practice bears the strong imprint of the domineering teacher, Rodrigo continues to evolve and grow in his own direction.

This capacity for growth was demonstrated when I finally relocated Rodrigo in Lima in February 1988. He had adapted his practice to the fast pace of urban life by abbreviating his ritual; and he had built an extensive network of friends, relatives, and clients. In his spare time he tinkered with stereo equipment, which helped him to relax. Although he lived in very modest quarters, he enjoyed the stimulation of life in the big city.

As we renewed our acquaintance in November 1988 and later in October 1989, I learned that Rodrigo often forms part of a curing trio along with his brother and sister. When he first came to Lima they held seven sessions on successive evenings in order to purify the mesa of any lingering influences of Rodrigo's teacher. Also, Rodrigo had made one more pilgrimage to the sacred lagoons in the early 1980s. He thereafter felt no need to return, contending that, once initiated, a competent curer should be able to tap the power of the lagoons in spirit. As he put it, "The flight of the spirit is direct."

López's Mesa

In the late 1970s the right side (Curandero) of Rodrigo's mesa (Figure 9), which governs the herbs and the San Pedro, was twice as large as the diminutive Ganadero to the left. However, the Ganadero was reinforced by a "counter mesa" in the open area beyond the

Figure 9 López Mesa, 1979

staffs. Also worthy of note was the fact that the container of San Pedro and the sword next to it, both located in the middle of the staffs, were treated in his rituals as true mediators: the San Pedro dominated the entire process, and the sword, with its cup-handle, was used by the healer to raise tobacco in activating both the San Pedro and the entire mesa. This *Espada Sorbetana* (Imbibing Sword), Rodrigo explained, is both black and white in nature and it is used in all curing rituals associated with both sides of the mesa.

In describing his artifacts, Rodrigo begins with the right side, delineating objects that have typical healing functions associated with positive herbal lore. The staffs at the head of the right side include (from right to left): a quince branch, four Aguaruna arrows, an Aguaruna bow, another arrow, his Bull Lance, his Aguaruna Lance, his Sword of Saint Gabriel, the Flier Sword, a Cimuro Sword, an Imbibing Sword, the Staff of the Ganadero King, the Sword of Saint Paul, the Ancient Shrine Staff, a Huayacán Staff, a Steel Snake, a Hoop Rapier, a Whistling Arrow, and another Aguaruna Lance. They either are used for cleansings (swords and staffs) or for defense (Aguaruna bow, arrows, lances).

Next come a series of *seguros* and flasks of single herbs, as well as a bottle of holy water and two bottles of perfume. Prominent among the *seguros* are *madrigueros* ("lairs"), used for the protection and regeneration of patients (see Jorge Merino's thorough explanation of the concept of *madriguero* in Chapter 12). Holy water and perfumes are used for spraying the mesa along with liquids from two of the flasks, while the remaining potions are used to make *seguros* to promote health, love, business, and good luck in general.

Stones constitute the largest set of artifacts, although they are small and occupy little space on the mesa. Individual stones represent powerful mountains that are loci for positive forces (including three crystals representing mines, minerals, and wealth), as well as representing body parts, flowers, and whirlwinds. Several are also chosen for their unusual shapes. These are all used in curing and cleansing rituals. In addition to the small individual stones, there is a round container holding special stones used to promote good luck.

A number of representations of holy personages, symbolizing the divine help of heaven, are found on the right side: a Saint Hillary statue for invoking the apostles; the Christ of Prague lithograph for curing children; the Virgin of Carmen (laminated print) for help in curing; two Saint Anthony statues (one plastic, one plaster-of-paris) to help find lost persons or objects; a laminated image of Sarita Colonia (a Peruvian folk saint); and an angel medallion. A small Cross of Motupe, a book of prayer, and a book on Oriental mysticism support the functions of these religious objects.

Star lore is expressed by a bronze sun (a "king") and a bronze moon (a "queen"). Luck and fortune are represented by a silver plate of amulets and a jar of minerals, which work in conjunction with the three large crystals already mentioned. A marble Venus (another queen) carrying a water jar is used for cleansing rituals linked to love magic.

The remaining objects on the right are the tools associated with heaven and the herbs. The most important tools are three rattles: the curer's gourd rattle used for the songs related to San Pedro and tobacco; the curer's bronze rattle used for songs relating to luck; and the right-hand assistant's gourd rattle which is used to accompany the healer during all his songs, but which is specifically related to the activation and maintenance of those powers linked to heaven and the herbs (a small set of pan pipes reinforces this function). A pre-Hispanic whistle is used to call back souls in cases of soul loss.

Serving and related implements include: a tin bowl for tobacco;

a plastic pail and three tin cups for San Pedro; a pair of shells (one a bivalve for imbibing, one a spiral for serving) used by the healer when he raises tobacco; a set of shells (four bivalves for raising, one spiral for serving) used by patients; two black male calf horns used by the two assistants for raising tobacco; two magnets for curing headaches; and a flashlight to aid in the preparation of the tobacco and herbal potions.

The smaller left side of the mesa is the locus of the negative forces associated with counteracting sorcery. The "staffs" here perform defensive functions. From right to left they are: the Swordfish Beak, two pre-Columbian staffs, a pre-Columbian bronze chisel, a deer's hoof, the Steel Snake, the Black Steel Bayonet, the Steel Rod, and a quince branch. The deer's hoof, when sprayed with cane alcohol, is used to drive off enemies, while the swordfish beak is used in cleansing rituals.

Rodrigo uses relatively few pre-Columbian pieces, with the exception of a monkey ceramic and a fish ceramic from the Huaca Chotuna, used to invoke this important site, as well as a stone axehead from Purgatory Mountain which is used to cure headaches caused by sorcery, and three ceramic faces (two felines, one human) for invoking pre-Columbian shrines.

As is characteristic of the Ganadero side, stone also predominates here. Rodrigo has seventeen stones, all used for cleansings and release rituals. Some of the stones are named after important mountains: Negro (two), Yatamero (two), Bronze (two), and Sanquelo. Four are "whirlpool" stones used for soul loss related to the sea. Three are fossils. Another indication of the focus of the left is a set of books on black magic placed there.

The remaining objects are implements for therapy: a gourd rattle used by the left-hand assistant to activate and maintain Ganadero power; two slugs of iron and bronze to cleanse these elements from patients who suffer from *antimonio de gentiles* ("antimony of the ancients" is a folk disease associated with the "airs" and "metals" of ancient tombs); four steel balls used in sucking rituals; a cigarette lighter and two flints for making sparks to drive off evil spirits; two shells for divining; three shells for raising tobacco to activate the left side of the mesa (used by the left-hand assistant) or for patients to raise Ganadero accounts; and two perfumes for spraying the left side of the mesa.

In the late 1970s the "counter mesa" in the space beyond the staffs consisted of a skull from a pre-Hispanic tomb wearing a *chullo* (a Quechua cap), two pre-Columbian staffs, and books on black magic. Its purpose was to ground or discharge the negative energies associated with sorcery attacks.

The San Pedro cactus plays a central role in Rodrigo's rituals. Initially it is invoked to activate the mesa. Then, later in the session, it is invoked again to activate the curing activities per se. The progression of the ritual is as follows:

1 Rodrigo "opens the charms" by spraying holy water around the general area of the mesa. He then petitions the "permission of God" to perform the ceremony, after which he sprays *agua cananga*, perfume, and *agua florida* to the four cardinal points.

2 At the head of the mesa with swords in hand, the two assistants raise tobacco five times each, moving from a kneeling to a standing position while Rodrigo sings a *tarjo*. The assistants spray their swords with perfume when finished. They then shake rattles while the healer raises tobacco with the cup in the handle of his personal sword. He also sprays it with perfume when finished. Raising is always done first with the right nostril, symbolizing the right side of the mesa, and then with the left, symbolizing the left side. These acts activate the San Pedro brew and the mesa.

3 Rodrigo and his two assistants sing the song of San Pedro. The healer drinks first (served by the assistant on the left), followed by the assistants (left-hand first) and then the patients (newcomers first), each drinking at the head of the mesa.

4 Rodrigo begins a song and the assistants join in, while all the patients dance in place. Occasionally, the assistant from the left carries the song alone, while Rodrigo moves out to the right armed with a sword. This allows the San Pedro to take effect in the participants' bodies.

5 Rodrigo sings the song of the queen of the Páramo Blanco Lagoon, interspersing the song with perfume spraying. The queen arrives on the right, where she works with San Pedro in activating the herbs on that side. She seats herself on the right and then activates the left, which builds an invisible barrier to protect the mesa.

6 Rodrigo then sings the song of the queen of the Mishahuanga Lagoon. She takes the same route as the first queen, embracing her companion once they are seated together on the healer's right. She also activates the left and the protective barrier.

7 The shaman sings a song inviting the spirit of San Pedro to arrive and heal his patients. The song is interrupted by the serving of tobacco, which is raised during the rest of the song, healer first. Then the mesa is sprayed with perfume and Rodrigo rubs

himself with his sword. The song is resumed while each patient
takes a turn dancing in front of the mesa.

8 Rodrigo sings the song of tobacco on behalf of the patients, who
all take turns before the mesa to raise tobacco.

9 The rest of the evening is taken up by the actual curing rituals,
which follow a standard format:

   a) *Rastreo* ("Tracking" or Diagnosis)—With the patient at the
   head of the mesa, the healer converses, divines, and sings a
   song intended to "pull" the patient's soul, transmitting it back
   into his or her body.

   b) *Destranca* ("Unbolting" or Release)—With Rodrigo's chants in
   the background, the two assistants, one in front and the other
   behind the patient, raise the patient from foot to knee, knee
   to stomach, stomach to heart, and heart to head, sucking the
   areas that are painful. During this treatment, the patient
   breathes into each assistant's shell of tobacco.

   c) *Limpia* (Cleansing)—An assistant rubs the patient from head
   to foot on all four sides with a steel lance.

   d) *Florecimiento* ("Flowering")—The patient is served a perfume,
   to be nasally ingested.

10 Rodrigo "closes the charm" by spraying the mesa with the three
perfumes used at the beginning.

I was not able to attend a session with Rodrigo in Lima until October 1989. At that time I noticed that the Curandero side of the mesa is now delineated by a white linen cloth and contains a new cavalry sword (the Female Guerrilla), while the Aguaruna arrows are gone, and the bow is on the wall behind the mesa (see Figure 10). The Ganadero side is marked by a striped red linen poncho and includes more pre-Columbian artifacts (of stone and wood) on the far left. Since the mesa is set against the east wall, there is no counter mesa. As a result, the two staffs from this sector have been moved to the head of the Ganadero division of the mesa, along with a new dagger.

In February 1991, besides participating in two more sessions, I was able to redocument Rodrigo's mesa. The major change in the Curandero division is the addition of a Bible and eleven laminated saints' images, which reflects the stronger emphasis on Christianity that Rodrigo has adopted since the late 1970s. Other new objects include a rattle ("of silver and gold") replacing one of the gourd rattles, two crystal balls for divination, a crystal bowl for holy water, two pieces of stainless steel, and a transparent plastic miniature white pyramid—all of which illustrate the emphasis on light and purity associated with this zone. Although Rodrigo still uses his

Figure 10 López Mesa, 1991

original gourd rattle to activate the Curandero accounts, its function is now reinforced not only by the new rattle but also by a brass bell and medallion used for communion and incense rituals.

Throughout the last decade the Ganadero sector has seen more elaboration than has the Curandero. Most of the new artifacts here are of pre-Columbian derivation. This is most apparent along the far left edge with the addition of (from top to bottom) five wooden pre-Hispanic statues (a *reina* [queen] *ganadera* with four males), four stone effigies (three Moche kings and one Moor [the largest]), and a bronze crucible. Three additional pre-Hispanic stone carvings line the lower border of the Ganadero division; from left to right they are a bird, a phallus, and a serpent's head. Along the upper border, at the base of the staffs, two ancient ceramics (a cylindrical pot and a king effigy) have joined the fish and monkey vessels. All of the pre-Columbian artifacts are used for defensive purposes and to "turn around" sorcery, especially the variety effected through the agency of the spirits of the pagan past. However, two additional wooden pieces, a small staff and a male effigy, are also used in divination and cleansing rituals.

Two spondylous shells and one conch were added in the 1980s. They are used to confuse sorcerers and to drive spells and curses into the ocean.

As in the past, stone continues to dominate the left half of Rodrigo's mesa. The numerous pre-Columbian lithics are supplemented by a larger cluster of flint stones (called "lightning") than before; these in turn are accompanied by two black "thunder" stones (one square, one circular). When added to the pre-Columbian, quartz, fossil, and "whirlpool" stones from the 1970s, the concentration is considerable.

Regarding his ritual, Rodrigo starts at a later time than before—now around midnight. He opens and closes with a lengthy series of Catholic prayers while spraying sectors of the mesa and the cardinal points with perfume. He now only has two major songs, one for San Pedro and one to muster the remaining forces used for curing. Before the first song, he and his two assistants raise the two sides of the mesa—Curandero and then Ganadero—and then everyone drinks the San Pedro. After the first song, the healer and the left-hand assistant raise tobacco in the bull horn in order to build a protective barrier against *espiritistas fumadores* ("smoking spiritists"), who according to Rodrigo are found in great numbers in Lima. A brief second song consolidates all of the powers of the mesa and of the "queens." Actual curing rituals for patients are the same as they were in 1980, except that, at the end of the session, while the patient raises a mild concoction containing no tobacco, an assistant sprays him in an upward motion with liquid from the healer's *seguro madriguero*. The closing rituals are a mirror image of the opening ceremonies.

8

Helmer Aguilar

First Meeting

The day after the first session with Rodrigo López I was working with Rodrigo at the home of his friend, Helmer Aguilar. Helmer took me aside and informed me that there was going to be another session that very evening. It seemed odd to me to have two sessions in a row, but since I was eager to verify some of the data collected the night before I said I would be there.

When I arrived at the house that evening, Helmer was the only person waiting for me. He said that Rodrigo had gone ahead and that we would meet him at the ritual site. However, when we arrived at the farm, there was no one there. Helmer then confessed that he had tricked me. He wanted to give me a private demonstration of *his* ritual without the distraction of patients. One reason for his deception, he explained, was that at the ripe old age of twenty-two he was "retired" from curing. Knowing that I was interested in researching curanderismo "in action," he was afraid I would not be interested in documenting his ritual since he could not provide patients.

I was tired. I had been up all night at Rodrigo's session and had only slept for a few hours that morning before following up on my notes and recordings from the ritual. But I was not about to miss a chance to document another healer's work. Besides, I had already thought of including Helmer in my research.

It was a very instructive evening. Helmer took me through everything from A to Z. He made every effort to explain each ritual and curing technique in great detail. His explanations that night and during the following days yielded the longest texts I gathered from any of the shamans with whom I have worked, before or since.

I was able to follow up with Helmer in June of the next year. As usual he was loquacious. I again saw him briefly in August

1981 and later, extensively, in February 1987 and November 1988. He was still retired. His artifacts, except for two (a plaster-of-paris head of Christ with a crown of thorns and a large conch shell), either had been given away, lost or stolen.

Some of Helmer's colleagues think that he does not use a mesa because he was hit by a major sorcerer's *golpe* (blow), which was so devastating that he was left with no desire to expose himself to such dangerous powers again. Whatever his reasons, he is still in retirement.

Biography

Helmer Aguilar Lázaro was born in Trujillo's port town, Salaverry, in 1957. The youngest of seven children, Helmer had five older brothers to look up to in this family of fishermen. (One of his brothers became a fishing specialist and another worked as a mechanical engineer for the port facilities.) Helmer was a very bright student, starting school a year early and skipping a grade later on.

At the age of seven, Helmer had a clear indication that he had the "second sight" (*vista* or *visión*) of a curandero. At that time the family owned three fishing launches. During a storm, one of the boats slipped its moorings and disappeared at sea. At 6:00 A.M. the following morning Helmer was awakened by a premonition that the boat was under full sail and entering Salaverry harbor. He reported that he could actually "see" the boat. At first he thought he was dreaming, but when he looked around he saw that he was sitting upright in bed. He ran to his father to tell him that the boat was safe. Although Helmer's father assumed his son had only dreamt the news, he went to the docks anyway. Sure enough, there was the boat, under full sail. It had been found by fishermen who sailed it back to port.

Helmer had a maternal uncle who was a curandero known as *Caballo Blanco*. This uncle worked in the highland town of Usquíl, where he and Helmer's mother had been born, but he occasionally traveled to the town of Moche, near Salaverry, to conduct curing sessions. The uncle was told about Helmer's vision. He immediately recognized the sign of a future curandero and took his nephew under his wing.

Since the uncle had poor eyesight, he began taking Helmer around with him to curing sessions to assist in the preparation of San Pedro and in setting up his mesa. Helmer dropped out of

school during the first year of this apprenticeship since he was regularly away from home when his uncle took him to sessions in the
highlands. When his uncle worked in Moche, one of his colleagues
from Trujillo would join him, which gave Helmer a broad exposure
to curers and their practices at a very early age.

When he was thirteen, Helmer's parents separated. Once again
his restless spirit began to stir. In his early teens he started working
with a healer from Ferreñafe. From this connection he met one of
the famous healers of the Chiclayo region. During his high school
years, taking advantage of the disruption in his family to leave
home, Helmer began working with this healer and with one of his
apprentices, the same person who became the mentor of Rodrigo
López and Roberto Rojas. Also, he had opportunities to make pilgrimages to Páramo Blanco, Mishahuanga, and Las Huaringas.

His adventures caused him to fall behind in his studies and, as a
result, he never completed high school. However, he felt that he
learned more important lessons at the lagoons. He brought back
three stones from each site, which provided "connections for one
to arrive mentally there. It's like performing divination and having
a photo of the person. . . . With the charm, by means of its connection, one projects oneself."

Helmer aspired to a profession, something like his brother who
pursued mechanical engineering. Healing started merely as an av-
ocation, something he did because he liked it. However, it began to
get into his blood. Although the strongest influence on him came
from one healer in particular, the idea of apprenticeship to only
one man never appealed to him. During his high school years he
met and worked with eight different healers.

When he was twenty, Helmer performed his first cure. A woman
with swollen knees came to him to request a session since she had
no money and no one would help her. It was not an easy case.
Helmer performed the ritual without assistants, a precedent he
followed until his retirement. After the session, Helmer prescribed
herbal poultices, a treatment which continued for two weeks with
noticeable improvement. For an additional two weeks, the patient
combined the herbal treatment with arthritis medication prescribed by her doctor. In a little over a month, according to
Helmer, her knees were completely healed.

Helmer was wary of practicing in the same area as one of his
mentors, the domineering shaman who constantly interfered with
the independence of Roberto Rojas. He took advantage of an

opportunity to travel with a northern healer who worked in the city of Arequipa, in the southern highlands of Peru. Once there, he resumed practicing on his own.

The exposure to the people and customs of the south considerably expanded Helmer's horizons. At this time he also had an experience which, like his vision at seven years of age, was a turning point in his life. Early one morning, toward the end of a session, something unusual happened as dawn was breaking:

> I had been thinking of God, of the idea of seeing Him—as it says in the Bible, "Lord, your will be done. Grant that I be allowed to contemplate the light of your face. . . ." It was daylight, but I opened my eyes and it was night and I was in a tunnel about three meters in diameter with a floor that seemed almost immaterial, like custard, and with sides similar to marble or rock that had been turned black from the smoke of innumerable candles. I could see at night. I saw infinity, an immense tunnel of lights . . . an infinity, but of small yellow lights in a single line. It seemed like a candle illuminating the depths. I literally pulled myself together physically, and—although it may seem like a lie to you—I felt that upon touching myself I became nothing.
>
> While I was looking for a way out, something—in place of God—something was calling me. Something absorbed me like air. Being close, very close to the end I couldn't see, but it seemed that, being in the tunnel, it seemed that there was a person there, that person had brought me there or had called me. Or rather it seemed that a current of air had brought me to that site and I felt that someone was there, but that person was telling me not to go on, that I remain there with him.
>
> At that point the tunnel resounded "pum-pum," as if something shook it up and the tunnel was illuminated by a beam of light that penetrated like this "sssssh" at an immense velocity right to the end. And whatever was there I wasn't able to see, but within my body I sensed that someone was there and that this person was hunched down.
>
> I wanted to go on, following where the light had gone. I wanted to go on, and it seemed—only in my mind because I couldn't see and I remained where I was—that there were other people at the sides of the tunnel and that they were hunched down. It seemed to me that they were inside the tunnel, not at the mesa, but inside the tunnel. I was conscious, but in my mind it seemed that there were other people at the sides when I wanted to go on. It seemed that they were arriving at the end.
>
> Puum! I saw it very clearly at my mesa. I saw myself inside the tunnel while at my mesa. When I finally realized what had happened it was 9:15 A.M., and some patients had left because I hadn't awakened. I had been like that for three hours and fifteen minutes.

This is how Helmer interpreted that experience during the session:

> Look, Purgatory Mountain [a coastal mountain and archaeological site invoked by healers] is a place where the curer opens the main doors and, if you have sight, you see that the mountain is a castle. It's a castle, a real castle, and one opens the main doors and inside there is a courtyard off of which you open smaller doors. There are smaller doors there like the labyrinth of a *huaca* [pre-Columbian shrine]. And you go along entering that charm. You have dominated it and you know where each small door is located, where each window is, where the ancients are located. You know what animals come out because you dominate that charm and you have that charm, you know it like the palm of your hand.
>
> That tunnel was the same. The curanderos of that area arrive, they arrive at the end by means of those tunnels, and at the end is the Inca, the god of the mountain or the power of that mountain. They arrive at the end and converse with him and tell him that they are going to cure someone or they are going to curse him. . . . I was able to enter that tunnel, but since I wasn't able to dominate it, I was found to be lacking.

The tunnel experience profoundly moved Helmer. He felt the need to get away by himself to put it into perspective. He therefore journeyed to the Lake Titicaca region to seek solitude on the cold highland plateau. At the same time he wanted to observe the practices of the local Aymara shamans.

After a year in the south, Helmer returned home. He felt he had mastered the curing art, but he was not motivated to pursue it as a regular vocation due to what he perceived as a bias against young practitioners. He said that in the two years that he had practiced on his own he constantly encountered the stereotype of a wizened old peasant healing his patients in a rustic setting. Although the vast majority of his clients were city dwellers, they still expected the shaman to conform to the stereotype. Helmer thought it was tough enough spending sleepless nights in the cold, battling sorcerers, without having to deal with patients' expectations that he could not meet.

Once he resettled, Helmer purchased his own boat and married a woman from Chimbote, whose family were all fishermen. But the marriage and the fishing both encountered rough seas. When I saw Helmer briefly in 1981, he informed me that he had divorced his wife, sold his boat, and was setting up a pig farm with his brothers. He felt that shamanism was something he would pursue later

Figure 11 Aguilar Mesa

in life. Even though he was still a loner and a rebel, he simply did
not feel like bucking the current.

   In February 1987 I spent a great deal of time with Helmer. In
the intervening six years he had fished up and down the Peruvian
coast, mainly with his brothers. For a brief period he also had
worked at a fish cannery in Ecuador and on an archaeological
project near Cuzco. At the time he had a temporary job with the
port authorities as "beach captain," that is, as a coordinator of the
fishermen, tourists, and owners of temporary beach restaurants set
up during the summer season. He was also attending night classes
in an effort to finish high school (which he accomplished a year
later). He still had no intention of resuming his curing practices,
but was getting very interested in politics. I had the impression that
this restless fisherman was like a ship without a rudder.

Aguilar's Mesa

As with the López mesa, Helmer's altar had a larger Yerbatero
right side than it did a Ganadero left side (Figure 11). He was ad-
amant about there being only two sides to his mesa, with no artifact

or cluster of artifacts forming a third sector. In discussing the interaction of the two fields of the mesa, he spoke in terms of energy:

> Look, I told you the dynamic. The negative of the Ganadero and the positive of the Yerbatero when they unite, they are transformed. When they unite, they are transformed into vibrations. These vibrations go from the positive pole to the negative, some to the human body and others to the brain.

Along with a can of San Pedro, a doll representing the spirit of San Pedro, and a plastic bottle filled with lagoon water, the right-hand Yerbatero side of the mesa was headed by an Aguaruna bow, arrow, and lance for defense, three hollow black staffs for raising tobacco, and a bamboo container containing ground herbs associated with the positive forces of the right side.

Stones were the most numerous of the ground artifacts, with a total of seventeen. Of these, the iron pyrites (six pieces), symbolizing riches, comprised the largest category. Sundry artifacts that reinforced the fortune stones were a bronze laurel branch signifying triumph or success and a large glass die. The early and pervasive influence of Helmer's uncle was revealed by four stones that represented Satapampa Mountain near Usquíl. Páramo Blanco was represented by three stones, while Mishahuanga was indicated by two. Located on either side of the head of Christ were two pieces of the same dark crystal used in divining, while the remaining stone was used for lowering fevers.

The roles of Páramo Blanco and Mishahuanga were further strengthened by Helmer's two large *seguros* containing herbs from these sacred power locales. The Páramo Blanco *seguro* was used to clear the mind and to raise or invoke lagoons in general, while the Mishahuanga *seguro* was used only for invoking lagoons.

Religious artifacts on the right side included: a cedar Cross of Motupe used for invoking this major north coast pilgrimage site; a bronze silver-plated paten for concentrating holy light; two plaster-of-paris heads of Christ symbolizing Helmer's love of God; a plaster skull and book representing wisdom; and a book about Saint Cyprian.

The remaining objects were therapeutic implements: four perfumes for spraying the mesa; *cananga* to control the Ganadero; cologne to sharpen the senses and heighten concentration; two florid waters to reinforce the Yerbatero; a tin cup for imbibing San Pedro; four pre-Columbian whistles for calling spirits; flint for making sparks to drive off spirits; a tin bowl for tobacco; a bivalve shell for serving tobacco; the healer's personal bivalve shell for raising tobacco on the Yerbatero; another bivalve shell used by patients to raise Yerbatero accounts; a small candle to use when mixing herbal potions; and a gourd rattle for activating the right side of the mesa.

Regarding the seeds in his rattle, Helmer related some curandero lore that he learned from his uncle which correlates with his concept of doors and tunnels in mountains and *huacas* and which helps explain why the curandero uses a rattle. According to this tradition, mountains and *huacas* are like houses with several doors. Helmer's uncle told him a story about an old curandero who played a guitar in order to enter mountains or *huacas*:

> Then, once inside, his spirit had to knock on each one of these doors because each one of those doors led to a room and each room had a spirit. Therefore, in order not to have to be bothered with knocking, he grabbed a rattle and said: "For each seed that it holds, I knock on a door." After that, upon sounding the rattle and moving each seed in the rattle those doors opened automatically.

The smaller Ganadero side of Helmer's mesa expressed the negative forces associated with the sinistral side of the healing art. The staffs at the head of this section were mainly small pre-Hispanic *chonta* daggers (five) used in counterattacks against sorcerers. This function was reinforced by a quince branch for driving off spirits, a small arrow, a swordfish beak symbolizing aggressiveness, and a large hollow staff used to raise tobacco when performing an exorcism ritual.

Shells (thirteen) and stones (six) predominated among the ground artifacts on the left. Among the former, five spiral shells were used for serving tobacco to patients; five bivalves were used by patients in raising; one bivalve was the healer's personal left-hand shell for raising; a pre-Columbian shell trumpet was used for invoking ruins and mountains; and a large bivalve, referred to as *pata de caballo* ("horse hoof"), was used with the skull or swordfish beak to provide a negative "kick" or charge against attacking sorcerers. Stones represented three powerful mountains (Yatama, Purgatory, and Mulatto), as well as a penis and two archaeological sites (La Raya and Marcahuamachuco).

There was only one pre-Columbian ceramic on the left; it reinforced the two pre-Columbian stones, the shell trumpet, and the pre-Columbian skull. Two books on black magic represented the infernal arts, while two poisonous cimuro herbs symbolized sorcery performed by placing potions in food or drink. A ceramic bull was used for charging sorcerers. A bronze key symbolized the opening of charms related to pre-Hispanic shrines, cemeteries, and mountains. A deer's antler was for speed in eluding sorcerers. Finally, two rattles activated the accounts of the left (the smaller one above and to the left of the gourd instrument related to house cleansings), while the brass bell reinforced the action of the left.

In contrast with Rodrigo López's team-player approach to ritual, Helmer, true to his independent nature, never worked with assistants. However, in other aspects, the stages of his rituals were very similar to Rodrigo's, except that he added two Ganadero songs before beginning the treatment of patients. This reflects the fact that both he and Rodrigo were initiated into the Páramo Blanco/ Mishahuanga tradition by the dean of the Chiclayo-region shamans, and that they shared the same disciple of this shaman as a mentor. Although Roberto Rojas also was trained by this disciple, he never made the pilgrimages to Páramo Blanco and to Mishahuanga, which might help explain the difference between his rituals and those of Rodrigo and Helmer.

Helmer's ritual followed these stages:

1 After the mesa was set up, Helmer prayed for permission from God to perform the session, while spraying the mesa (perfume for the right, *cananga* for the left).
2 Following a song for San Pedro and the mesa, Helmer raised tobacco to activate the brew and all artifacts.
3 A song for the San Pedro brew was sung before the healer drank it. The song was then sung for the patients as they drank San Pedro and danced.
4 Next came the song to call the queen of Páramo Blanco, who entered on the right, activating first the Yerbatero and then the Ganadero.
5 The queen of Mishahuanga was invoked in song. She followed the same Yerbatero-to-Ganadero course as did her counterpart.
6 A second song for San Pedro was sung, this time to invite its spirit to the session. After the song, the healer raised tobacco on behalf of the spirit of the plant.
7 A Ganadero song for a pre-Columbian skull from the ruins at Marcahuamachuco in the highlands was sung.
8 A Ganadero song for another skull, designated "the stutterer" (*tartamudo*) was sung. This skull aided in divination.
9 Curing rituals for patients followed the same pattern used by Rodrigo López, except that Helmer performed all of the assistants' duties himself.

10 After all present raised perfumes and were refreshed, the account was closed and the session concluded.

As with Rodrigo's ritual, the prime mover, San Pedro, dominated the major stages of the session. In addition, Helmer symmetrically paired or balanced rituals, each addressed to the opposite sides of the mesa—that is, two queens for the right (Paramo Blanco and Mishahuanga) and two skulls for the left (Marcahuamachuco and *Tartamudo*).

9
Víctor Flores

First Meeting

While I was busily engaged with Roberto, Rodrigo, and Helmer, an opportunity to meet an older healer presented itself thanks to my colleague Varvara Ferber. By early November 1979 Varvara was finishing over one year of study in Peru, working with two female herbal vendors who had stands in one of Trujillo's markets, the *Mayorista*. In the course of her work she met a Trujillo shaman, Víctor Flores, through an acquaintance with one of his assistants. She offered to introduce me.

During a break in my work with the young trio, I accepted Varvara's offer. Víctor was an expansive, well-connected entrepreneur. He knew everybody who was anybody in Trujillo and kept a notebook filled with the well-preserved business cards of his wealthier clients. While he attended to the needs of clients from all strata of society, rich and poor alike, he used his network of influential people to trade favors in order to carry on his work.

We arranged to meet at a small beach community on the outskirts of Trujillo where Víctor performed rituals and stored one of his three mesas.[1] Donald Skillman accompanied me to the meeting. It was obvious to us both that Víctor was ill at ease as he laid out his mesa on a reed mat and allowed me to take pictures. When I asked to take his picture, he declined until I suggested a photo of the two of us together. Víctor's reticence diminished only after Don and I attended one of his rituals; from that point on our rapport was excellent.

Víctor later confided that when I introduced myself as an *investigador científico* (scientific investigator), all he heard was investigator! (Víctor is partially deaf.) This triggered a very bad recollection from his youth when he saw a healer harassed by the police. They put the curer in jail, where he was beaten and then forced to drink most of the San Pedro brew that had been prepared for a session.

I saw Víctor again in July 1980 and was able to fill the gaps in the research of the previous year. The lacunae were abundant since my 1979 research season finished just as our work together was starting. A seven-year hiatus followed the 1980 visit before I began working with Víctor again in August and September 1987 and in February 1988. This is what I learned from Víctor during our intermittent encounters.

Biography

Víctor Flores Capuñay was born in Monsefú in 1932, the fourth of six children. His father was a merchant who traveled a great deal. When Víctor was old enough, he was allowed to accompany his father, particularly on trips to Salas in the early 1940s. Although his formal education suffered because of these journeys, he was exposed to the healers and lore of this famous center of northern healing during the impressionable years from eight to ten.

In 1942, the family settled in Túcume, where Víctor received all his formal education—four years of primary school. His exposure to folk healing continued, however, since Túcume was the home of some notable northern healers. One in particular had just begun his practice and was famous for making the spirits of the mountains manifest themselves at his ceremonies. The spurs on the spirits' boots and the rattles they danced to could be heard during sessions, and they would speak through a skull on the mesa, divining the causes and cures of patients' ailments.

Both of Víctor's parents were avid followers of the healing tradition, so he continued to be exposed regularly to the work of local shamans. He dreamed of becoming a famous healer himself, and even practiced with some crude staffs and *seguros*. When the time came for his church confirmation, an old friend of the family, a curandero, was selected to be his godfather. Víctor told the man that he wanted to follow in his footsteps.

In the late 1940s, during his teens, Víctor's right hand became swollen and painful. It felt like he had been bitten by something. He approached the healer who worked with the mountain spirits and the skull, and, since his family was known to the shaman, he was invited to the next session. That night, between 1:00 and 2:00

A.M., the curandero and another colleague removed the pain and stopped the swelling. Víctor was told that he had been the victim of *daño* or sorcery instigated by a schoolmate whom Víctor had punched—with his right fist.

Víctor recalls that in 1949 he overheard a conversation in the Chiclayo market. Two young men were discussing the fact that successful curanderos could actually earn more than physicians and were certainly more popular. Thinking about how far behind he was in school and how poor his father was, Víctor resolved someday to become a renowned healer: "Then I dedicated myself to curanderismo, to think of it with love because I wanted to be a man who was esteemed."

A year later Víctor was drafted into the Peruvian army. As often happened in those days, the recruiters simply went through the streets rounding up those who were eligible and shipping them off with nothing but the clothes on their backs. Víctor ended up in Tumbes. For the next two years he served in posts along the entire border between Ecuador and Peru, ranging from the dry coastal plain to the dense jungles of the upper Amazon. Like Víctor Neyra, he had the quality of leadership and finished his service with the rank of sergeant.

After his discharge, Víctor returned to Monsefú, where he tried to learn the trade of typewriter repair. This did not work out, however, so a year later he returned to the border area and found employment with the state-operated *Estanco de Tabaco* as a water pump mechanic on the international canal near Zarumilla and Aguas Verdes, an area noted at the time both for its tobacco and for its curanderos. The work was not hard, so Víctor was able to labor nights as an *alzador* (curer's assistant). Besides learning curing rituals, Víctor gained a wealth of knowledge of the extensive herbal lore of the region.

In 1957, Víctor met a woman from Tumbes and brought her to Chiclayo, where the couple planned to settle and raise a family. Víctor could not find work as a mechanic, but his curing experiences in the jungle served him well when he became the assistant of a local shaman with a large clientele. The two men got along well and the healer became the godfather of Víctor's first child, a daughter born in 1958. At about the same time that he began to work with the Chiclayo healer, Víctor learned that his godfather had died during his absence and had willed his mesa to him. By

1959, Víctor's teacher allowed him to place his inherited artifacts beside the principal mesa, and the two men would work together through the night.

In 1960, friends of Víctor's sister approached her about persuading Víctor to perform a guinea pig diagnosis for them. By rubbing the animal over a patient followed by vivisection and entrail divination, curanderos determine if an illness is the result of sorcery or organic causes. Víctor consented. His sister's friends were pleased with the results and asked Víctor to conduct a mesa on their behalf at their home in Chimbote. The principal patient was a relative who had been bedridden for a month and who suffered from lapses of memory. In one session Víctor cured the man and successfully launched his career as a curandero, at the age of twenty-eight.

Víctor's practice grew as word of him began to spread in the markets among the merchants. A family from the town of Paiján (between Chiclayo and Trujillo) asked Víctor to visit them and try to cure a relative whom neither the local doctor nor another curandero had been able to help. The enthusiastic young curer was successful, which further enhanced his growing reputation. He decided to set up a practice in Paiján because the townspeople there began to flock to him.

In 1963, Víctor caught a cold that drained his energy and would not go away. He coughed day and night and was unable to hold sessions. He had made it a point to get to know all the local notables, including the doctors. They were unable to help him. As a result, Víctor and a group of doctors resolved to make a pilgrimage to the famous Las Huaringas lagoons in the northern highlands near the town of Huancabamba. Besides the special curative properties of these waters and the herbs that grow nearby, the healers of the region are reputed to be among the best in Peru.

The pilgrims found their way to the home of the famous curandero of the Black Lagoon. Unfortunately, at the time he was just as sick as Víctor, suffering from what he thought was pneumonia. The doctors gave him a checkup and concluded that he did not have pneumonia. It appeared that both he and Víctor had maladies brought on by the envy of other healers.

Given such a meeting of minds between traditional and modern healers, a session was certainly in order. It was a momentous occasion for Víctor. The veteran healer not only cured both their ailments, but he also made *seguros* for Víctor, taught him new herbal

remedies, and baptized his most prized power object, a Moor figurine, telling Víctor that it would make him a famous curandero.
Since that day, Víctor has returned to Las Huaringas at least once
every year, spending most of his time there with the healer of the
Black Lagoon. He eventually also met healers at the Shimbe Lagoon in 1975 and again in 1980.

Once back in Paiján, Víctor was inspired to rededicate himself to
the healing art. His fame spread and his clientele increased. During this period he became acquainted with a local landlord who
also owned an important northern bus line headquartered in Trujillo. Víctor helped the man solve problems related to his business.
Afterward, the client became deeply involved in folk healing and
often attended sessions to assist Víctor and to accompany his
chants on the guitar.

This amateur healer also assisted Víctor to become a successful
curing entrepreneur. He was very well connected; and on his rec-
ommendation wealthy clients, including civil authorities and foreigners, began to flock to Víctor's sessions and to request mesas set
up in their homes or places of business. Víctor was soon so successful that he was able to open a small bar and restaurant, run by his
wife, in Monsefú and to rent quarters for himself in Paiján and
Trujillo, thereby facilitating his itinerant approach to healing.

Víctor's success was not without its personal toll. In the late
1960s, because of his constant travel, his wife left him, taking their
five children with her. Full of remorse, Víctor gave up healing and
became a taxi driver in a town near Tumbes, hoping that his wife
would invite him back. The invitation never came.

Eventually, Víctor resigned himself to the loss of his family,
found a new companion, and resumed his practice. His current
mate lives in Sullana and the couple have two children who have
recently joined their father in Trujillo to finish their education.
Víctor owns a house in Trujillo, not far from the city's center, as
well as land near Moche.

In recent years Víctor has recognized the need to pace himself.
In fact, for a time in the early 1980s, as his hearing problem grew
worse,[2] he stopped his practice altogether. When he returned to
work, Víctor limited his assistants to two reliable people (he formerly had a whole backup team) and also began reducing the
number of clients treated at sessions.[3] He apparently is learning to
balance his professional and personal lives.

Figure 12   Flores Mesa, 1979

Flores's Mesa

The first time that Víctor set up a mesa (Figure 12) for me to document, he did not have all of his artifacts on hand. In addition, it
was near the end of one of my field seasons when we met; time was
short and he still did not fully trust me. I also learned that Víctor
has three different mesas in three separate communities and often
mixes artifacts from one location with those from another. I felt
that with such a flexible format there would probably never be an
ideal time or place to document his *materia medica*. Fortunately, I
was able to persuade Víctor that a partial and hasty documentation
was better than no documentation at all. The following is what
emerged from my first effort.

Víctor's mesa is divided into equal halves, Gloria on the right and Ganadero on the left. However, the small number of artifacts and open space of the Gloria contrasts markedly with the large number of objects and density of the Ganadero. Víctor does not have a clearly delineated middle field, but to balance the contrast of Gloria and Ganadero he has three mediating artifacts: a gourd rattle, which "moves the whole mesa" and works in conjunction with Víctor's "first [first acquired] artifact for curing and defense," the Moor figurine (originally paired with a sword, which was absent in 1979), and Víctor's second artifact, the King Inca of Las Huaringas Sword, that he calls "the center of the mesa" (see Figure 12, the sixth object-staff from the left). This sword and three others (named for folk saints Juanita Rosilla and Carmen del Rosario on the right and for Maria del Rosario on the left) were gifts forged for Víctor by a Huancabamba blacksmith and baptized by a famous shaman who worked at the Black Lagoon of Las Huaringas. They are his primary cleansing and curing tools.

In terms of symbolic importance, the swords and staffs at the head of the mesa compensate for the heavy weighting of ground artifacts on the left side. First of all, there are seven to the right of the King Inca of Las Huaringas (from right to left: his Steel Reed, Lemon Sword, Officer's Sword, Morisco Sword, Juanita Rosilla Sword, *chonta*, and Carmen del Rosario Sword), all designated as Gloria. Also, of the remaining five to the left of the king, one (the Maria del Rosario Sword) pairs with the two on the right having a similar shape and is designated Gloria, while another Officer's Sword pairs with the same kind of sword on the right and "can work on both sides." The remaining three staffs (named after snakes) are linked to the Ganadero and are used for defense and to cure soul loss caused by snakes.

Within the two fields of the mesa, artifacts are generally grouped in horizontal rows or layers. For example, within Gloria, the top "layer" consists of four *seguros* (two for the healer, two for patients) and a bottle of white wine used for spraying the mesa. The middle layer has seven perfumes (four *canangas* for spraying the Ganadero, flanked by two *floridas* for spraying the Gloria side, with a cologne above them for the healer), a glass for San Pedro, and a shell for serving tobacco. The bottom layer is made up of three rattles, two of bronze for Ganadero accounts and a gourd for Gloria accounts and for the mesa as a whole.

The concept of layers continues on the left, with three main categories of objects: five pre-Columbian ceramics (top), thirty stones (middle), and eighteen shells (bottom; all used for raising tobacco). The five ceramics (two kings, one man, one woman, one bridge spout) are used in curing soul loss or bad air ailments caused by pre-Columbian ruins. Sixteen of the stones from archaeological sites reinforce the functions of the ceramics (Víctor could only remember two of the sites, Chotuna and La Bandera). Two magnetized stones and four mineral stones are for good luck. A cluster of six light-colored flints from the mesa of Víctor's original mentor is used for driving off spirits and to enhance the curer's *vista*. Finally, there are two lagoon stones from the bottoms of Black Lagoon and Arrebiatada. The latter is used to fend off sleepiness in the early morning hours, while the former is used to charge the *seguros*. Among the stones there is also a bronze Saint Cyprian statue, a deer's hoof for driving off spirits, and several artifacts used in curing soul loss (two bronze snakes, a fish head, and a sea lion's jawbone).

The second time that I had an opportunity to document Víctor's mesa was eight years later (Figure 13). Good rapport had been established, and we were not rushed. All of his Trujillo artifacts were available and were laid out in a careful, systematic fashion. As before, the mesa showed a sharp contrast between the uncrowded right and the dense left sides.

On this more recent mesa eight swords on the right and three short staffs (right to left: Saint Anthony for cleansings, Wooden Dagger for reinforcement, Saint Cyprian for curing children) delineate the smaller and more open area of Gloria. The two Officer Swords are now paired, while the Juanita Rosilla and Carmen del Rosario swords are still on the right side of the King Inca of Las Huaringas sword. Three new shorter swords are the Spanish Sword (far right) for raising luck, the Snake Sword (second from the right) for curing soul loss, and the Steel Greyhound (fifth from the right) for curing bad air from archaeological sites.

Continuing, the crowded left has eighteen *chontas*, handed out to patients for self-cleansing or for purification rituals, and two serpentine swords at the far left,[4] one used for cleansing (Steel Reed, the shorter of the two) and one for defense (Lemon, the longer). Immediately to the right of this pair is a black *chonta* used for defense against sorcerers and a double-headed pre-Columbian *chonta* used to raise patients for their protection.

Figure 13 Flores Mesa, 1987

Ground artifacts are not quite "horizontally layered," but the same clusters are still present. For example, within Gloria, *seguros* are still at the top right but are now accompanied by two magnets for attracting good luck in business. Also placed at the top right: a cross from Motupe used to cure and invoke the spirit of Padre Guatemala; a small, fluorescent statue of the Virgin of Fatima; and a plastic image of the Virgin of the Gate of Otuzco (a famous northern highland pilgrimage site), both used in support of opening and closing prayers. The gourd rattle governs the right side and rests close to the *floridas* and perfume, as before. Replacing the white wine is whiskey (against the cold night air) and cane alcohol used in the tobacco mixture.[5]

Moving to the densely packed Ganadero, the shells (ten spiral-shaped, used in conjunction with the fish head for curing soul loss caused by water, and five bivalves for imbibing) line the left side of this zone (not the bottom as before). To the right of the shells, the nine pre-Columbian ceramics (two kings, two felines, bridge, bottle, face, *cholo*, man/woman) and six pre-Columbian stone figurines still form a horizontal layer at the foot of the staffs. Below the figurines and to the right of the ceramics, the natural stones from pre-Hispanic ruins still form a partial second layer and are joined by a bronze bull and a bronze lion, for frightening evil spirits. Two rattles (one bronze, one ceramic) govern the powers of this side, along with tobacco. Missing from the setup was Víctor's most important power object, the Moor, which he had left in Sullana. Its companion, a brass-handled sword, *La Espada Ganadera* (see Figure 14), which Víctor found with the Moor in a pre-Columbian ruin and considers his second most powerful artifact, was also in Sullana. Both dominate the left and, along with the King Inca Sword, control the entire mesa.

On the evening of a session, at about 7:00 P.M. people begin gathering in Víctor's home in Trujillo. Some have consultations in Víctor's small office. At about 10:00 P.M. several taxis arrive, offering a reduced group rate for the round-trip to the site of the ritual. By about 11:00 P.M. everyone has been transported to the site in the countryside near the town of Moche. Groups vary in size from about twenty-five to fifty people (they were even larger in the past).

The site is a field just outside of Moche where Víctor has built what his *alzadores* call *La Fortaleza*—a very large walled enclosure specifically designed to serve the needs of patients during sessions. The walls are two meters high and they enclose a large rectangle of about forty meters by ten meters. There is an open section for the ritual; at the back of this section are benches and an overhang where patients can rest. There is also an open area in the back where plants are growing, as well as a section where a series of rooms were being finished for patients to stay before and after the ritual. It is a very comfortable complex and effectively shields participants from the cold night winds.

By about midnight, Víctor's assistants, in 1987 one of whom was a young woman, have set up the mesa. They then circulate among the group collecting the equivalent of about $1.00 per person from those who want to receive the San Pedro and participate in the curing ritual. Many of those present usually are friends and relatives of patients, or members of a group of Víctor's followers who simply come to participate in the ritual without taking San Pedro.

The session progresses as follows:

  1 Víctor's opening invocation (including a salute to the four cardinal points) is sung about midnight.

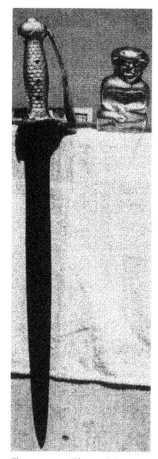

Figure 14 Flores Mesa,
espada ganadera and *moro*
(1987)

2 A general call for San Pedro is issued, and all who will participate come to the head of the mesa and receive their glasses of
San Pedro.

3 Patients receive their staffs and begin rubbing their bodies. An
assistant instructs everyone to turn to face the left wall (from the
shaman's perspective seated at the mesa).

4 Patients form a semicircle in front of the mesa and repeat Víctor's invocation while he stands in the middle.

5 The assistants then serve tobacco to those who will take it. At
their own pace, patients take the tobacco, first inhaling with the

left and then with the right nostril, while the assistants go around the circle monitoring the activity and offering more tobacco as needed. Víctor also circles, singing and shaking his rattle in front of each person (head down so that his face, under his broad-brimmed hat, is not visible).

6 Patients are brought one by one to stand facing the main mesa, where the two *alzadores* perform a *levantada*, or raising of the patient, from the ground up. Both assistants chant before they imbibe each dose of tobacco.[6] Meanwhile, Víctor wanders around the group singing, occasionally drawing near the patient being raised to sing a diagnosis.

7 After the *levantada*, each patient is taken away from the circle, where he/she faces the left wall and is cleansed by both *alzadores*, one with a sword, the other with a stone sculpture. This time the work is done from the head down and includes hits against the patient's chest, pulling of the patient's knuckles as arms are held outward, and constant invocation. During the cleansings, the rest of the patients remain standing in the circle and are encouraged by Víctor to stamp their feet in time with his singing. Eventually those who have been cleansed are allowed to sit down.

8 When all patients have been raised and cleansed, Víctor resumes his seat at the mesa. Meanwhile, the *alzadores* raise and cleanse each other.

9 At about 2:30 A.M. there is a quiet period. Víctor remains seated at the mesa.

10 At about 3:00 A.M. all the patients return to form a semicircle and receive more tobacco to raise.

11 The final stage is a *florecimiento* performed on each patient in turn in front of the mesa. Víctor sprays liquid from his *seguro* directly at the patient.

12 After this has been completed, the staffs are collected, some divinations using clothing that patients have brought are performed, and Víctor sings a closing song.

The ritual is performed with a sense of openness and friendly warmth. Talking is constant; Víctor does not hesitate to turn on his flashlight in order to find something on the mesa, and there is no suggestion of a rigid structure or a stringent code of ritual behavior.

10
Nilo Plasencia

First Meeting

I met Nilo Plasencia during my first session with Rodrigo López in early November 1979. That evening Nilo had served as one of Rodrigo's assistants. Since I took a turn in front of the mesa along with Rodrigo's clients, I had a chance to assess Nilo's abilities as a curing assistant. He was excellent. He had learned the techniques very well and performed with flair and great energy. It was obvious to me that he was an uncommon *alzador*.

Nilo was present in June 1980 when I followed up on my research with Rodrigo and Helmer, at the latter's house. He sat quietly through two days of intensive interviews, yet his presence was very supportive and contributed a great deal to the atmosphere of positive rapport and cooperation.

I did not see Nilo again until August 1987. At that time Donald Joralemon and I needed another healer in order to broaden the scope of our work with the patients of curanderos. It was then that I remembered Nilo. I knew that he had been practicing cautiously on his own when I first met him as Rodrigo's assistant in 1979. When I saw him again in 1980, there had not been time to investigate his activities; I was too busy filling gaps in my information about Helmer and Rodrigo. The time had finally come, seven years later, to get back to him.

It was not hard to find Nilo. He lived a few blocks from Helmer. Don Joralemon and I found him at home, smoking a cigarette on the couch of his living room. Curly hair framed his chiseled features. He was as agile and lean as I remembered him. He gave me a quizzical, half-smiling look as he slyly asked why it had taken me so long to come back to see him.

I excused myself on the grounds of having had only short stays in Trujillo during the intervening years. He responded with a hearty chuckle and then began a jovial narration of our first meeting and some of the events that followed. In particular, he reminded me of an incident that had occurred during my first session with Roberto Rojas, which I had related to him years earlier. In dealing with the attack of a sorcerer, Roberto's counterattack had been so ferocious that he broke the skull from his counter mesa with a blow from his iron serpent staff.

After recounting old times, I told Nilo about our current research and asked if he would be willing to participate. He seemed a bit reluctant, but gave us his consent.

The next night I attended the first session with Nilo alone since Don had to attend a session with Víctor Flores. Any doubts I had entertained about Nilo's willingness to work with us were soon eliminated. The high energy I recalled from years before was as strong as ever. He worked hard the whole night through, totally immersing himself in every detail of the ritual while at the same time endeavoring to explain things to me.

In the next weeks, between sessions with Víctor and Nilo, I gradually documented the latter's mesa and ritual, while piecing together the following details of this rugged fisherman's life.

Biography

Born in 1944 in Huanchaquito, a fishing village near Trujillo, Pedro "Nilo" Plasencia Vergara was the fifth of seven children of a couple from the highland town of Contumazá. He grew up and was educated on the huge coastal sugar estate of Casa Grande, where his father was an employee in charge of inventory at the hacienda's branch office in Sausal. It was a stable but unchallenging existence, and Nilo's natural intelligence and ambition led him to depart for the more worldly ambiance of Lima when he was only fourteen. In the capital he worked and studied, finishing high school in 1961. Following his graduation, he worked for four years as an employee of an advertising firm.

In 1965, Nilo returned to Sausal. At the age of twenty-one, he already had seven years of experience in the big city, but he was tired of being away from his family. After working for some time on a *chacra* (small farm) granted to his father by Casa Grande, a friend persuaded Nilo to try fishing in the port town of Chimbote where one could make good money. The first boat that he shipped out on was called "Nilo."

After two years of work in Chimbote, opportunities opened up in Salaverry, closer to Nilo's home. He first worked with a Spanish crew, who gave him the nickname *Chavalo* ("Kid"). For the next decade, Nilo earned a living either as a fisherman or stevedore, according to the availability of work. In 1970, he married and began raising a family, which eventually numbered six children.

Nilo was exposed to folk healing from an early age. His father was a curing assistant and his maternal uncle was a curandero who diagnosed by taking the patient's pulse, a highland tradition. However, it was not until the mid-1970s, when he was thirty-one, that Nilo began to consider healing as a livelihood. At that time he met the tyrannical sorcerer who so profoundly influenced Roberto Rojas. In between stints as fisherman and stevedore, Nilo joined the group of aspiring healers who gravitated to this sorcerer. In particular, he and Rodrigo López began to emerge as a team of competent assistants who worked for the *maestro*. They became known as *los tigres*, the tigers.

Through the late 1970s the team matured. On one occasion they were instrumental in deflecting the *golpe*, or attack, of a shaman which had weakened their mentor. A colleague of the *maestro*, who treated him after the attack, acknowledged the invaluable service the two had rendered. Nilo was quick to point out, however, that the tyrant for whom they worked would never have given them any credit. He was not, in Nilo's mind, a teacher by any definition. What they learned from him was learned only by observation and by being ordered around, not by any instruction. In addition, they learned from the contacts they made with other healers and from their own personal experiments performed while working for this difficult practitioner.

By about the end of 1978, Rodrigo was slowly initiating his own practice. Nilo worked briefly as his assistant, but by 1979 he was operating his own mesa. The night I attended my first session with Rodrigo, Nilo worked as the assistant on the Ganadero side of the mesa, but it was apparent by the vigor with which he worked that he was much more than a simple aide.

When our contact was renewed in mid-1987 Nilo was almost a ten-year veteran. In the interim period, although he practiced mainly in the countryside near Moche, he had also worked occasionally in the highlands inland from Trujillo, as well as in Lima, where he and Rodrigo worked together as partners, operating both of their mesas at the same time. His own family roots in the

Andes helped him to develop a large pool of clients, eventually resulting in a regular flow of patients from this region to his rituals in the Trujillo area.

Nilo is a very independent, strong-willed individual. In this regard, it is instructive to note how he made the final break from his mentor, especially in comparison to the difficulty Roberto Rojas has had in the same undertaking. As Nilo tells it, in the early 1980s the sorcerer invited Nilo to have a beer with him. During the ensuing conversation his mentor told Nilo that he felt that Nilo did not know a thing about healing. To this Nilo replied that once a pupil graduates he goes on to become a professional, while the teacher remains a mere teacher. Nilo went on to point out that he had "graduated" and gone on to acquire his own experience with two famous northern healers, one from Ferreñafe and the other from the Shimbe Lagoon, where he had bathed and collected herbs. Both had cared enough to baptize his power objects and to teach him about herbs and how to prepare *seguros*. The Shimbe healer had even cured him of *golpe de espiritismo* (spiritist attack) and shown him how to cure all of the varieties of *daño* ("harm" by sorcery) as well as *susto* (soul loss).

An argument ensued and the two men came to blows. Not one to be pushed around by anyone, Nilo struck the sorcerer. The man later filed a legal suit, but it was dismissed (the judge was one of Nilo's relatives). Nilo has not been bothered since.

In the late 1970s, just before his break with the sorcerer, Nilo had an experience which revealed that he was destined to become a healer. He was in the highlands near Santiago de Chuco on the feast day of the patron saint of the town, Santiago (Saint James). He was experimenting on his own with his incipient mesa. His patient's family believed it was a case of devil possession. Just after midnight a huge black cat appeared, hissing and growling. The family's livestock bolted, the patient fainted, and everyone present developed serious headaches. Nilo went down on his knees and prayed to Santiago for their salvation, offering to hold a Mass for the saint if they came through this experience unharmed. It was a typical sierra winter night—cold, clear, and star-studded. Suddenly, Santiago, the warrior apostle, appeared in the sky, riding his charger with his brilliant, shining sword in hand.

Another experience confirmed Nilo's conviction that it was his destiny to be a healer. After he had set up his mesa for what later turned out to be his first cure (of a woman who experienced chills and blinding headaches), Nilo was praying with one of his swords in his hand when:

> I saw a light that spoke to me in my thoughts, no? In the lucidity of my sight it told me that I must call the sword "Lance of Light." Therefore, it has the name you have there in your notes. It is called Lance of Light, and in this fashion it was practically baptized, but in the thought of a ray of light, a nebula out in space.

At one point in our conversations, Nilo, reflecting on this lance and the shells of the Ganadero side of his mesa which support it, connected his fishing background to his work as a curandero:

> All of the shells come from the sea; as you well know three-quarters of the earth is composed of water. . . . As a fisherman, I said that I was going to follow a special line. Everybody works with mountains, charms, *huacos* [archaeological objects]. All the bad leaves. And why not the good also? The good also goes because at times there are pearls, there are jewels, there are ships that sink and treasures that go to the bottom of the sea. Well, given the qualities of the sea, they are all turned into water there under the sea. There I take the edge off your ills, your bad luck, all your pains. There they go losing their edge every time we turn them around into the sea below.

From August to mid-September 1987, and later in February 1988, I worked intensively with Nilo since he had become actively involved in our study of patients. As a result of our project, he came to the attention of Europeans staying at a newly completed hostel built by Eduardo Calderón. They had traveled to Peru to learn about Eduardo's practices, but whenever Eduardo was out of the country many of them gravitated to Nilo, who welcomed the increased exposure. Nilo also participated in a local congress on traditional healing in mid-1988, and has had an article about his work published in a Peruvian popular magazine (*Gente* 1988, No. 653, pp. 68–70). He has seen the number of patients seeking his help swell, at least in part as a result of his increased notoriety. It will be interesting to see if Nilo becomes the same kind of curandero celebrity as Eduardo in the years to come.

Plasencia's Mesa

The two fields of Nilo's mesa (Figure 15) are very clearly delineated by placing each on its own separate cloth. The larger Banco Gloria on the right is the side of the herbs and saints. The Banco

Figure 15 Plasencia Mesa

Ganadero of the left is about half its size, and it is associated with rituals of *volteando* ("turning around") and *botando* ("throwing away") the curses placed on Nilo's patients by sorcerers. Although there is no middle field on the mesa, there are balancing artifacts, especially the aforementioned Lance of Light, which, together with its neighbor, the Aguaruna Staff, and a crucifix, form the "center" of the mesa. Speaking of the sword, which he calls the "commander of the mesa," Nilo says:

> All is focused there. That is for diagnosis from the moment that you begin to work with the blessing of God and with the permission of Our Lord Jesus Christ. You have to take hold of yourself and of the sword. In other words, that is the gift that it gives you, that is the gift that you shouldn't lose for anything.

The sword works with the herbs, "the little sisters" who are "decreed by the Providence of Our Lord Jesus Christ . . . born by the Providence of Our Lord; no one plants them, no one fertilizes them, no one waters them, no one cultivates them." Adopting a nautical metaphor, Nilo explains that the herbs and the sword, with the support of the numerous shells on the Ganadero side, serve as the "rudder of the ship."

The "staffs" at the head of Gloria serve the customary cleansing and protective functions usually associated with the right side. They include (from right to left): an Imbibing Lance with a cup in the handle used by the healer to activate the power of Gloria with tobacco (only part of the blade shows in Figure 15); a *chonta*; a Saint Cyprian Staff to dominate and control curses; a pair of *chonta* branches for whipping away evil; a Sword of Saint Gabriel the Archangel, used with the Lance of Light to cleanse patients; another *chonta*; two additional pairs of *chontas*; the central Lance of Light; the Aguaruna Staff; and two Blood Staffs used in curing curses performed through spiritism. Beyond the staffs on the right are (from right to left): a bag of herbs, a cup of San Pedro, an herbal mixture used to induce vomiting, and a container of San Pedro.

Objects on the ground on the right side include most of the standard positive artifacts used in healing: three framed images of holy personages (Christ, the Virgin, and a folk saint, Sarita Colonia); a crucifix; a prayer book; four major *seguros* called *madriguero* ("of the burrow, den, lair"; see Chapter 12) belonging to the healer; patients' *seguros*; a white rose; *agua florida*; two perfumes; tobacco; *refresco*; two gourd rattles; a harmonica; shells for serving and raising tobacco; a crystal ball for divining; two minerals for luck; and two heart-shaped stones for curing heart problems. Somewhat unusual is a set of stones used to "enchant and disenchant" (*encantar y desencantar*) as well as a set of pre-Columbian relics placed on a cap and used to "bind" (*amarrar*) enemies.

At the head of the Ganadero there are five "staffs" (from right to left): a large *chonta* used in cleansings; an Aguaruna arrow used to *rayar* (i.e., create lightning to counter sorcerers); a deer's foot to drive off attacking spirits or sorcerers; and two swords, the Female Guerrilla to "turn around" curses and the Steel Sword for creating lightning.

Some ground artifacts on the left have animal referents; they include a brass bull (upper left) and two snakes (one in stone, the other in steel) used to "turn around" curses. In the lower left-hand corner are two pre-Columbian pots (not shown in Figure 15) used to cure *antimonios*, a sickness brought on by the dust of pre-Columbian ruins. A gourd rattle, resting on a book about sorcery, is used to activate the Ganadero accounts.

The remaining larger part of the left side is dominated by a set of shells used to serve and imbibe tobacco to activate this side of the mesa and to "turn around" curses. Once again, Nilo uses marine imagery in describing the shells as the medium by which all curses and evil accounts are washed away and swallowed by Mother Sea.

The night of a session all participants are transported to a *chacra* near the Rio Moche. The ritual takes place in the backyard of a small farmhouse of some friends and former patients of Nilo.

The ritual sequence is as follows:

1. *Recordar el remedio* ("Remember the remedy"). At midnight, staffs are sprayed and Nilo chants an opening song to activate San Pedro and the mesa as a whole. During the chant, Nilo focuses first on the Banco Gloria and then on the Banco Ganadero.

2. San Pedro. Nilo first serves himself a cup, after blessing and touching mesa objects with it. Then, while shaking his rattle, he talks into the cup, speaking his own name and referring to various body parts. After he drinks, he repeats the invocation in the name of his assistant. The patients all follow, each drinking San Pedro in front of the mesa. When everyone has been served, Nilo sprays the mesa with perfume.

3. *Jalar la yerba* ("Pull the herb"). Nilo sings a *tarjo* for San Pedro and the herbs so that they will enter into the bodies of the participants. In the middle of the chant, he stops and sprays perfume on the mesa.

4. *Tabaco* (for healer and assistants). Nilo sings into the tobacco bowl, orienting himself to different parts of the altar. After preparing *tabaco*, he invokes and touches each of the major shells on the left with a serving of the mixture. He then sings a *tarjo* for *tabaco*. Everyone stands while he and his assistant, swords in hand, invoke and then ingest the tobacco mixture through their left nostrils. A similar procedure is repeated with their right nostrils. As everyone sits, Nilo sprays the mesa and then sings, turning to the left side and raising his knife toward the altar. Then, back facing the center of the mesa, he again sings into the tobacco bowl.

5. *Tabaco* (for patients). One by one, patients repeat after Nilo a series of invocations. They take staffs and go out toward the left to ingest *tabaco* through their left nostrils. Nilo again sings at the left side. The patients return for a second dose, and the same invocations are repeated. They then imbibe through the right nostril at the left side of the mesa. Those who do not take the tobacco mixture receive perfume in their hands and are told to inhale it deeply.

6. *Jalar el espíritu, Destrancar* ("Pull the spirit, Unbolt"). Nilo takes each patient around the corner of the house, to the right of the mesa, and conducts a divinatory conversation or *rastreo*. At the

beginning of the discourse, which he calls a *juego* (game, set, or "playing"), he tells the patient to look at his face and then asks if he looks normal. He then lowers his head to catch the shadows in a fashion that transforms his face into an ugly apparition, and asks patients what they see, cuing them to say "a mask" or "a monster." If he is successful in engaging the patient, he can usually nudge or encourage the person to project onto his (Nilo's) face the features of the perceived adversary. This achieved, he proceeds to coach the client through a verbal attack on his "enemy," during which much suppressed emotion may be released or acted out. After this, Nilo ingests tobacco and sends the patient back to his/her seat.

7 *Baile, Limpia* ("Dance, Cleansing"). After everyone has had a *rastreo*, each patient comes before the mesa to perform a dance to the rhythm of Nilo's rattle and *tarjo*. The process proceeds with Nilo raising the client from feet to head, using a shell of tobacco into which the patient has breathed. This is followed by a *tarjo*, a series of invocations, and the imbibing of more tobacco by the patient. Nilo then takes the patient to the right for a *limpia*; that is, he rubs the patient's four sides with his two swords and then sprays him/her with liquid from his *seguro madriguero*.

8 *Seguro* ("Herb Bottle"). Nilo mixes a *seguro* and then sings and plays a harmonica over it before delivering it to the patient across the mesa. He rings bells over the mesa, sings, and tells the patient to dance. The patient then gets a thorough spraying with perfume.

9 *Florecimiento* ("Flowering"). Nilo has each patient stand before the mesa to be sprayed with perfume.

10 *Cerrar la cuenta* ("Close the account"). By about 6:00 A.M. Nilo calls everyone in front of the mesa for a final closing song. Halfway through, he stops to spray the mesa with liquid from his *seguro madriguero*. At the end of the song, he closes with a "Good morning," and tells everyone to shake hands with each other.

Another aspect of Nilo's practice involves undoing sorcery that has been performed by the burying of a possession, article of clothing, or likeness of the victim along with a hex or spell. This sorcery bundle is called an *entierro* (burial) and requires special attention. If Nilo detects this kind of sorcery, he recommends that the patient accompany him to the south to a town near Barranco where a specialist in *entierros* who works with coca, alcohol, and cigarettes is reputed to be able to make the sorcery bundle manifest, thus neutralizing its effect. Nilo says that this is the only way to undo such curses.

I I

José Paz

BY DONALD JORALEMON

First Meeting

Douglas Sharon's published work on Eduardo Calderón served as the departure point for my first fieldwork in Peru (October 1980 to September 1981).[1] Interested in the degree to which Sharon's informant was representative of Peru's north coast curanderos, I wanted to document in similar detail the practice of a curer whose biography showed fewer acculturative influences. It was not long after I took up residence in the beach community of Huanchaco, just a few miles from the large urban center of Trujillo, that I made contact with my ideal informant. Huanchaco's Catholic priest, Padre Rufino E. Benitez Vargas, referred me to José Paz Chaponan, a sixty-five-year-old curandero, who came to town every week to hold ritual healing sessions.

Patients could find José either in the small town of Lambayeque, twenty minutes from Chiclayo, or, on Wednesdays and Thursdays, in Huanchaco. Surrounded by houses in various stages of construction, his home had a fresher coat of paint and evidenced more careful upkeep than most of the others in the community. The front door was usually open, a line of wooden chairs just inside for those awaiting consultation. We spent most of our time together here, squeezing in interviews between the almost steady stream of patients. His forceful personality and digressive conversational style made formal, direct questioning almost impossible. In addition, he was initially suspicious of my motives and would offer evasive responses before going off on tangents of his own. Thus, I acquired bits and pieces of his life history over a long period of time, including some last details from his widow, Nérida Cacél de Paz, after his death in 1985.

Biography

José was born in 1915 in the small town of Túcume, about forty kilometers north of Chiclayo. His father was a fairly wealthy land-holder and silversmith who served as *gobernador* of Túcume for eleven years. His mother was from the nearby community of Mo-tupe. She died when José was ten. José had two sisters, a small fam-ily by the standards of rural Peru. As a child José was expected to work on his father's *chacras* and, as a result, he only finished the second year of elementary school.

It is clear that José's father was a very important figure in his life, a fact that is not surprising given the early death of his mother. His memories recalled his father as a powerful, confident man who won the respect of all his neighbors for his stern but fair leader-ship. For José, the personal power of his father assumed almost su-pernatural proportions, as indicated by the following story he told me one evening.

It seems that one day José and his father (also named José) were returning on horseback from the town of Morope to their home in Túcume when they came across a certain Manuel Vidraure trav-eling in the same direction. Vidraure was a *brujo* (sorcerer), a dis-ciple of the powerful Juan Rojas ("*gente de peso*," or powerful men, in José's words), who was so skilled in the evil art that he could kill people with nothing more than the force of his will. Overtaking Vidraure, the senior Paz blocked his way and, with profuse insults, demanded that the evildoer turn back and never again set foot in Túcume.

When Vidraure's teacher, Rojas, learned of the confrontation between the two men, he visited his disciple to chastise him for the incident. Admonishing his student never to cross Señor Paz again, Rojas explained that "he is the master of us all." As punishment, Vidraure was required to serve José's father on a later occasion when the elder Paz participated in a ritual performed by Rojas. In José's mind, this humiliation of the sorcerer was the ultimate dem-onstration that his father held sway even over those who had mas-tered the most potent of evil forces.

Knowing of José's deep feelings for his father, I was not overly surprised to learn from him that one of the two human skulls he placed on his protective mesa was that of the senior Paz. José claimed to have had the assistance of a doctor when he opened his father's coffin some years after his death. He believed that he could call on the spirit (*ánimo*) of his father to strengthen and protect him during rituals. The two other spirits on which José relied in his sessions were famous, powerful shamans, Santos Aventara and Santos Crisantos.

José also inherited from his father a strong belief in the importance of respect. Among his favorite topics of conversation was the increasing lack of respect shown by new generations of children to their parents. In his own homes, José demanded and received total deference from his own offspring as well as from the two children from a previous marriage of his wife. They waited on him, obeyed his every command, and maintained strict standards of conduct in his presence. His wife treated him almost as lord and master, to the extent that she even sugared and tested his tea for him.

José confessed that he had lived an irresponsible life until his early thirties. He worked in the fields in the mornings and drank all afternoon. Although he was married and had seven children (two of whom died), he described this period of his life as a reckless time. The sudden deaths of his wife and father within a short time caused him to reevaluate his life-style. He went into construction as steady employment and for two years cared for his children by himself. It was at this time that he also began practicing as a curandero; but he was always vague about the exact circumstances surrounding the beginnings of his practice.

In 1968, José married his second wife, a native of Trujillo. He considered her two children as *hijos políticos* (adopted children), but nevertheless had a kind of visitor's status in this family's Huanchaco home since he spent a majority of his time in his first house in Lambayeque. There, an elder son, Santos Paz Acosta, with wife and child, as well as another adult woman and her ten-year-old son, shared a two-story structure which, like the house in Huanchaco, stood out from neighboring homes for its size and quality.

When I asked José how he learned to be a curandero, he said that at age thirteen he had observed and participated in a few ritual sessions performed by some of his father's peons. However, it was not until many years later that he actually began to practice. He claimed that he had no specific teacher and that he learned about herbs through personal experimentation. His training was a process of personal elaboration on his informal childhood experiences rather than a strict apprenticeship to a practicing curer.

By the time I met José, with approximately thirty-five years as a practicing curandero behind him, he was obsessive about his full-time role as a curer. His conversation rarely strayed from related themes and he even had dreams about herbs and patients on a regular basis. He was fond of pointing out that he was not interested in the pecuniary rewards of his profession, but rather in the exercise of his God-given talent for the benefit of others. This altruistic commitment, however, did not stop José from maintaining a reasonably careful accounting of debts.

It is hard to imagine how a person less convinced of his vocational calling could have adhered to the kind of schedule José maintained for so many years. For twenty-three years he worked only in Lambayeque and averaged one session every week without fail. For the twelve years since he took up residence in Huanchaco he had added to his weekly Lambayeque rituals at least three more a month in his new home. As a rough estimate, José had led close to 2,300 curing rituals up until 1980. It is unlikely one would subject himself to such physical and mental punishment without a basic personal commitment to curing.

José's dedication to curing was intimately tied to his religious faith. That he considered himself deeply religious is illustrated by the Catholic icons that adorned both of his houses, the religious images he included on his curing altar, and the orthodox invocations he employed in his ritual. He had a tattoo on his right forearm that showed a crucifixion figure above his own initials. He told me repeatedly that he was able to cure because "God helps me."

The way that José perceived the relationship between his religious faith and his shamanistic art was most clear in his use of the word *"vista"* to describe the basis of his curative capacity. Literally, *vista* is sight, or vision, but for José the word more accurately implied an intuitive grasp or comprehension. The following comments by José illustrate his use of the concept:

> *Vista* is the ability to see, to recognize. You have to have *vista* to cure. . . .
> Not everyone has *vista*. Some people can see but they don't recognize what they see. . . .
> When the herbs appear [in a session], they go by fast, like a film. I have to be able to recognize them and to know which patient they will cure. This is *vista*. . . .
> When I am old, too old to do sessions, I will still cure. I don't have to do them now; I do them only because I enjoy them. Before the session I already have an idea of what is the cause of each patient's sickness and which herb will cure it; I do the session just to be sure. Because I have *vista*, I don't really need to do it. . . .
> God gives me the *vista* to cure.

Vista, then, is a God-given intuitive ability to "read" an individual as well as to comprehend the meaning of what is visualized in the course of a ritual session. On one occasion, José used the word *tele-patía* (telepathy) to describe this capacity, explaining that from the moment he saw a person he knew what kind of an ailment he/she was suffering from. José considered *vista* the key to his ability to heal.

It is important, however, to recognize that for José *vista* was not a kind of divine gift at birth, but rather was a contingent reward for ongoing faith. He told me that he would light candles at his home altars and pray because otherwise he felt he would lose the assistance of God and the saints. He clearly considered his relationship to these supernaturals a matter of constant reaffirmation, and the power that resulted from it a conditional endowment. This is a crucial point because it differentiates José from the tradition of shamans whose power is seen as a personal gift, a capacity present from birth. In José's view, *vista* was available to anyone, if the right kind of faithful relationship to the sacred world of the saints and God was established. This conception is consistent with popular Catholicism, in which acts of faith can be expected to produce beneficial results.

José's religious faith and sense of having divine assistance were key elements in his personal confidence in his ability to heal. This confidence had to be strong enough to stand up under the pressures implicit in the marginal, unorthodox status of the curandero. Not just for himself alone, but also for those who came to him for help, it was essential to present an assured and authoritative image. It was, after all, as recently as the 1950s and early 1960s that Peruvian society disparaged and even persecuted curanderos, a fact that José often recalled with an ironical resentment. He would say, "The police would come to harass me one day, and the next be there waiting for me to cure them!"

In addition to his declarations of religious devotion, José also used extended narrations of his past cures to underscore his authority. These stories almost always involved one of two themes: "I am a powerful person," and/or "the world is filled with liars, cheats, and disrespectful (ungrateful) people." There were many stories about other curanderos who were really frauds and sought only to rob their clients, as distinct from José, who had no interest in money at all. Other stories concerned people who were openly critical of him but who invariably requested his help when sick;

these included medical doctors from Lima, foreigners, high-ranking people in the military, and, as mentioned above, local police. Another series of stories revolved around persons involved in dishonest, violent, or merely disrespectful acts. These stories were told as illustrations of the general degradation of contemporary Peruvian society, in contrast to what José considered a more moral past.

When José was an actor in one of his stories, he would recount dialogue and action in which his part was always proud and authoritative, while others ended up humbled and meek before him. For example, a lower echelon civil guard tries to extort money from him in return for not arresting him for practicing without a license. José plays along, coolly, and then levels his adversary with a "who's who" in the civil guard who have been his patients. In another story, José squares off against a medical doctor in the diagnosis of a young woman's complaint and wins the competitor's admiration by correctly identifying, on the basis of the woman's pulse alone, a pregnancy combined with a temporary state of blindness. His repertoire of stories was impressive.

His storytelling was not just for the benefit of anthropologists. When friends came by to share a few beers, José pursued the same conversational tack as he did with patients while waiting for the time of the session to begin. Whether or not the tales were basically accurate, José's embellishments as well as his relentless repetitions were clear indications of a strong emotional attachment to the underlying message: I am a good, powerful man in a world full of hypocrites and evildoers.

When I returned to Peru in June 1987 I had already learned of José's death. It occurred on New Year's Day, 1985, when José had left his Lambayeque house to walk the short distance to the home of another woman whose company he kept. There had been a party in his house the night before and he had slept late into the day. According to his wife in Huanchaco, the woman who shared his home in Lambayeque had only recently abandoned José, causing him worries on top of his longstanding liver and prostate problems. The day was very hot, as summer was just beginning, and José paused to rest along the side of the road. He was found at that spot soon after, dead of a heart attack.

José's Huanchaco wife, whom I know as Norma, speculated openly about the "real" cause of his death. Still angry over the fact that she only belatedly learned of José's death from a former patient who happened to stop by the house in Huanchaco, instead of from anyone in the Lambayeque family, she is sure that he had been improperly cared for by the woman who lived with him, and that his new "*querida*," a twenty-four-year-old, had also caused him trouble. She suggested that there may well have been sorcery involved, the result of jealousy between the two women in Lambayeque. Thus, for Norma, José's heart attack takes on greater significance as it is contextualized in terms of sexual competition. While speaking openly of José's other companions, she was also quick to note that she was the only one to whom he was legally married. She also took pride in the fact that she did not place any demands on his estate, over which relatives in Lambayeque fought for years after his death.

José's legacy did not end with his death. Some six months before José's death, his eldest son, Santos, had begun to take an interest in curanderismo and had served as an assistant to another curer in Lambayeque. After a respectful six months of mourning for his father, Santos started his own practice, using the altar José had employed for sessions in Lambayeque. In addition, Norma soon began to do sessions using the second of José's altars in Huanchaco.

However, Norma did not perform rituals unassisted. Rather, she arranged with Santos to arrive every Wednesday, carrying herbs from the special markets near Chiclayo, to work with her. They did ritual sessions inside the Huanchaco house, because Norma felt that it was no longer safe to use José's outside location in nearby Huanchaquito. Santos took the central position seated behind the mesa and did most of the chanting during rituals. Norma and her son, Luis ("Lucho"), took primary responsibility for managing the patients and doing the tobacco raising. It is interesting to note that Santos's songs were taken word for word from José's rituals, thanks to a tape recording Santos had made before José's death. Indeed, the ritual performed by Norma bore a striking resemblance to José's in every sense.

Despite the appearance of Santos's central role in Norma's rituals, she noted emphatically that she was the curer. She did the "suspending" and "cleansing," as well as all the consultations before and after the ritual. Norma insisted that she was the one with *vista*, that only recently had Santos begun to "*despejarse*" (to become clear-sighted). Predictably, Santos had a different view of his association with Norma. He agreed that she had the primary role in working with the Huanchaco patients, but he also insisted that fewer and fewer clients came to Huanchaco once they learned that he was working in Lambayeque.

At the end of the last field season (December 1988) I returned once again to Norma's house in Huanchaco. The family had opened a stationery store alongside the house and appeared to be quite prosperous. Norma said that she no longer did ritual sessions, but quickly added that her former patients still came for ritual cleansings and consultations. She also said that Santos was still practicing in Lambayeque.

Paz's Mesa

José worked with two largely independent sets of mesa artifacts, one which he kept in Lambayeque and the other which he stored in Huanchaco. He considered the Lambayeque artifacts to be more powerful—necessarily so since the sorcerers of that region were more powerful. He pointed to the substantially greater number of objects on the mesa in Lambayeque as evidence of its greater power; the Huanchaco mesa was substantially smaller (for more detail on these mesas see Joralemon 1984).

In both locations José used two altars: the main mesa, which he described as "pure luck and heavenly glory," and a second, defensive mesa, the *mesa de afuera* (outside mesa), which would be set up about twenty feet in front of the main mesa. José conceived three banks or fields in the structure of the main mesa: from left to right, Banco Ganadero, *banco guayanchero* (Bank of the Herbalist, Specialist in Love Magic), and Banco Curandero. The secondary mesa was symbolically associated with the left field of the main mesa, the Ganadero, and had few artifacts: two human skulls, a stone carving of a snake, and some shells.

The left side of the mesa (Figure 16) was associated with the powers of the sorcerer, with negative, life-taking powers. Here were placed objects of the ancestors (*"los antepasados," "los gentiles"*), such as pre-Hispanic ceramics, stone carvings, and shells found either at archaeological sites or at other places of power. Dangerous herbs were also placed on this side of the altar, plants used in sorcery to poison or control a victim and given names such as: *cóndor* and *toro misha, león, tigre,* and *gato cimora.* Like the names of these plants, which José explained were linked to the form each took during visions, other artifacts on the left side were also associated with the wild, such as small figures of owls, snakes, and felines.

Figure 16 Paz Mesa, Banco Ganadero

Books of black magic and a small statue of Saint Cyprian situated
between two spent shotgun shells were also on this side.

The central part of the mesa, the Banco Guayanchero (Figure
17) was seen by José as the location of luck. In fact, José called the
central line of artifacts of the mesa the "generator of luck." Images
and small statues of Christ, including crucifixes, and of the Virgin
Mary dominated this field. Another statue of Saint Cyprian was included, this time alongside the Virgin, as well as a group of small
magnetic stones and crystals. A line of bottles containing herbs ran
from front to back. In one large bottle in the center were herbs
that José conceived as his own personal *seguro*. All the herbs of this
field took the form of beautiful flowers in José's visions. His glass
of San Pedro and the container in which the liquid tobacco was
kept were also found in this field.

On the right side, in the Banco Curandero (Figure 18), were artifacts associated with the healing art: more images and statues of
Catholic saints, as well as shells, stones, and bottles of herbs used in
curing. These latter appeared in José's ritual visions as the actual
plants themselves, passing by his eyes like a film as he concentrated
on each individual patient.

Figure 17 Paz Mesa, Banco Guayanchero

Figure 18 Paz Mesa, Banco Curandero

In addition to the many objects placed on the mesa's mat, there was a line of wooden staffs and metal swords thrust into the ground immediately in front of the altar. José indicated that each one had a specific place where it worked best and that the metal swords and staffs belonged to the right side. Those placed to the left were of wood and had certain defensive properties. One staff (bejuco), placed at the exact center of the mesa, was especially important for José. He explained that he could use it to control uncooperative patients; the staff would direct the power of José's mind toward the person over whom he wanted to exercise control.

Drawing from many of José's enigmatic responses to mesa-related questions, it was clear that he understood the role of artifacts in terms of the processes of defense, diagnosis, and cure. He saw the objects as relational sets; certain of them worked together in one or more of these processes. Although the objects of each field had a quality in common, as suggested by the general associations to sorcery, luck magic, and curing, it was as subsets within each field that they fulfilled their role in rituals.

In their defensive capacity, certain objects served José as an early warning system, vibrating when an attacking force manifested itself. He explained that this was the primary function of the outside mesa; when he saw the objects there begin to tremble he would sally forth, armed with a sword from the main mesa, to repel the interfering force. A curandero who was insufficiently powerful or vigilant could easily be overcome or even die if these forces were not countered. José had seen such an incident when another shaman tried to perform a ritual while drunk and was overwhelmed by the power of a rival.

The diagnostic role of the mesa artifacts was involved with José's ability to relate the visions he had for each patient to symbols on the mesa. For example, he once "saw" a large bird of prey on a patient's shoulder, pecking away at the individual's heart, and associated this vision with the poisonous herb which has the visionary form of a condor. During one session, he visualized something which he associated with a small stone carving of a pregnant woman with a tortured facial expression that was placed on the left side of the mesa. José's diagnosis was a depression resulting from a past miscarriage. Sometimes the message of the vision was made intelligible to José through a combination of associations with mesa objects, rather than a single item providing the key. Interpreting the vision in terms of the mesa artifacts was a central element in José's notion of *vista*, discussed above.

Mesa objects also contributed to the cure of patients, not only through visionary identifications of the proper curative herb for each patient's sickness, but also by their use in cleansing rituals. Early in the ritual each participant received a staff from among those in front of the main mesa, with instructions to rub it all over his or her body at each interval in the session. José explained that in the process the staff absorbed the patient's sickness.

As is common with other curanderos, José's understanding of his mesas was more pragmatic than philosophical. He was poor at providing didactic explanations for the many artifacts on his altars. He was interested in how each object would "work," not in what each meant in some intellectual sense. He said that before placing a new object on a mesa he would converse with it, during a ritual, to determine where it was from and what was the nature of its power.

José's rituals were well-orchestrated affairs, managed with the help of two assistants. Performed outdoors, on the beach near Huanchaco or in a field near José's home in Lambayeque, the major stages were as follows:

1   Opening rituals. First there was a thorough fumigation of the ritual area with incense. Opening invocations were then sung, to the rhythm of rattles, and the mesa was orally sprayed with perfumed water.

2   San Pedro (for the curer). José would pour himself a glass of San Pedro and, after reciting the Catholic blessing, "In the name of the Father, the Son, and the Holy Spirit," drink it in a single gulp. He said that he would then "converse" with the spirit of the plant to learn where it grew and how it would work in the session.

3   San Pedro (for assistants and patients). The two assistants and then each patient, one by one, would take a glass of the San Pedro, while José chanted: "*Bien nombrado, bien contado*, (reciting the patient's name), *por tu sombra, por tu suerte, por el Padre, Hijo, y el Espiritu Santo, y con el permiso de Dios* (Well named, well accounted/told, for your name, for your 'shade,' for your luck, for the Father, Son, and Holy Ghost, and with the permission of God)." Once emptied, the glass that had held the San Pedro was rubbed in circles on the patient's head by one of José's assistants (three times in each direction). A staff from the main mesa was handed to the patient with instructions to leave the enclosure and rub it over his/her body, from head to foot.

4   *Tabaco*. First, the two assistants nasally ingested several doses of tobacco, served in shells, for each patient (who were treated in pairs). The shells were first touched to the individual's feet, then knees, waist, and head, symbolizing the process of raising. Before ingesting the liquid, the assistant repeated the invocation quoted above ("Well named, well accounted . . . "). Next, the patients ingested doses of tobacco (left nostril first, then the right) while facing the *mesa de afuera*. Sent outside afterward, patients could be heard vomiting in the darkness. During this time, José, seated behind the main altar, took repeated doses of tobacco.

5   *Juego de la mesa de afuera* (Game of the defensive mesa). This phase of the session entailed the imbibing of more tobacco, but this time performed in front of the outside mesa. First, José would perform raisings for selected patients involving four doses of the liquid for each. The entire group then was given second doses of tobacco, after a circumambulation of the outside mesa (three times counterclockwise, three times clockwise). While this was happening, José would return to his seat behind

the main mesa, leaving his assistants to direct the patients. He told me that while the patients circled the secondary mesa spirits of the ancestors would appear around them, turning the whole area cold. Sometimes these spirits would try to cause trouble, which he had to stop by threatening them with his sword. He saw this as a pleasurable time: "It is very pretty; I like it a lot. But only those with *vista* can see them." Also, during this phase of the ritual José would begin to experience visions indicating the sources of his patients' illnesses.

6 *Juego de la yerba de la suerte* (Game of the luck herb). While the patients rested, José would concentrate on the herb bottles of the middle field, visualizing the combinations which would serve as *seguros* for clients who sought luck in business ventures or in love relationships. Individual patients would be called before the main mesa during this segment of the session.

7 *Rastreo* (Tracking). Two more tobacco raisings by patients were then performed in front of the main altar, first individually and then by pairs. José remained seated behind the mesa and, while calling out the name of the patient, would throw two shells onto the right side of the altar. He said that this was a process of cross-checking the conclusions he had reached about the proper cures for patients. After each tobacco dose, patients would leave the ritual area for more rubbings with their staffs.

8 *El florecer* (The flowering). By about 3:00 A.M. all patients had finished taking their fourth dose of tobacco. José's assistants would bring the whole group to the front of the main mesa, four abreast, women in front and men to the rear. Row by row, the patients received perfumed water in their cupped hands, which they were instructed to inhale and then rub over their necks and faces. After this, they were sent out once more for a staff rubbing and then given a short rest.

9 *La última oportunidad* (The last opportunity). The assistants called patients back before the main mesa, by twos, for a final dose of tobacco. Meanwhile, José, from his position behind the mesa, reached toward each patient with one shell in each hand and then tossed the shells onto the right side of the altar. If they landed any way but open side up, he knew that the herb(s) he had identified was (were) not the correct remedy. Concentrating on another possibility, he would repeat the procedure until both shells landed face up.

10 Closing rituals. A repetition of the previous perfumed water offering would close the ritual just as dawn was about to break, this time with José standing behind the altar singing of his herbs, of sacred lakes, and saints. Sometimes José would spray patients with perfumed water; other times he would leave this to

his assistants. Patients returned their staffs, which the assistants would spray with perfumed water. José offered his closing invocation and sprayed the mesa one last time with the scented water. It was important that the mesa be packed away before the sun appeared. Back at José's home, private consultations were held with patients to explain what the ritual had revealed about the causes and cures of ailments. Remedies were prepared and payments accepted.

12

Jorge Merino

BY DONALD SKILLMAN

First Meeting

I first met Jorge Merino in August 1985 by way of a mutual friend, Pedro Guerrero, a Franciscan parish priest whose territory included the Salas-Penachí-Cañaris-Incahuasi region of the Department of Lambayeque. For more than thirty years Father Guerrero had travelled the Lambayeque sierra on horseback performing Mass for outlying Quechua communities. He had been trying to convince the church authorities in Chiclayo to replace him in the mountains with a younger priest because he was not well and wanted to devote his remaining years to his own community of Salas and to his nearby *chacras* (farms). Yet, here we were, he having invited me, preparing to travel on horseback from Salas to Penachí, where he once again would officiate for more than a week at the annual Fiesta de Penachí, which takes place at a famous pilgrimage site high in the sierra.

Father Guerrero had been operated on previously for gallstones, but the problem persisted. The journeys to the highlands were especially painful to him, and he did not think he would survive another operation. Instead, he had sought relief from a master herbalist he knew and was somewhat pleased with the results. Before leaving for Penachí it was necessary to replenish the supply of herbs used in his *remedio*, and to do this we paid a visit to Jorge Merino. It is interesting to note that while Father Guerrero knew perfectly well that Merino was a curandero in the full sense of the word, it was Merino's herbal knowledge that brought him to the curer's door. As a good Catholic priest he was unable to approve officially of the role that the curandero plays in society, yet he is also a practical man and recognizes value when he sees it. His introduction began my long association with Jorge Merino.

Biography

Jorge Merino Bravo is somewhat unique as a Peruvian healer. Although his method of curing falls within the broader category of curanderismo practiced along the north coast of Peru, it is more specifically related to the type of traditional healing that has evolved in the highland Ayabaca province of Piura (Polia 1988), the border areas of southern Ecuador, and the tropical rain forests of the departments of Loreto, Amazonas, and Cajamarca. Like Víctor Flores, Jorge makes use of healing traditions that represent the four geographic zones of Peru: *costa* (coast), *sierra* (high mountain), *montaña* (low mountain), and *selva* (jungle).

Jorge was born on April 23, 1937, in the District of Montoro, Province of Ayabaca, Department of Piura. Originally there were six brothers in his family, but only three survived into adulthood. Jorge's father died when he was thirteen; he was then sent to live with an older cousin on his mother's side of the family. He ostensibly was to work as a laborer in his cousin's fields but, as it turned out, the cousin's real motive was to have the youngster help him with his curing altar, or mesa. The cousin was a curandero.

Shortly after arriving at his cousin's home, Jorge was asked to participate in a ritual session. The only patient present was a *compadre* of his parents. That night Jorge was given his first taste of San Pedro. Within a short time, a vision appeared to him. It was the image of a small child, barely fifty centimeters tall, with yellow hair and two burning stars for eyes. Jorge wanted to sing, but the child told him that it was wrong to sing; he should pray to God instead. And so Jorge began to pray.

Later that night, another vision came to Jorge. This time he saw the patient lying beside the mesa, covered by a white sheet and surrounded by a ring of burning candles. Jorge thought this strange because the patient was still where he had originally been seated, away from the mesa. At this point, Jorge's cousin, the curandero, asked him what it was that he was seeing. Jorge did not respond because the child forbade him to speak.

Later in the session, yet another vision appeared. This time it consisted of two men chasing a chocolate-brown cow through a dry wash. Again, his cousin asked Jorge what he was seeing, and again he did not respond. The curer insisted. Suddenly, the child appeared once more, telling Jorge to stand up. He obeyed. His cousin asked once more what he was seeing. This time Jorge began to describe the cow and the men chasing it. He saw them rope it and take it back through the same dry wash. Upon hearing this, the patient perked up and declared that this was a cow that had been stolen from him a year before.

The visionary child began to dance in a circle. He pulled Jorge by the hand and told him that the patient would die in eight days, on a Friday at 10:00 A.M. On the eighth day after the session, the patient passed away—exactly as the child had predicted.

The morning following the session Jorge felt as if he had received a blow to the head. He lapsed into unconsciousness for the remainder of the day. Not long after, he began to form his own mesa, conforming to his observations and experiences during that fateful night. Thus, at the age of thirteen, he set out as a curer and has never abandoned his mission.

During his first years as a young curer Jorge found it necessary to work as an agricultural laborer. As is the case with many healers from rural areas, this combination of agriculture and healing has been the norm for most of his life.

Jorge was twenty-two when he was inducted into the Peruvian army. He was stationed for two years as a radio operator in Tumbes, near the Ecuadorian border. By his account, he enjoyed army life. He evidently had more than his share of freedom after he met an enthusiastic captain who befriended him and encouraged his work as a curer. Jorge wound up spending his time in the military as a sort of unofficial curandero to his regiment, much as did Víctor Neyra.

Jorge left the army in 1961 to live in Jaen (Cajamarca). There he married and spent the next ten years working as a curer and farmer. In 1971, he moved his young family to Chiclayo (Lambayeque), seeking better educational opportunities for his children. He continued to support them, working primarily as a curandero. He relocated again in 1983, this time north of Chiclayo, in the countryside near the town of Salas, a move motivated by sheer economic necessity. Jorge staked out one hundred hectares of desert and began all over again. At the age of fifty-one, he became a father for the seventh time.

In the four decades that Jorge has worked as a curandero he has occasionally found it necessary to acquire new mesas, giving the old ones to disciples. He has done this because, as he puts it, his mesas have a tendency to become capricious with use. They have been known to try to strike back (*golpear*) at an adversary without Jorge's direction. He figures that through the years he has assembled about twenty mesas for this reason. They have all conformed to the same general configuration—especially with regard to a spatial layout in symbolic zones or fields. There has been little deviation from the organization of his first mesa.

Jorge is essentially a self-taught curer. He has never felt the need to apprentice himself to another *maestro* since he has always believed that God is his teacher. He has remained a curer all his life because he has a firm conviction that he has a mandate from God and that he is particularly good at what he does. In spite of his lack of formal education—he scarcely completed three years of primary school—Jorge is intelligent, well informed, and extremely articulate. He enjoys his work and believes that his services and skills improve with the passage of time.

Merino's Mesa

In the course of his all-night ritual Jorge concentrates, in succession, on four different symbolic zones of the mesa. As a result, communication is established between all sectors of the mesa. It is through the medium of the *encanto* that the sections of the mesa are connected. Before describing Jorge's artifacts and their spatial arrangement, it is necessary to elaborate on this vital concept.[1]

Encantos are free-flowing forces of nature that exist relatively uncontrolled and unaffected by other nonhuman powers. The goal of the curandero is to call forth and dominate an *encanto*, after which it serves as a companion to the mesa. For every mesa artifact there is a companion *encanto* that has to be brought under control. Jorge sees the objects of his mesa as representations of things from daily life, powerless until the *encantos* associated with them are activated by ritual. From the very start, he programs the artifacts to serve him, each and every piece with a very specific mission in mind. And it is through their *encantos* that these artifacts come to life and are able to act. Collectively, these *encantos* comprise the *encanto* of the mesa, just as the artifacts make up the mesa zones, which in turn constitute the mesa.

The *calicanto* is another force of nature that exists somewhat independently. It is composed of all the shadows (*sombras*), or spirits, that are called to a power spot and then are deposited there. It too must be dominated by the curer before it can be of any use to him. The *calicanto*, once dominated and assigned to a particular place, stays put. It is then available to receive the *encanto*.

The *encanto* flows randomly but is particularly drawn to spots where *calicanto* forces are found. This can be a curer's mesa, where that force is then under control, or it can be a mountain. Mountains that have an *encanto* project an image called a *genio* ("genie," see Vidarte's concept in Chapter 5) that is perceived by the *vista*, or psychic sight, of the healer.

A general feature of Jorge's mesa worthy of mention is the preponderance of what he calls *cerros* "mountains," (that is, power stones), in all sectors. This is similar to the mesa of Roberto Rojas (see Chapter 6). Since mountains are the most common loci for *encantos*, stones far outnumber other classes of artifacts on Jorge's mesa, as they also do on the altars of many other healers.

The concept of *madriguera* also figures importantly in Jorge's ritual and relates to the ideas of *cerros* and *encantos*. Literally, the term refers to an animal's lair, burrow, den, or cave. For Jorge, *madriguera* denotes powerful mountains (*cerros*) that are capable of dominating the evil that approaches the mesa by way of the *encantos* of hostile sources. The concept expresses both defense and offense in that a *madriguera* represents protection/defense for the occupants, but also a place from which attacks are mounted and in which prey is trapped.

A further connotation of *madriguera* for Jorge is that it is a place of renewal and rebirth. As we have seen, Rojas (Chapter 6), López (Chapter 7), and Plasencia (Chapter 10) apply the term to bottles of magical or powerful plants (*seguros*) collected at sacred highland lagoons, the healing waters of which regenerate those who bathe in them. These *seguros*, thought to be impregnated with the power of the lagoons and their associated mountains, serve a dual purpose of regeneration and protection.[2] This is reminiscent of the Quechua term *pakarina*, a mountain cave of origin associated with highland lagoons and springs. Such caves are considered to be sources of life.

With the foregoing concepts in mind, let us now turn to Jorge's mesa (Figure 19). The following is a list of its symbolic zones. His mesa is actually comprised of four mesas, each independent of the others and yet interdependent at the same time.

Figure 19 Merino Mesa

1 *Mesa de respaldo.* This is actually two mesas in one, the *mesa blanca de respaldo* and the *mesa negra de respaldo.* The first is on the outer right side (staffs, San Pedro, bottles) and the other is on the outer left side (staffs, tobacco, boulders, bottles). Their primary function is to reinforce (*respaldar*) and defend (*defender*) the entire mesa. This includes maintaining order throughout the divisions of the mesa.

2 *Mesa blanca curandera.* The primary purpose of this inner, right-hand division composed of stones is the performance of flowerings (*florecimientos*), that is, closure, good luck, and purification rituals performed at the end of a session.

3 *Mesa negra gentileña incaica.* The primary function of this inner, left-hand section composed of stones is to attack (*golpear*) and counterattack (*contrarrestar*). It is also useful for curing, defense, and cleansings (*limpias*).

4 *Mesa de centro*. The purpose of this middle zone, found at the foot
of the four Christian lithographs, is to reinforce both the Mesa
Blanca Curandera and the Mesa Negra Gentileña Incaica, whenever there is such a need. The function of this sector is to mediate
(*promediar*) or balance (*balancear*) the other two. For example,
Jorge may find it necessary to unite the Mesa de Centro with one
of the other two when he feels that it is lacking strength. It is also
important in the defense of and the support of the patient.

Artifacts of the Mesa de Respaldo reflect the "reinforcing" and
"defending" nature of this all-encompassing and facilitating division. Most of the curing agents or their ingredients are present
here. On the right side are herbs, San Pedro, perfumes, talcum,
vinegar, and disinfectant; on the left are flowers, sugar, limes, holy
water, and alcohol (rum, wine, port, maize beer). Also, the artifacts
and tools used in cleansing belong to this zone; they include a steel
auger/digging tool, *ajojaspe* staffs, a Longinus "lance," quince
branches with *chontas,* a cross-shaped tire iron, and a pair of scis-
sors, all on the right. On the left are other tools: another steel au-
ger, more *ajojaspe* staffs, a round *chonta,* a flat stick, a bowl, a
strainer with spoon, and a drinking glass. Each side has one large
stone related to a pre-Columbian shrine: white ruin on the right,
"Chinese" ruin (*Huaca China*) on the left. These two rocks are the
most powerful artifacts on the entire mesa. They work together as
well as with other power stones on the respective sides to defend
the entire mesa. Other stones on the left include a flashlight-
shaped rock used to reveal black magic and two defensive worked
stones of pre-Columbian origin: an axe-head and a mortar called a
whirlpool. In general, cure-enhancing herbs (including San Pedro)
and perfumes predominate on the right, while defensive power
stones and alcoholic liquids are most prevalent on the left side.

Stone dominates the white (inner right) and black (inner left)
mesas, particularly the cluster of contrasting white and black
mountains at the head of each. The smaller luck-enhancing white
mesa also features two additional stones (turtle to impede thieves,
and sun's rays for warmth—working with the sun circle on the central mesa), a vulture feather to "dispatch" (*despachar*) evil, and several artifacts that are paired with similar objects on the black mesa:
a deer's foot to foil thieves, a stone weight used in cleansings, and
three pre-Columbian *tumi* knives used in cleansings for cases of
soul loss.

In addition to the artifacts paired with similar ones on the white mesa, the defensive black mesa contains a bronze pre-Columbian rattle used exclusively to activate the powers of this side. Other objects found here include two pre-Columbian ceramic whistles (duck, nightingale) kept in a bivalve shell and used to attract powerful magical charms, a small stone weight used against sorcerers' whirlwinds, three power stones (black plateau, snake, mountain) for the personal protection of the healer, and a cluster of defensive mountains with designations like lair, whirlwind, greyhound, snake, and plateau. The black mountains at the head of this mesa are divided into "standing" and "lying" subtypes, with an intermediate type between them.

The central sector is the largest division of the entire mesa, a fact consistent with its role as reinforcement for the smaller white and black mesas. Like the other divisions, it contains many power stones, the largest concentration of which are small, regenerative lairs. These are supplemented by other named stones: a pair of cattle fertility stones, a sun circle for warmth, an earth circle for soul loss caused by the earth or ruins, an Inca stone to transport the healer's thoughts, a shell for courage in raising, a soldier used against headaches, twin peaks for cleansings, stairs for soul loss caused by mountains, a skull for soul loss caused by the dead, a yellow stone for eye problems, and two "matches" (flints) paired with two stones called "rays of light" to promote courage and illumination with the help of summoned magical charms. These stones are found in the lower left corner of this central division.

Above the power stones are two rows of spiral shells. The top row, which includes the healer's personal shell on the right, is used to raise tobacco in support of cleansing rituals with staffs. The lower row is used for raising tobacco to promote good fortune. Near the lower right corner of these two rows of spiral shells are bivalve shells, two of which are used to support animal cleansings, while the remainder are used to raise wine at the end of the session, or to raise tobacco while dispatching negative forces at the end of a cleansing. To the right of the two rows of shells is a set of bivalve shells laid out in the form of a cross. These are used for serving a special purgative remedy to the patients who are most critically ill in the early morning hours after a session.

Along the very top of the central mesa are images of Catholic saints symbolizing divine aid: framed lithographs of Jesus, Saint Hilarion, the Virgin Mary, and the Peruvian Saint Martin of Porras, along with statues of the Virgin, Saint Cyprian, and four images of Saint Anthony, who helps locate lost or stolen property. In the top right corner of the central mesa, next to the staffs, is a replica of the famous healing Cross of Chalpón. At the bottom corners of this division are two large bowls of tobacco, used as a catalyst in rituals. The accompanying gourd rattle is used exclusively to activate the powers of the central mesa.

Following an Ayabaca tradition, a number of artifacts associated collectively with the entire mesa are hung on the east wall, against which the mesa is positioned. These are: a rosary of the Holy Virgin to facilitate Jorge's prayers, the curer's hat used as a defense, a handwoven cow's-hair rope to stimulate depressed patients, a framed painting of Jesus in captivity (especially venerated in Ayabaca), and two long iron auger/digging tools placed for defensive purposes on either side of the door in the east wall (to the right of the mesa).

It is worth mentioning that the concept of "balanced dualism" appears to pervade Jorge's ritual, and to serve as an underlying premise for the operation of his mesa. This is seen on the macrolevel in the positioning of the Mesa Blanca Curandera (inner right side) and the Mesa Negra Gentileña (inner left side) with the mediating Mesa de Centro between them. It is also evident in the division of the Mesa de Respaldo into two complementary sections — the Mesa Blanca (outer right) and Mesa Negra (outer left), encompassing the entire mesa like two halves of a whole.

On the micro-level, there are artifacts in the individual zones that are paired with their dualistic counterparts either within the same or in a different zone (similar to the mesas of Navarro, Chapter 3, and Vidarte, Chapter 5). Examples of the first kind of pairing within the Mesa de Respaldo are the two interacting augers, the two large stones, and the two pairs of staffs (ajojaspe). Paired interaction also occurs within the Mesa Negra Gentileña Incaica, between the standing (parado) and lying (echado) mountains. A constant dialogue is maintained between these power stones. In the case of the mountains, the dialogue is facilitated by an additional small mountain.

Examples of the second kind of pairing, i.e., between symbolic divisions, are the mountains, the stone weights, the tumi knives, and the deer hoofs, found on the Mesa Blanca Curandera and the Mesa Negra Gentileña Incaica. Here, the interaction involves balance and reciprocity between the zones.

Further evidence of balanced dualism is found in the distribution of lairs or *madrigueras*. Except for the inner right mesa (Blanca Curandera) and the outer right (Mesa Blanca) of the Mesa de Respaldo, there is an association of *madrigueras* with all other parts of the mesa. This implies a sense of "renewal/rebirth" that, while integral to the Mesa Blanca Curandera, is nonetheless found outside of that sector, in zones whose primary functions are quite different or even opposed to its functions. In effect, a balance of the notion of renewal/rebirth is achieved between the Mesa Blanca Curandera and the rest of the mesa through the medium of the *madrigueras*.

Finally, balanced dualism is expressed in the interaction of the *encanto* with the *calicanto*—the notion of opposites attracting one another. This is seen throughout Jorge's ritual, which is, in effect, the catalyst that brings into meaningful interaction the paired, complementary artifacts and the functional divisions of the mesa. Ultimately, it appears that this dynamic interplay of opposites is a symbolic cipher for the resolution of conflicts in the lives of the healer's patients.

Jorge's rituals are performed indoors, and, while there is a definite sequence of events, the precise timing of each segment is variable and inexact. Jorge maintains that time has nothing to do with controlling or regulating his mesa; only the number of patients he has to contend with on a given evening influences the schedule. Jorge normally prefers to start a session at 10:00 P.M., but he has started as early as 7:00 P.M.

In the past, Jorge held sessions only on Tuesdays and Fridays. Now, because of all his other activities, he limits his practice to Fridays, and to only those Fridays that fall outside the first five days of a new moon. His reason for this is that the first days of the new moon are too cold and the San Pedro does not act as strongly then as it does otherwise.

Jorge begins a session with a lengthy series of prayers to activate the different sectors of the mesa. He then administers the first drink of San Pedro to the patients, interspersed with more prayers. From approximately 11:00 P.M. to 3:00 A.M. the session is almost entirely given over to performing the ritual cleansings or *limpias*. These are the most important acts of the session. Each and every participant is taken outside and rubbed from head to foot with a staff. This includes the assistant(s), as well as the *maestro* himself.

After the *limpias* are concluded, the *suspendidas* ("suspendings" or "raisings" of tobacco) begin. The primary functions of the *suspendidas* are to cleanse and defend. Jorge insists that these actions be performed in moderation; one shell full of liquid for each nostril is sufficient.

After the *limpias* and *suspendidas* comes the period of the session devoted to *florecimiento* (flowering), a raising of tobacco whereby individuals seek to enhance their luck, increase their fortune, improve their livestock, do better in their work, et cetera. This is followed by more *suspendidas*, done this time with sweet wine (*vino de misa*) instead of tobacco.

By 6:00 A.M. most other curers would have finished the process of dismantling and storing the mesa. Jorge does not do this—his mesa is always left assembled inside against the east wall. The first rays of sun never strike it, which is a concern of most curers. Jorge's sessions have, on occasion, lasted until 8:00 or 9:00 A.M. This may happen when there are many patients, or when Jorge requires many to take his special remedy at the end of the ritual (see Skillman 1990 for a list of the ingredients). In the latter case, the selected patients are sequestered for twenty-four hours. Jorge also differs from other curers in that he does not sing songs during the ritual. Instead, he employs prayer, proverbs, anecdotes, and advice.

As the session progresses, Jorge focuses on different symbolic zones of the mesa. First, he opens with prayers while concentrating on the right side of the mesa. Next, he turns his attention to the left side, while he also spends a signficant amount of time performing the curing/cleansing acts. Then, after the *suspendidas* of tobacco, he redirects his attention to the right, moving first to the central section of the mesa and then, while performing the flowerings and raisings, back to the right where he started. Thus, in the course of the evening, Jorge's ritual journey traces the shape of the letter U, tipped on its side, through the symbolic zones of his mesa.

13

Curanderismo: Occupational Considerations

BY DONALD JORALEMON

Becoming a Curandero

Diverse paths led our twelve informants to the occupation of curandero, but there are important similarities in their accounts as well as in the constellation of factors that predisposed them to the curer's trade.[1] Paramount among these is a familial link to practicing curanderos and/or parental approval of curanderismo evidenced by recourse to its practitioners in times of sickness. Seven of the curers had one or more close family members actively engaged in curanderismo, and in all twelve cases encounters with the curing/sorcery complex are remembered as central childhood experiences. Curanderismo was neither foreign nor particularly exotic to these healers as they grew up; it was a part of the accepted and normal world of their childhoods.

The idea of special selection is operative in the stories our informants tell of their lives, of childhood or early adulthood experiences that foretold an unusual talent for curing. For some it was a prophetic dream, for others a unique ability recognized by a curing specialist. Like curanderos elsewhere in Spanish-speaking regions (Trotter and Chavira 1981:16), Peruvian curers refer to "*el don*"—the gift for healing. This "gift," considered by most to be a God-given capacity of only a select few, manifests itself in the special sight, or *vista*, by which a curer comes to know the causes and cures of illnesses. In one way or another, each of our informants found in his past evidence that curing was not so much an occupation as it was a special calling.

A long period of apprenticeship, usually entailing work as a ritual assistant, or *alzador*, is the course most of these men followed. It is not unusual for an apprentice-curer to learn from several specialists, nor for there to be long interruptions in the training while the novice pursues other employment. It appears that for most curanderos learning is a mixture of imitation and experimentation, with relatively little directed teaching on the part of a mentor. There are also several other common elements in the early years of our informants' practices which merit attention.

Pilgrimages to sacred sites were important initiatory experiences for most of the curanderos. These were usually to highland lagoons, especially those known as Las Huaringas (near Huancabamba), which are "power spots" in the classic shamanistic sense of the word. Baptismal experiences, the learning about and collecting of herbs, visionary encounters with powerful supernatural forces, as well as cleansings and healings by the famous curanderos who live near these places, all figure in the learning process for curers. The curing lore acquired during pilgrimages, together with artifacts collected which can evoke the power of the sacred places, become permanent features of a curer's practice. Indeed, periodic returns to these powerful locations is a pattern in the healing practices of a number of our informants.

Vivid encounters with the devil during the early stages of the careers of four of the curanderos (Navarro, Guerrero senior, Vidarte, and Rojas) recall the central association between Satan and illness found and documented throughout Latin America (Kiev 1968:38; Taussig 1980a,b; Trotter and Chavira 1981:27–28, 33, 62; Ingham 1986). In the following chapter, consideration is given to the relationship between the devil's connection with the symbolic structure of the mesa and the colonial roots of the idea of an evil incarnate. In the present context it is important to stress that for these curers Satan is a very real presence, not merely a metaphor for evil. Visionary engagements with him are experienced as actual, face-to-face confrontations. They are remembered as pivotal moments in the moral development of the novice curer, who must weigh the Tempter's offer of power against the loss of spiritual autonomy entailed by being "*compactado*." Satan is a frightening figure to these healers, but his power can be resisted or even turned around to help contribute to a cure.

A third commonality in the beginning of our informants' practices relates to their first solo cures. In four cases (Calderón, Guerrero senior, Vidarte, and Rojas) the curer performed his first unassisted healing ritual for a relative; for another (Flores) the first patient was the friend of a relative. Drawing clients from close kin provides a fledgling curandero an opportunity to test his knowledge and abilities in a less threatening, familial environment. Just as importantly, it can serve as a base from which to attract more patients as family members begin to refer friends. Given the size and importance of extended family links in Peru, this referral network can quickly establish a curer's reputation. Also, given the dispersal of Peruvian families due to work-related migration, the resulting pool of potential clients can reach across the country and require the kind of hectic travel schedule seen in the practice of Víctor Flores.

The Threats of Repression and Competition

The above observations about the strategic usefulness of a familial base for a beginning curandero raise the important and often neglected fact that curanderismo is a business, a source of revenue in a country plagued by astronomical levels of underemployment and unemployment. Most of the curers in this study depend for their livelihood on the income generated by their curing. They employ similar tactics to protect against the two most significant threats to their ongoing financial success: official repression from church and state, and intense competition from other healers of all types.

Repression has been virtually a constant in the experience of Peruvian folk healers, from the early colonial campaigns against "idolatry" (Sharon 1978:25–26) to far more recent condemnations from both church and civil officials. A number of the curers with whom we have worked recall encounters in which police confiscated their herbs, threatened them with imprisonment, and demanded bribes. Physical assaults on curers by the police and military were common until recent decades.

Maintaining a practice in the face of such official repression is difficult enough, but competition for clients from other curanderos can be just as formidable an obstacle to a successful curing trade. While visiting a curandero not included in this study, Santos Cajusól Vidaurre of Túcume (outside of Chiclayo), I participated in a session performed in the backyard of his home. During the night I could hear the singing and rattle-playing of several other curanderos also conducting rituals in the same neighborhood. In fact, this small section of the town had numerous practicing curanderos. A similar proliferation of curers characterizes nearby

Lambayeque, the well-known town of Salas, as well as other communities in the region. Further data is necessary to determine whether the number of practicing curanderos is influenced by broader economic forces.

In the larger urban environment of Trujillo not only are there many curanderos but there is also an impressive diversity of other curing specialists, including Tarot card readers, herbalists, pulse readers, a variety of religious healers, and even one individual who has erected a two-story-high pyramid in his courtyard to harness the curative force of the ancient Egyptians. In subsequent chapters we will discuss how patients often move from one healer to another, shopping in what sometimes seems to be a supermarket of healing options.

In considering the economic or business side of curanderismo, and in particular the defensive methods our informants use to guard their practices, it is worth noting that Peruvian folk healers participate in what Hernando de Soto (1989) terms the "informal" or "non-formal" economy. Like street vendors (*ambulantes*), unlicensed taxi drivers and bus operators, and workers in unregulated, small-scale factories, curanderos exist outside the law. As representatives of the "formal sector" vacillate between unofficial tolerance and coercive police action in their relations with "non-formals," the latter adopt characteristic precautions. Principal among these maneuvers, as documented below for curanderos, is the search for pseudo-official status and the formation of close and even kin-like relations with persons who have position and power in the formal sector.

Several curanderos with whom we worked carried printed business cards that identified their occupation as *"herbolario"* (herbalist). Jóse Paz explained that this professional designation was used because one can acquire a license as an herbalist, but not as a curandero. His license, which permits the collection and sale of medicinal herbs, hung on the wall of his consultation room. He claimed to have used it on more than one occasion to escape police shakedowns. Curanderos use the herbalist license as a covering credential, a formal sector permit which can help to protect them from official harassment.

Like the business card and framed license, our informants also sought to imitate some of the other accouterments of parallel formal sector professions, namely those of doctor and priest. In several instances, the consultation rooms of curanderos were clearly patterned after those of medical doctors, with a variety of framed titles and letters on the walls and, in one case, a gray steel desk and swivel chair. Similarly, the prominent display of religious icons, sometimes presented on full altars, was undoubtedly meant to convey to clients the sense of an affiliation with the Roman Catholic Church. The mimicking of Catholic liturgy in the rituals described in earlier chapters is also designed, consciously or not, to establish a link with orthodoxy and gain the official legitimacy that accompanies it.

These efforts to create the appearance of official status are supplemented by a second protective strategy—namely, forming friendship alliances with members of the formal sector to whom the curandero can turn for support. Víctor Flores maintained a notebook full of the business cards of the wealthy and powerful clients he had served, and he also displayed on the walls of his office photographs of himself with them. José Paz frequently told stories of the police and military officials he had cured, some of whom were social visitors to his home. Many curers invest substantial effort and incur significant costs in the cultivation of social ties to persons with standing in the "official" world.

Relationships with formal sector representatives can also be solidified through the system of *compadrazgo* by asking wealthy and/or well-connected persons to serve as a godparent. The use of fictive kin ties to attain economic advantage is a common practice throughout Latin America and reflects the pattern of personalism which John Gillin (1955:493) long ago identified as basic to the "ethos" of Latin American culture. It is also a technique frequently employed in the nonformal economy of Peru as a counter to the uncertainty faced by businesses without legal standing, including curanderismo.

The competition curanderos face also encourages the strategic use of kin-like relationships with all patients, whether or not they are better positioned in the formal sector. The ideal situation for a curer, especially in the early stages of a career, is to form close, personal connections with patients, not only so that they are more likely to refer others but also so that they will become repeat customers. In subsequent chapters we discuss how curanderos often have a core group of long-term clients who consider themselves as much friends as patients of the curer. Extremely loyal, this group is as important to a curandero as are the "regulars" to any business.

In recent years a new element has been added to the curandero's career, influencing both the relations with the formal sector and the dynamics of competition. The interest of academic investigators, Peruvian and foreign, in the curanderismo complex has had a major impact on the lives and occupations of curanderos. It is essential that this not be omitted or overlooked in a consideration and study of the contemporary curer.

The "Researcher Effect" on Curanderismo

Academic researchers appear to have been "good for business" among curanderos, both for those curers who have actually participated in research projects and for those who have never met an anthropologist or a social psychologist. The case of Eduardo Calderón, who has gained international fame largely as a result of his "anthropological discovery," is exceptional only in the degree of his success. The simple presence of non-Peruvian researchers at rituals performed by Nilo Plasencia contributed to an impressive increase in his clientele, from just a couple of patients to more than thirty a session in the space of several months. Víctor Flores, who liked to introduce the investigators in a loud voice during sessions as "doctors from the great universities of the United States," saw our presence as a public relations boon; a letter of recognition he requested from us was added to the framed testimonials on his office walls.

Research on curanderos has also helped to confer on traditional medicine a new kind of cultural legitimacy, communicated to the general Peruvian population via popular magazine and newspaper coverage of research projects and academic congresses, as well as through documentary films on folk healers shown as "shorts" before feature-length movies in popular theaters. Respected and influential Peruvian scholars, including Carlos Alberto Seguín and Fernándo Cabieses, have become advocates for the official recognition of the value of Peru's traditional medicine and for its integration into biomedical practice. This move toward a new legitimation of folk healing in Peru parallels the internationally higher profile of traditional medicine resulting from promotions by development agencies such as the World Health Organization.

It may well be the case that the level of official repression experienced by curanderos has diminished as their academic fame has increased. The effect of formal sector attention, in this case coming from universities and research institutions both in Peru and in foreign nations, has certainly given curanderos a new respectability. It remains to be seen whether this change in status is temporary or permanent, or, for that matter, whether or not it is actually in the best interest of curers to risk being co-opted by the formal sector in the process of gaining legitimacy.

One thing is clear: the investigator has "contaminated" the object of study. The occupation of curandero in Peru, especially in and around the larger cities, is not what it once was. Curers with whom we spoke were almost universally aware of the *"famoso Tuno"* (the famous Eduardo Calderón, nicknamed Tuno), and many hoped that contact with foreigners would bring them the same wealth and reputation. One individual, a very poor and unsuccessful curer in the town of Cartavio (twenty kilometers north of Trujillo), explicitly saw cooperation with our project as an avenue to reestablish his failing practice. Another, the above-mentioned Santos Cajusól, inquired about the commercial feasibility of selling a tape recording I had made of his ritual songs. In short, many curanderos are aware of the opportunity a researcher represents and want to profit from the relationship. Of course, the same is true of how the researcher thinks of the curandero!

A nostalgic preference for the "pristine" anthropological context might lead one to see this as an unfortunate situation. It is no such thing. Curanderos have been in the business of adapting to dramatic cultural changes for centuries, and the occupation has survived precisely because those who have practiced it were sufficiently pragmatic to keep themselves open to opportunities while also remaining defensive against threats. The first time a researcher came to a curer's door, curanderismo was no longer "traditional." Change began the moment the researcher's presence caused the curandero to begin calculating the significance of this new turn of events. The investigator quickly became a new consideration in the business of curing, one of the many to which curanderismo has in the past and will continue in the future to adapt.[2]

14

The Metaphysics of Curanderismo and Its Cultural Roots

BY DOUGLAS SHARON

Twelve Curers — a Shared World View

We began this survey of the lives and practices of twelve Peruvian healers in order to discover whether or not they shared a common cultural ideology. In looking back over the empirical data, we see that all twelve curers set up the power objects of their mesas in a spatial configuration which expresses the Curandero/Ganadero dualism that is then explicitly applied in their therapy and rituals. With minor exceptions, certain broad classes of ritual paraphernalia consistently have similar symbolic associations and are assigned to the same mesa zones.

At the end of the chapter on Eduardo Calderón I hypothesized that during a night session a unilineal left-to-right curing movement might be encompassed in a more comprehensive right-to-left-to-right cycle. A review of the data on the thirteen healers' rituals (including those of the younger Guerrero) reveals that nine clearly follow this cyclical progression. Four (Navarro, Guerrero senior, Flores, and Paz) do not overtly appear to open their sessions on the right side before undertaking left-to-right/cleansing-to-luck acts. The fact that two of the four (Flores and Paz) begin with rites to activate San Pedro, which is placed on the right side of their mesas, possibly indicates an initial orientation to that side. However, this is not clear from the data. Guerrero senior places San Pedro on the right, but opens with songs which are very general regarding the powers invoked. Navarro, as a result of his pact with the devil, reverses mesa fields but does not seem to correlate specific rituals with mesa sectors.

The fact that a majority of the healers in our sample follow a three-part ritual format suggests that their therapy replicates a shamanic journey in the classical sense, as described by Barbara Myerhoff (1976:102–3) in a seminal article on equilibrium and the shaman's calling:

> The shamanic journey is in three phases. The shaman sets forth from the realm of the mundane; he then journeys to the supernatural and returns. Always the passage involves these three destinations or locations. . . . The shaman travels to the edge of the social order each time he undertakes these journeys. He enters non-form, the underlying chaos of the unconceptualized domain which has not yet been made a part of the cosmos by the cultural activity of naming and defining. With each crossing over, he gains power, as do all persons who travel to the edges of order, for . . . such contacts with the boundaries of conceptualization are sources of power as well as danger. Shamans are liminal people, at the thresholds of form, forever betwixt and between.

As we have noted in prior chapters, Curandero/Ganadero dualism frequently translates into Christian versus pagan, that is, good versus evil, or, to put it in societal terms, order and stability versus chaos and disruption. In effect, a ritual movement from the right, with its predominantly Christian icons and healing herbs, to the dangerous left, with its pagan, antisocial overtones, can be perceived as a journey beyond the status quo, or natural order, into the supernatural. The elaborate battles with spirits and ritual "cleansings" aimed at "throwing away" or "turning around" sorcery signal the incredible power being marshalled in this murky realm inhabited by ill-defined forces and beings associated with unbaptized (i.e., unnamed), anti-Spanish heathens (e.g., Incas, *gentiles, moros*). This domain may not be "unconceptualized" in the full sense intended by Myerhoff, but it has certainly been rendered amorphous and marginal by colonialism's efforts to extirpate the indigenous world view from Peruvian culture. The term *ganadero* is thus most appropriate for the ambiguity prevalent on the left (see Introduction, note 2).

There is an adversarial quality found in the accounts of curanderos' lives and therapeutic philosophies as sketched in the preceding chapters. Our informants express an oppositional view of the world they live in, a black-and-white struggle between forces of good and evil. Whether in recounting a perilous encounter with enemies, human or supernatural, or in discussing the structural symbolism of the altars around which their rituals are organized, these men voice a shared conception of the human situation: that life entails confrontations with those who would cause harm, thereby necessitating recourse to those who would cure it. To be "in harm's way" is unavoidable in human existence, but the curandero, because of a special "gift," is capable of furnishing both protection and revenge. (See Giese [1989:12] regarding "the fluid border between the 'good' curandero and the 'bad' *brujo*.")

Despite the adversarial tone of the encounter between good and evil, in actual practice, the curandero deals with both sides of the therapeutic equation during a curing session, bringing the opposites together in some meaningful fashion. In this regard, Joralemon (1984a:10) describes the symbolic logic underlying both mesa and ritual as a mediation between life-giving and life-taking forces:

> The mesa, as it is understood by the shaman, is a game-board, a symbolic paradigm against which the ritual is played. It represents the struggle between life-taking and life-giving forces, between left and right. But this struggle, this opposition, becomes a resolution, by the shaman's re-affirmation of mastery over *both* the left and the right. . . . [The shaman] is a balancer in the contest between opposing forces [while the ritual], which the mesa presents in concrete symbols, is a balancing act performed by an individual who stands above the contest by mastering both sides. It is thus that struggle—opposition—becomes passage, and cures are accomplished.

Reflecting on the sources of this symbolic logic, Joralemon (1985) draws attention to the relationship between the San Pedro-induced hallucinations of the curandero and the significance of mesa artifacts. The explanations provided by our informants confirm his observation that "mesa objects are representations of visionary imagery experienced by the shaman as a result of ingesting the mescaline-bearing San Pedro potion" (Joralemon 1985:21). Serving as a kind of "visionary map," the mesa anchors the curer's visions and helps him control them. Furthermore, as Joralemon argues, the left/right associations of mesa symbols are consistent with what would be expected based on the neurophysiological effects of mescaline.

The physiology of mescaline experiences, however, does not alone account for the symbolic content of curandero ritual. In an important caveat, Joralemon (ibid.:25) points out that, neurochemistry aside, shamans draw on a set of culturally appropriate symbols in harnessing the effects of the hallucinogen to the goal of curing:

> While the reactions to mescaline may be organic responses, they become cultural events by the imposition of meaning. The symbolization of the physical experience in Peruvian healing rituals is an irreducible cultural phenomenon; investigating the physiological effects merely helps to illustrate the bounds within which the symbols are generated.

It is therefore necessary to consider the cultural roots of the dualistic philosophy that curandero mesas express. In the following, after discussing an interpretation of mesa dualism suggested by the German ethnographer Claudius Giese, I consider the obvious relationship between mesa ideology and Roman Catholic teachings. Then, the influence of Andean cosmology on mesa symbolism is studied, suggesting potential pre-Columbian antecedents for the ideology shared by our informants.

Opposition and Balance

In the work mentioned briefly in the Introduction, Claudius Giese (1989:151–54) argues that "absolute confrontation," not mediation, is the message communicated through the symbolic logic of mesas. He also offers some insight into Joralemon's association of the mesa fields with "life-giving" and "life-taking" forces, and he argues that the mediating or balancing function I found in Eduardo Calderón's central mesa field is "not sufficiently supported by the ethnographic data" (ibid.:151).

In a discussion of Joralemon's interpretation of the right and left sides of the mesa, Giese (ibid.:154) points out that the curandero's use of the powers of the left side to free a patient from the clutches of a sorcerer suggests a mitigating life-giving, not an exclusively life-taking, association for this symbolic field. His informant, Don Ruperto, sees this liberation of the patient as "the act of curing" (el acto de curar), the first phase of a session, and associates it with the left side of the mesa. Don Ruperto distinguishes the curing act from "the act of raising the luck" of the patient (el acto de parar la suerte), the second phase of a session, which he associates with the right field of the mesa.

Giese's informant describes his entire mesa as a mesa curandera (curing mesa) and, in contrast to Eduardo, does not refer to the left side as "evil." Nevertheless, many of the artifacts of the left side of his mesa also possess a negative, aggressive character which the healer must "tame" to achieve his aims. It is Don Ruperto's mastery of life-taking forces that enables him to channel the sorcerer's power to the goals of curing. This ability to control and even reverse (recall Plasencia's rituals of *volteando*, "turning around") the harmful powers concentrated on the left mesa field is a key feature of the cure directly related to the "defensive" nature of the Ganadero field.

In a similar fashion, the overall association of Don Ruperto's mesa with curing does not eliminate the connection or link between curing and the right side of the altar. In treating his patients, Don Ruperto orients himself to the Christian religious sphere as well as to the sacred lagoons and magical plants, all of which, while relating to right-sided, luck-enhancing associations, can nonetheless be marshalled to control or defend against hostile powers. Here too there appears to be a mitigated but explicit left/right logic consistent with that found among other curanderos.

Turning to the central sector of the mesa, Giese (ibid.:151) notes that Eduardo Calderón compared the function of the middle field to the role of a "judge" (that is, one who weighs both sides of an issue) or to a "needle in a balance," and explained that the central field is the "place where the chiefs, the guardians, those who command, those who govern present themselves" (Sharon 1978:90). Giese cites these comments as evidence that Eduardo associated the central field with "the commanding authority," but did not directly "speak about 'mediating' or 'balancing' the two fields" (Giese 1989:151). Yet in another publication (Calderón and Sharon 1978), which Giese also cites, Eduardo offered the following comments:

> In other words, there has to be a *balance* between the two forces, good and evil, because Saint Cyprian is always in the center or the middle part [of the mesa]. . . . Saint Cyprian plays an important role within the syncretic religious field, in that, before being a saint, he was a sorcerer (ibid.:99, italics added).

In a chapter dealing with his ritual Eduardo described the "accounts" or powers governing the three fields of his mesa in a way that also involved the idea of mediation:

> The twenty-five thousand accounts come to be the union between the twelve thousand accounts that govern the Field of Justice and

the thirteen thousand accounts that govern the Field of the Sly
Dealer realized by the *mediation* of the Middle Field that is governed
by the twenty-five thousand accounts (ibid.:106, italics added).

However, just because Eduardo uses these concepts, do they apply to the mesas and rituals of other curers? According to Giese
(1989:151), north Peruvian curanderismo does not entail the balancing of polarized powers, but rather "the targeted calling out of
determined beings and powers" ("*das gezielte Einsetzen bestimmter
Wesen und Kräfte*"). For him the left is the side of "absolute confrontation," used for the protection and defense of patients against the
attacks of sorcerers. It is also used to ward off, to fight against, and
"throw away" (*botar*) the negative beings and powers associated
with the left, and in some cases to return negative powers back to
the sender. Only after the removal of all negative influences from
the patient by a curing or "cleansing" ritual performed on the left,
can the powers of the right side be called upon for a luck "raising"
ritual conducted on the right mesa field.

Giese contends that "the opposition of the powers remains in existence during the entire ritual, at no time is it resolved . . . , which
is shown only by the function and use of the *artes* [power objects]
during the entire ritual" ("*Die Gegensätzlichkeit der Kräfte bleibt während des gesamten Rituals bestehen . . . , was sich allein an der Funktion
und der Verwendung der 'artes' während des gesamten Rituals zeigt*"). Don
Ruperto conceives the middle field as a "command center" from
which he has access to and control over all areas of the mesa. He
compares this sector to a centrally controlled state, like Peru, or to
a monarchy.

Giese's model may well account for the fairly fixed sequence of
rituals by which the forces of the mesa are activated; however, subsequent healing acts are often far less lineally structured. Many
healers, after charging all sectors of the mesa and associated beings
and powers, proceed to perform "cleansings" and "raisings" with
objects (mainly staffs) drawn from the left, right, or center in accordance with the dynamic interaction they perceive that occurs
between the concentrated forces of a fully activated mesa, which
includes those "called" (*llamado*) as well as the psychic vision of the
curandero. On many of the mesas documented in previous chapters, as well as on Giese's informant's mesa, some "cleansing" paraphernalia (e.g., quince branches, or *chontas* in Don Ruperto's case,
see Giese 1989:95) are specifically placed on the right side, along

with "defensive" weapons and "protective" *seguros*. We have already seen that the largely "defensive" nature of artifacts on the left side of Don Ruperto's mesa is mitigated by the "cleansing" aspect of curing. In fact, some healers contend that the left only provides a defensive function, while both curing and luck are associated with the right.

In short, although I think that Giese's "command center" analogy for the middle sector of the mesa is correct, I do not feel that the ritual process is as unilinear as he seems to suggest, nor is artifact symbolism as unambiguous. Not all healers maintain Don Ruperto's clear separation of "cleansing" as a strictly left-hand function distinct from luck "raising" as a largely right-hand ritual as documented by Giese (1989:100-106, 139, 148, 151).

Although our informants do not use the term themselves, I still think that the ritual process they direct is dialectical in nature and that the idea of balance is a key to a successful cure. I do not think that Giese's "command center" analogy obviates the dialectic since the central field of his major informant's mesa, like those of Calderón, Paz (Joralemon 1984a:4–6, 18–19), and the informants of Polia (1988:149), contains artifacts with both right and left associations. For example, the staff of Saint Cyprian positioned in his mesa's central field is explained by Don Ruperto, as by Calderón and Paz, as relating to Cyprian's double nature: once a sorcerer, later a saint (Giese 1989:81–82). Don Ruperto's entire mesa is governed by two staffs—the king and queen—located at the head of the central section and expressing a union of opposites, i.e., male and female. The way these staffs work together is an example of "sexual complementarity," a classificatory principle that pervades the highland Andean world view. American anthropologist Catherine Allen (1988:84–86) demonstrates how a highland Quechua *despacho* (burnt offering) illustrates the "relativity characteristic of Andean thinking—the continual enfolding of male and female principles that both contain and exclude each other" (ibid.:83). She elaborates:

> Thus, while each man or woman is a complete individual with both male and female qualities, the two unite to form another individual of a higher order: a *warmi qhari* [literally woman-man], nucleus of the household [ibid.:85]. . . .
> Thus, dialectical opposition in ritual draws upon tendencies of action and thought that have already been ingrained in participants.

... Cosmos, community, household and individual are felt to attain existence through the fusion of opposites like the *warmi* and *qhari*, each of which contains the other [ibid.:208].

The king of Don Ruperto's mesa is also the symbolic "axis," representing a line of union between the upper and lower levels of the Andean cosmos, which (as I show later in this chapter) Giese correlates with the right and left sides of the mesa, respectively. This shamanic *axis mundi* is intimately related to the indigenous concepts of *sami*, a force penetrating the three spheres of the universe in a vertical line, and *tinku*, a living line of force symbolizing the "encounter" of a variety of opposites (Giese 1988:12–14; 1989:78–80, 157, 171). Allen (1988:207) contends that *sami* "resembles the Polynesian *mana* and our own concept of energy," while *tinku* is "a mixture of different elements that bring something new into existence . . . [which] is endowed with vitalizing force."

Tinku is the Quechua word for the juncture of two rivers, but it is also the name of a ritual battle which promotes fertility, moral equilibrium, and the resolution of boundary disputes. American anthropologist Joseph Bastien (1989:76) describes the objective of a *tinku* as "a way of uniting opposite sides in a dialectic that clearly defines and recognizes the other as well as establishes their interdependence" (see also Harrison 1989:103). For Bastien, what distinguishes this Andean dialectic from the Western version is the fact that it neither negates the "other" nor dissolves the opposition into a synthesis (and resultant new form) as in Marxian dialectics. "Rather, this dialectic accentuates the opposites into a whole while establishing their independence as reciprocal units" (Bastien 1989:76).

Bastien (ibid.:82) demonstrates that a highland Aymara curing ritual is modeled after the *tinku*,

> where oppositions are crossed into conflict, mediated, and transformed into complementary terms of reciprocal exchange. The process is one of dialectical structuralism wherein conflict is used to communicate in a traumatic way that temporarily resolves conflict by group catharsis. The conflict attains such levels of gravity that the opposing sides readily assume their structural distance and recognize the necessity of collaboration. . . . The goal is toward maintenance of balance and symmetry.

Perhaps Giese's "opposition" and my "balance" are not so far apart. In this regard the remarks of American anthropologist Barbara Myerhoff (1976:102), in an article on shamanic equilibrium, seem relevant:

> Shamanic balance is a particular stance. It is not a balance achieved by synthesis; it is not a static condition achieved by resolving opposition. It is not a compromise. Rather it is a state of acute tension, the kind of tension which exists ... when two unqualified forces encounter each other, meeting headlong, and are not reconciled but held teetering on the verge of chaos, not in reason but in experience. It is a position with which the westerner, schooled in the Aristotelian tradition, is extremely uncomfortable. Unlike the view of highest good as the golden mean, this view gives us few guidelines for action. Unfortunately, we westerners have come to feel that enduring this sort of tension is not really necessary, that somehow it is possible to allow one pole to exist and prevail without its opposite. We seek good without evil, pleasure without pain, God without the devil, and love without hate. But the shaman reminds us of the impossibility of such a condition, for he stands at the juncture of opposing forces, and his dialectical task is continually to move between these opposites.[1]

Christian Moralism and Native Dialectics

As noted earlier, when verbalized by healers, the mesa dialectic is most frequently articulated in terms of Christian moralism, that is, as a struggle between good and evil. This is a logical expression in an overwhelmingly Catholic country with a colonial history that included church campaigns to "extirpate idolatry" and convert the native population to Christianity. American anthropologist Irene Silverblatt (1983), in a discussion of female witchcraft in the colonial period, provides insight into the historical process involved. She describes the medieval Christian world view brought by the Spaniards to Peru, which

> divided the universe into two clearly defined and opposing spheres: the world of virtue and the world of vice. On the one hand Christians—the servants of God—were upholding a moral order of goodness against onslaughts made by the servants of the Prince of Darkness. Within this conception of the world, the devil, the incarnation of evil, was ever-energetic in his perpetual attempts to overthrow God's kingdom. We should not forget that the devil was a real and familiar figure to the inhabitants of Late Medieval Europe, as tangible and known to them as the patriarchs and saints (ibid.: 415).
>
> In the earliest records of Spanish observers we discover that they viewed native religion as merely one other vehicle through which

the devil manifested his attempts to overthrow God's kingdom. Indigenous religion was devil worship. . . . It was not a great step from
the discovery of idolatry to the discovery of witchcraft. Since witchcraft in terms of the logic of Western thought involved a complot
with the devil, and the devil was already speaking to the *indios*
through idols, witchcraft must also be rotting Andean society. If
witchcraft was present, then there must also be witches with whom
the devil could consort (ibid.:417).

The Spanish created witches in Peru where none existed before.
It was the Spanish who decreed that witchcraft and idolatry were in-
distinguishable. And from the perspective of native society witchcraft, the maintenance of ancient traditions, and conscious political
resistance became increasingly intertwined. If the Spanish declared
witches outlaws they also transformed them in indigenous eyes into
legitimate representatives, the defenders of traditional culture
(ibid.:425).

Thus it should come as no surprise that in most mesas encountered in this study pre-Columbian artifacts are identified with
sorcery/witchcraft and placed in the Ganadero zone, the side of the
devil, while Christian icons and artifacts associated with the triumph of good over evil are placed in the Curandero sector, also
called Gloria, the side of God.[2] Even when the standard left/right
organization of the two fields is reversed in the case of Ruperto
Navarro, these associations are maintained. As anthropologist
Michael Taussig has pointed out in several publications, the moral
dualism of Spanish culture preserved the hierarchy of colonial
class relations in Latin America by stipulating an equivalence between evil and that which was native (see Taussig 1980a:251;
1980b:169–81; 1987).

Reinforcing my suggestion that there was a colonial source for
the moralistic dualism of contemporary curanderos is Silverblatt's
contention that native Andean cosmology had no "notion of evil or
an embodiment of a Satanic-like force which was comparable to
Western conceptions" (Silverblatt 1983:417). The indigenous ideology, as Silverblatt sees it, "entailed a dialectic vision of the universe in which dualist forces were viewed as reciprocal and complementary" (ibid.:418), while "balance in the universe as a whole was
intrinsic to reestablishing the health of an individual" (ibid.:420). A
similar point is made by John Ingham (1986:109–10) for pre-
Columbian religions in Meso-America, although in this case potential native precursors to the Spaniard's Christian theological devil
are also identified.

Thus far it appears that our informants' verbalized interpretations of their mesas are directly inspired by Catholic colonial moralism—that is, the battle between God's servants and the agents of the devil. However, while mesa symbolism is explained in these terms, the rituals themselves unfold as *tinku*-like dramas that juxtapose paired opposites in complementary and reciprocal encounters capable of resolving conflict. Within this structural framework the good/evil dichotomy is assimilated along with a host of other pairs: Curandero/Ganadero, Christian/pagan, curandero/brujo, saint/sorcerer, Christ/Satan, health/sickness, right/left, white/black, life/death, up/down, and so forth. Many of the oppositions are Christian, but the manner in which they are handled is Andean. It is useful in this regard to recall Allen's (1988:84) characterization of relativistic Andean thinking as the "continual enfolding of . . . principles that both contain and exclude each other."

I believe the relativistic, dialectical nature of north coastal shamanism is what accounts for its successful adaptation to the black-and-white moralism imposed by colonial Spanish Catholicism. This intellectual achievement is particularly noteworthy given the fact that the Christian doctrine of good versus evil, philosophically and historically, has never been amenable to dialectical thinking. In practical terms, the kind of action it inspires seeks to drive the opposites apart or, in the most extreme case, to annihilate one side of the equation. This contrasts radically with the Andean dialectic, which promotes a course of action similar to that developed in the *tinku* where the opposites are brought together without being absorbed. Both models are dualistic and both generate conflict; however, the reciprocal complementarity inherent in Andean thought engenders dialogue and interaction. On the other hand, the dichotomous absolutism of the medieval version of Christianity is categorically incapable of this type of give-and-take.

I do not mean to give the impression that concepts of good and evil are unprecedented in native thought, however. In fact, ethnographers have documented numerous cases of the good/evil dyad throughout South America among groups sufficiently isolated and unacculturated that they are able to discount missionary influence. However, what distinguishes the aboriginal good/evil pair from the Christian model is a Manichaean worldview best typified by the Kogi who inhabit the northern Andes of Colombia. According to anthropologist Gerardo Reichel-Dolmatoff (1974:295–96) the Kogi contend:

In order to guarantee the existence of Good, it is necessary to fo-
ment Evil because if the latter should disappear—finding no
justification—the principle of Good would disappear as well. It is
deemed necessary that a person should occasionally commit sins
which bear witness to the active existence of evil.

Anthropologist Peter Roe (1982:308) sees the Kogi case as simply one illustration of a cultural ideology which is the correlate of a
cosmologic model shared by the contemporary tribal peoples of
lowland South America. He characterizes this cosmology as rooted
in what he calls a kind of "Hegelian Taoism" which "translates
strictly defined dyads, each pair representing dualistic manifesta-
tions of a single concept into a continuum model based on the notion that life is death and death, life." In the myths that support
this world view, the two key symbols are the reptilian dragon and
the were-jaguar who form the primary oppositional dyad from
which numerous other pairs are derived. Both mythic beings have
positive and negative qualities that are juxtaposed in complementary double dyads. However, "instead of four static cells of a
square, a dynamic system is constituted by weighting one element
of each set of dyads." In this fashion the two features of the two
mythic beings are "equated and interpenetrate to keep the model
in perpetual movement." The result is "a continual process of thesis, antithesis, and synthesis that transforms, by the overlapping of
the major figures' aspects, what might at first appear to be a static
oppositional system into a dynamic scheme of endlessly ramifying
transitive relations."

Roe argues that there is a respectable antiquity for the contemporary cosmologic model in both the lowlands and adjacent highland areas of South America. In seeking precedents for the complex symbolism documented in the ethnographic present, he starts
with South America's pristine state: Chavín in the Peruvian highlands. He suggests that the early stages of Chavín art, dating to
about the early first millennium B.C., "depict uniquely lowland
fauna in ways that make it unmistakably clear that they were used
as structural symbols in a cosmological scheme of uncanny resemblance to the modern ethnographic one" (ibid.:274).

From the foregoing, it appears that the cultural ideology shared
by the twelve healers in this study represents an adaptation to—not
an adoption of—the Christian ethos. Upon close inspection, the dialectical nature of the philosophy the healers hold in common is
much more congruent with Andean thinking and with lowland

South American cosmology. In the following sections Andean cosmological notions of considerable antiquity are explored, and it is suggested that they play a strong role in, and provide cultural continuity for, contemporary north coastal Peruvian shamanism.

Cosmology and Mesas

In *Wizard of the Four Winds* I attempted to place Eduardo Calderón's shamanism into a larger cross-cultural context by reviewing the literature on mesas and related cosmological beliefs elsewhere in the Andes and in other parts of Latin America (Sharon 1978:76–90, 174–96). That survey revealed the use of microcosmic healing altars throughout the region.[3] It also demonstrated an underlying Amerindian cosmology, summarized best by American anthropologist Peter Furst (1973–74:40):

> The universe . . . is stratified, with an Underworld below and an Upperworld above . . . each with its respective spirit rulers and other supernatural denizens. There are also gods of the principal world directions or quarters, and supreme beings that rule respectively over the celestial and chthonic spheres (for example, sky gods, lords of the dead, etc.) . . . The several levels of the universe are interconnected by a central axis (*axis mundi*).

In his article on Aymara curing rituals of highland Bolivia, Bastien (1989) shows how the shaman represents the earth and mediates between the powers and beings of the upper and lower spheres (*pachas*) of the three-tiered indigenous cosmos. Crucial to the cure is the retrieval of the patient's soul from the ancestors of the netherworld.

Among the Quechua of the southern Peruvian highlands, who share the same cosmological notions as their Aymara neighbors, the shaman plays an identical role as mediator between up (*hanan*) and down (*hurin*) on behalf of the humans inhabiting this world (*Kay Pacha*). The cure also involves bargaining with the ancestors for the patient's soul. (See Sharon [1978:76–90] for a survey of the literature on Quechua and Aymara shamanism, mesas, and cosmology.)

The comprehensive and all-encompassing nature of the Andean *hanan/hurin* cosmological dualism is indicated by Anne Marie Hocquenghem (1985:9, cited in Giese 1989:148):

The world is classified on the basis of the recognition of a unity, formed of two opposed and complementary parts, defined as *Hanan* and *Hurin*. . . . *Hanan* and *Hurin* seem to be two notions that permit the ordering of the world, establishing between the different parts and halves of a whole a set of correspondences and oppositions. The moment one recognizes the double list of that which is *Hanan* and *Hurin*, of that which attracts and rejects, it is possible to comprehend the system of classification and the organization of the Andean world.

Summarizing the information on the Inca ceremonial calendar transmitted by the early colonial Spanish sources, Hocquenghem (1987:26–45) elaborates on the paired oppositions derived from *hanan/hurin*. In this cosmology the male sun moves through the upper world from east to west each day. Every month the female moon moves in the opposite direction, being born in the west and disappearing in the east. In the lower world their courses are reversed in what Hocquenghem calls a "double inversion." This cthonic "world in reverse" is the realm of the ancestors who govern fertility and reproduction. Structurally, Inca cosmology has much in common with the cosmologic model of the contemporary tribal groups of lowland South America (see Roe 1982:271–73).

The Inca calendar illustrates a classificatory system which divided space (the empire), time (the year), and society into two complementary parts that were in turn subdivided into halves, resulting in four quarters, four seasons, and four social groups. It also imposed a hierarchy in this world (*Kay Pacha*), with *hanan* components dominating *hurin* categories—for example, with the sun, king, males, higher ranks, and the elderly on the right in ritual and social contexts, while the moon, queen, females, lower ranks, and the young were on the left.

Hocquenghem contends that the ceremonial calendar has regulated and assured economic production and distribution in the Central Andes for 4,000 years and that it still serves this function today in the highlands in the form of the Catholic calendar of *fiestas*. As she sees it, the relations of authority and production have been, and continue to be, dominated by religious activity, specifically the cult of the ancestors, adherence to which organizes the interaction between the human and natural realms and assures reproduction and continuation. One is reminded of the critical role played by the ancestors in contemporary Aymara and Quechua curing rituals, as well as that of the *gentiles* in northern Peru.

Building on Hocquenghem's work, Giese (1989:152–57) establishes a direct relationship between north coastal mesas and these Andean cosmological concepts. He correlates the three sections of his major informant's mesa with the three levels of the traditional Andean cosmos: left with *Ukhu Pacha* (underworld), center with *Kay Pacha* (this world), and right with *Hanan Pacha* (upperworld). He demonstrates that "cleansing" rituals are performed on the left side of his informant's mesa, while luck-"raising" rituals are performed on the right. "Cleansing" involves "throwing away" negative influences by rubbing the patient in a downward motion (i.e., into the underworld). *Tabaco* taken as a part of this therapy is absorbed through the left nostril. Good-luck rituals, or "raisings," quite literally involve an upward motion (i.e., into the upper world), as assistants move their shells containing the tobacco mixture from the feet to the head of the patient before ingesting it through the right nostril. All rituals are directed from the healer's "command center" midway between the left and right sides of the mesa.

Further reinforcing the mesa/*pacha* correlation is the fact that the left side contains objects from below the surface of the earth (e.g., pre-Columbian artifacts from ancient burial grounds), or from the bottom of the ocean (e.g., shells)—all associated with "down," *hurin*. On the other hand, the right side contains materials from highland lagoons (e.g., herbs), or objects linked to the sky (e.g., saints' images)—all associated with "up," *hanan*. Giese demonstrates how the metaphysical connotations of light and darkness are clearly related in curandero terminology with the upper and lower worlds, respectively, as well as with the right and left sides of the mesa. The central sector of the mesa, like the earth's surface, is the place where these dualistic forces are expressed in human life, in this case through the instructions of the curandero as he receives information from the right and left (or up and down) and then directs the concentrated forces of the mesa.

Giese's identification of the indigenous cosmological component in north coastal mesa symbolism is confirmed for the northern highlands as well. Polia (1990:109) demonstrates that the right and left sides of the curing mesas of that region correlate with the upper and lower worlds, respectively, of the Andean cosmos, while the central sector correlates with the earth's surface, specifically with the sacred lagoons and magical flora for which the area is famous.

Identification of the relationship between mesas and cosmology leads to speculation about the roots of this component in contemporary Andean shamanism. However, defining this contribution is a difficult task. The following discussion of cosmological conceptualizations of dwellers of the lowland tropical forest and of the higher Andes attempts to show some connections.

Desana and Inca Cosmologies

Given the absence of written records, the history of Andean cosmology will probably never be fully known. However, the work of archaeologist William Isbell (1978) in interpreting the cosmological order expressed in prehistoric Andean ceremonial centers sheds some light on this history and its relationship to native South American religious traditions. I have already noted Peter Roe's identification of the structural similarity between highland and lowland cosmologies of considerable antiquity. Isbell begins with an interpretation of the cosmology reflected in Inca architecture—an interpretation based on Reichel-Dolmatoff's (1971) ethnographic material on the shamanism and cosmology of an Amazonian people, the Desana of the Vaupés region of Colombia.

Isbell describes the way in which the Desana longhouse (*maloca*) functions as a cosmic model in replicating the structure of the cosmos. Forked or U-shaped posts called "red jaguars" symbolize the vaginal passage as well as the entry to other levels of the tiered Desana cosmos. They divide the *maloca* into masculine and feminine areas which correspond to different cosmic levels. They also define the main activity areas as those between the legs of the jaguar.

The central long beam of the roof symbolizes "the cosmic axis bone which gives strength and synthesizes masculine and feminine." It "has the meaning of 'ladder' which penetrates and unites cosmic levels" (Isbell 1978:281). In Desana cosmology, the axis runs from the masculine solar zenith through all levels of the universe into the female primogenic underworld (ibid.). At the intersection of the long beam and the middle U-shaped post, "a center is created where communication between cosmic levels is possible" (ibid.:283). Here the Desana shaman places his bench, the symbol of wisdom, in order to promote concentration and insight. This is the place from which he guides members of the community on hallucinogen-induced religious journeys (ibid.:283).

Isbell compares the Desana microcosmic *maloca* with the layout of Cuzco, capital of the Inca empire. The city was built in the shape of a puma. Between the legs of the puma lay the city's three-sided main plaza (*Huacaypata*) which had the form of an inverted U, open at one end. Buildings at the closed apex of the U-shaped plaza were dedicated to Viracocha, the bisexual creator-god of the Incas, while buildings on the left and right sides of the plaza were associated with female and male activities, respectively. Commenting on the buildings at the apex of the U, Isbell points out that they represent "a synthesis of the right and left axes" (ibid.:275).

Isbell discusses two other structures in the center of the U-shaped plaza. One, the *Sunturwasi*, was the focus of important rituals dedicated to the sun and ancestral Inca emperors. The other, the *Ushnu*, was the throne of the Inca, which symbolized the solar axis. Regarding these two structures Isbell (ibid.:278) points out that they

> established communion between the living and the deities or spiritual powers of other cosmic domains. Living Incas were united with the sun, their mythical progenitor, and with the deceased ancestors as well. Lying between a masculine and feminine axis on opposite sides of the *Huacaypata* Plaza, these central buildings were the foci for communion between the living and the spiritual, belonging on the central synthetic axis with Viracocha the creator.

Isbell (ibid.) goes on to show that the ideological structure expressed in the main plaza of Incaic Cuzco is illustrated in the cosmological model drawn by Santacruz Pachacuti Yamqui in his depiction of the main altar and associated icons in the Temple of the Sun, located at a *tinku* or juncture of two rivers, also in Cuzco:

> The drawing is enclosed by an inverted U shape open at the bottom. At the apex is the creator Viracocha. Two columns of figures descend from Viracocha. Those on its right are masculine. . . . On the left are feminine figures. . . .
> Within the inverted U and on the central synthetic axis with Viracocha stand a man and a woman. They are apparently the descendants of the cosmogonic kinship chart and represent the new synthesis of the parallel axes and descent lines in human marriage and procreation.
> The position is analogous with that of the *Sunturwasi* and *Ushnu* which bring together the human and spiritual worlds.[4]

After comparing Desana ethnographic data with ethnohistorical information on the Inca, Isbell concludes that in both societies "the relationship of humans to the cosmos, and the means of gaining spiritual power are communicated by mapping this ideological structure into community form" (ibid.:284). He finds the same ideological structure behind both "ground mappings," which he defines as a U-shaped configuration, manifesting a left/right opposition and encompassing a central axis which focuses ritual activity. It serves as a "mediating space between cosmic domains." The two sides are "opposed and complementary principles" representing the forces necessary for "dynamic cosmic equilibrium," while the apex represents the synthesis or unification of these oppositions. The axis is a mediating cosmic axis for rituals which provide "sources of contact with and access to spiritual power" (ibid.:284–85).

Pre-Inca Antecedents

Isbell (ibid.:286–95) uses his model to interpret archaeological data from prehistorical Central Andean ceremonial centers, which first appear shortly after 2000 B.C. Between 1500 B.C. and 500 B.C. these centers were concentrated on the north and central coasts and the north highlands of Peru, where they frequently took the form of three-sided rectangles. Isbell emphasizes that "the examples are so numerous that the form cannot be fortuitous" (ibid.:286). He focuses his analysis on two major centers, Chavín de Huántar in the highlands and Garagay on the coast, since they have been studied in sufficient detail to allow comparison with the cosmological configuration shared by the Desana *maloca* and the Inca plaza. His contention is that, if the same configuration is present, it may be inferred that the two archaeological sites communicated the same meaning as the Desana and Inca examples and that "the ideological structure expressed in the architecture ... was another mapping of the structural pattern already defined" (ibid.).

Without repeating Isbell's detailed discussion, suffice it to say that he effectively demonstrates that at both sites the components of the cosmic model are clearly present and maintained themselves through time despite modifications that occurred when they were in use. An interesting feature that Chavín de Huántar and Garagay have in common with many other sites of this period is a sunken circular court in the plaza framed by the U. Isbell concludes that "these ceremonial centers from the early first millennium B.C. communicated the same meaning and cosmological structure expressed in 16th century Cuzco and the modern Desana *maloca*" (ibid.:295).

We will probably never know the specific details of the myths that were ritually portrayed 4,000 years ago in U-shaped compounds encompassing a central cosmic axis. But the general contours can be gleaned from the art and architecture of Chavín de Huántar. According to American archaeologist Richard Burger (1992:275), this ceremonial center, built like Cuzco's Sun Temple at a confluence of two rivers "can be interpreted as embodying the *tinkuy* [or *tinku*] concept and linking the local landscape to the underlying dualistic cosmology expressed in the art and architecture." Chavín's ceremonial architecture was "a stage for ritual" and "a tool for focusing and directing supernatural power" (ibid.:267). The temple itself was "a cosmic center in which opposites were mediated and balance was maintained through the performance of appropriate religious ceremonies" (ibid.:277). The principal cult image (the Lanzón), depicting a fanged anthropomorphic being, was carved in a pose that, according to Burger (ibid.:271), expressed the deity's role as "a mediator of opposites, a personification of the principle of balance and order." Its placement in the middle of a cruciform gallery illustrated the "concept of centrality," and its penetration of the roof and floor of the chamber demonstrated its role as "an axis or conduit connecting the heavens, earth, and underworld" (ibid.). Burger (ibid.) interprets a design element (cruciform with central depression) of the Lanzón as

> a cosmogram, representing the world with the four cardinal directions and indicating the sacred center by the depression. A version of this cosmogram appears on most major Chavín sculptures, and its configuration is mirrored by the layout of the Old Temple's circular court, which reiterates the role of the ceremonial center as the place of mediation with the heavens and the underworld.

An insightful early interpretation of Chavín lithic art comes from one of the pioneers of Peruvian archaeology, Julio C. Tello (1961:185), in his comments on the obelisk which now bears his name:

> The figures represented in the obelisk described are two diverse aspects of a single divinity whose power or principal attribute is to grant to humans the nourishing fruits; thus it bears said fruits in its claws. In its first aspect it bears the fruit inside its body and in its genitals the seed that should reproduce them.

Under the action of other powers of nature . . . this divinity produces fruits and seeds. But when the animal destroys or devours the secondary animals that symbolize said powers, then the seeds germinate, grow and flower; no doubt because they have diminished or deadened said powers.

The first aspect of this divinity could signify the agent that originates the dry or hot season, that is to say, when the florescence disappears and only the seeds remain.

The second aspect signifies the dark and rainy periods of winter in which said seeds germinate and grow. . . . All these different elements that here appear reunited in a complex and mysterious whole form part of a mythological cycle related to the powers of nature which directly influence the conservation or destruction of socioeconomic values of humanity.

Archaeologist John Rowe (1967:83) identified the mythical monster or dragon in the Tello Obelisk as the cayman, the impressive South American crocodile-like reptile. Archaeologist Donald Lathrap (1971; 1985) has also interpreted the iconography of this monument. He argues that, like the Lanzón, the obelisk constitutes an *axis mundi*, or archetypal pivot, of the four quarters.

[It is] a powerful pivot precisely because it is such a complete and detailed model of the cosmos. The whole cosmos is represented by a Great Cayman who is also the Master of the Fishes. This supreme entity is unfolded into the Great Cayman of the Sky, marked by the harpy eagle affix . . . and the Great Cayman of the Water and Underworld marked by the *Spondylous* and *Strombus* affixes. . . . The two entities are separated by a membrane . . . on which mundane life takes place. The jaguar [located on the membrane] is clearly in a subsidiary position and is the channel through which mediation among the various parts of the system takes place. The key cultivated plants are always seen emerging from the nose and mouth of the jaguar (Lathrap 1985:249–50).

Lathrap (ibid.:251) also discusses the circle within a notched square (Burger's cruciform with central depression) that appears on the obelisk adjacent to the jaguar on the central membrane:

This circle represents an orifice in the membrane between the upper and lower halves of the universe through which is allowed the flux of supernatural power. . . . Further, it represents the circular depressed courtyard within the rectangular arms of the ceremonial center. . . . As a point where the power potential of the cosmos can be activated, it becomes a switch in the cosmic circuitry.

For another sculptured relief from Chavín de Huántar, the

"Smiling God" (a fanged, clawed Medusa-like figure holding two shells), Lathrap (ibid.:241) contends that the deity is "maintaining the balance of the cosmos" by

> balancing the male principle of order and culture, represented by the conch, held in his right hand, against the female principle of chaos and regeneration, represented by the spondylous, held in his left hand.

In the early 1970s a lithic depiction of the "Smiling God" was found in the sunken circular court encompassed by the rectangular arms of the Old Temple at Chavín. Of particular significance is the fact that the deity holds the San Pedro cactus. This is the earliest archaeological evidence for pre-Columbian use of the cactus in a context of obvious religious importance. It is the beginning of an uninterrupted archaeological sequence demonstrating ongoing native use of this hallucinogen in northern Peru, from the formative Chavín horizon through all subsequent regional cultures to the colonial period.

A sculptured relief from the New Temple at Chavín de Huántar, the "Staff God," is important since it is generally accepted that it depicts the central cult deity of the late phases of Chavín development. It recurs in the iconography of the south highland Tiahuanaco and Huari cultures of the mid to late first millennium A.D. Related motifs occur in north coastal cultures (especially the Moche and the Chimu), where staffs are replaced by weapons or food plants and the being holding them is framed on occasion by a two-headed serpent in the shape of a U. Rowe (1967:86) suggests that the highland staff-bearer is a sky or thunder god, "like the Inca deity Illapa, who was pictured as a man holding a club in one hand and a sling in the other." Isbell (1978:290) offers the following interpretation:

> On the elongated Raimondi Stone a sexless [or half of a male/female pair; see Lyon 1979:99] humanoid with feline attributes is depicted with a tall headdress which gives the being a columnar or axis-like appearance. The upper headdress portion is depicted as issuing from jaws and includes elaborate projecting rays that might represent the visible sun at the solar axis, while the sexless figure below represents the creator deity of which the visible sun is but a projection or manifestation. The humanoid being on the Raimondi Stone also grasps a vertical staff in each hand which would seem to represent the two axes expressed in the "legs" of the temple and synthesized in the apex and central axis of this humanoid itself.

Mesas and Structural Continuity

Returning to our point of departure, the mesa, it can be seen that, although this ritual rectangle is not literally an architectural construct, it does share in common with ancient religious sites the fact that it structures space in a fashion that facilitates human ritual activity. Also, although it does not have a U shape, it often positions participants in a U-shaped formation, that is, with the healer at the apex and the patients along the left and right sides (see Giese 1989:13 for more on this configuration; see Urton 1992:249–52 for seating of Quechua work parties). However, there is a great deal of variation on this pattern, with patients frequently clustering on whichever side of the mesa offers the most protection when outdoors, or behind the shaman when indoors, or even encircling the shaman (Flores).

In a metaphorical sense, when seated at the mesa, the shaman— like the "humanoid being" on the Raimondi Stone—embodies the cosmic U—that is, with the trunk of his body as apex and his limbs forming the left and right sides.[5] From this perspective, the mesa is an extension or projection of the U formation, with the positioning of artifacts clearly delineating a left/right opposition and central area where the two forces meet in complementary ritual activity embodied in the shaman's hands. As the popular saying puts it: "One hand washes the other."

An axis is not apparent until one realizes that the Christian cross, which is found on most curing mesas, can function as a pivotal "center" or *axis mundi* (Eliade 1964:268–69, 489n.). In other cases, a central sword or *vara mayor* (major staff) serves the same function (e.g., the seven-coiled "Serpent King" on Don Ruperto's mesa, Giese 1989:80, 157). The axis as ritual locus and the apex as synthesizer are evident from the shaman's use of pivotal artifacts to balance the two mesa fields from his seat of power at the apex.

Since the characteristics of the mesa conform to the cosmological configuration defined by Isbell, it seems reasonable to assume that this ritual prop expresses the meanings signified by the cosmic model. That is, the mesa, as a reflection of Andean cosmology, is a mediating space between levels of the cosmos with the sides (Ganadero and Curandero) representing the two primary cosmic forces and levels, while the apex (the shaman's seat) represents the unification of opposed principles linked to a central, mediating cosmic axis (cross). In effect, to use Isbell's expression, the mesa provides "sources of contact with and access to spiritual power" (Isbell 1978:284).

From the foregoing, it appears that the manner in which the mesa organizes and defines space is the contemporary, transformed manifestation of a 4,000-year-old cultural configuration. In spite of the fact that the Spanish Conquest eliminated the native political and religious institutions through which these cosmological concepts found spatial expression, associating them with the work of the devil, nonetheless, these ideas have maintained themselves at a grass-roots level. This has occurred because the dialectic governing Peruvian mesas and curing rituals is a profound expression of a folk wisdom and tradition which has practical as well as symbolic value. In addition to integrating two distinct historical and ethnic traditions—Spanish Catholicism and indigenous animatism—the mesa dialectic provides a code for the problem-solving activities entailed in curing. The pragmatic side of the mesa dialectic emerges in the experiences of curandero patients, to which we now turn our attention.

PART II:

Curanderismo from the Patients' Viewpoints

BY DONALD JORALEMON

Part I set forth the theoretical and symbolic presuppositions of curanderismo, as well as the personal characteristics and life stories of a sample of its practitioners. We now turn to the actual practice of this healing art. Our course may be compared to having just learned from a group of cancer specialists how they came to their occupation and the basic theory about tumors that underpins oncology, and we are now ready to depart on clinical rounds with our informants to see how that theory is applied. However, these "rounds" will take us through ritual performances, not bedside visits, and we will be listening mostly to the patients rather than the clinician.

Unlike recent patient-focused work in medical anthropology (e.g., Kleinman 1980; Kleinman and Gayle 1982; Ness 1980; Finkler 1985), this exploration of patients' experiences is not primarily directed toward a clinical assessment of therapy outcome or a translation of symptoms into biomedical and/or psychiatric diagnoses. Instead, we are concerned with what the relationship between patient and curandero tells us about the conceptions of suffering they share as well as about the connections between those conceptions, the ritual therapy built on them, and the patient's lived experience.

Joralemon's analysis of the social impact of curandero practice draws inspiration from recent critiques of medical anthropology, especially from the critical perspectives of Merrill Singer (1989, 1990) and those of Margaret Lock and Nancy Scheper-Hughes (1990). These scholars have pointed out that issues related to health must be considered "in light of the larger political and economic forces that pattern interpersonal relationships, shape social behavior, generate social meanings, and condition collective experience" (Singer 1990:181). They call for a synthesis of "the macrolevel understandings of political-economy with the microlevel sensitivity and awareness of conventional anthropology" (ibid.).

With these priorities in mind, Joralemon develops from the testimony of individual patients and their conversations with curanderos an analysis of the sociocultural and economic reality which is the wellspring of patient suffering. Because the majority of patients relate their symptoms, either directly or indirectly, to conflicts between men and women, special attention is paid to the politics of gender in Peruvian society. His analysis is consistent with the anthropological view of sickness expressed so elegantly by Lock and Scheper-Hughes (1990:71):

> Sickness is not just an isolated event or an unfortunate brush with nature. It is a form of communication—the language of the organs—through which nature, society, and culture speak simultaneously. The individual body should be seen as the most immediate, the proximate terrain where social truths and social contradictions are played out, as well as a locus of personal and social resistance, creativity, and struggle.

15

Curandero Clients and the Experience of Daño

A Patient's Journey

On a Thursday morning in January 1980, a father, daughter, and son-in-law boarded a bus bound for Trujillo. The twenty-year-old woman, pale and frightened, was unresponsive to the two men's reassurances as the vehicle wound its way up the hill, leaving the port city of Chimbote behind. During the two-hour trip she alternately wept, screamed in terror, and slept.

In Trujillo, the three made their way through the crowded market area to the corner from which a line of reconditioned vans and mini-buses generally departed for the nearby coastal town of Huanchaco. Unfortunately, a strike had halted this service and they were forced to hire a much more expensive taxi. With the young woman so ill, they had no choice.

The fifteen-minute ride ended as the taxi pulled up to a well-kept, single-story house some five blocks from the ocean. The two men had to half drag their charge from the backseat, where she cringed against the door like a terrified child. A voice called from within the house, instructing them to enter and be seated. A row of wooden chairs lined the wall just inside the door.

The room they entered had a set of plastic-covered chairs and sofa, a coffee table with a pitcher of plastic flowers, and a prominently displayed painting of an older man with a woman at his side. A new curtain separated this room from a dining area with a large wooden table and an old console television. Above the curtain hung a hammered-metal reproduction of the Last Supper. Two large dogs quietly watched the three strangers.

Before long a woman came from the back of the house. Though heavier and not as regal-looking in person, she was clearly the companion of the man in the living room painting. The father rose to greet her and asked if Señor Paz was at home, explaining that he had brought his sick daughter from Chimbote on the advice of family members who had been cured by the aforementioned Paz. The woman looked at the man's daughter sympathetically and responded that her husband had not yet arrived from his other home in Lambayeque for his weekly two-day stay in Huanchaco. She explained that if he had not arrived by Wednesday night he would not come until the following week. She then asked what was wrong with the daughter.

The older man, his voice showing the strain, told Señora Paz that his daughter had been sick for about a week. Increasingly fearful of people and noises, she refused to eat and had hardly slept for days. She complained of terrible pains in her head and would sit in the house crying for hours on end. At unpredictable moments her quiet sobbing would turn to ear-splitting screams, and she would stare wildly at her family as though they were about to kill her.

Señora Paz expressed her sympathy for the daughter's plight and then asked her age and if she was married. The father, pointing to the younger man, explained that his daughter was now married to her second husband, although she was only twenty years old. Her first husband had abandoned her and their two children a year before, and there was now also a six-month-old baby from the second marriage. She had become incapable of caring even for the infant.

Acknowledging the seriousness of the woman's condition, Paz's wife assured them that her husband could help. She suggested that they continue their journey north to Lambayeque, where Paz could treat her during his Saturday night curing session. Or they could return the following week when he was sure to come to Huanchaco for his usual Thursday night session. She spoke firmly and showed great confidence that Paz could heal the daughter.

The two men were deliberating when I came to the door. Surprised to see a foreigner, their conversation stopped and their eyes followed me as I entered to greet Señora Paz. She explained again that her husband had not arrived, noting that these people had come all the way from Chimbote to see him. She urged me to take this opportunity to visit José's Lambayeque home and then left us briefly to find paper and pen to write the directions.

At this early stage in my research I had done nothing more than exchange pleasantries with my informant's clients. Here was a chance to learn from those who sought his help. I spoke with the father, explaining that I had come from the United States to study the practice of curanderos in Peru. I mentioned how much I respected José's knowledge of herbal remedies and his success with his patients. The gentleman listened intently and then asked, "You believe in *brujeria* (sorcery)?"

"I believe people can do harm to one another in many ways I don't understand," I replied. "I know I have seen many patients of Señor Paz who have been very sick and whom he has helped."

My answer seemed to satisfy the father and his son-in-law, both of whom noticeably relaxed and began to converse more freely with me. With two sets of directions, we left together and walked back to the center of Huanchaco. The daughter lagged behind, walking as if in a daze, so there was ample time for us to talk about our pending trip. We parted at the central square, where they found a taxi to take them back to Trujillo. They would spend the night in a cheap hotel in the city and then father and daughter would proceed to Lambayeque the next morning. The son-in-law would have to return to Chimbote.

The next afternoon we met again, this time in José's two-story house on the outskirts of the small community of Lambayeque. While José attended to a steady stream of patients, the father and I chatted, first casually and then more personally. He had lived in Chimbote most of his life, though he was originally from the mountains. He and his wife had only three children, two daughters and a son, but a lack of money had required all to go to work after finishing primary school. He described his own work as *particular*," a common expression for the state of underemployment or unemployment faced by the majority of Peruvians.

To understand fully the life circumstances of this family, one must have to at least have passed through Chimbote. With air polluted by a noxious combination of a steel mill's smoke and the stench of fish-meal factories, the city is exceptionally unpleasant even by the standards of Peru's coastal urban centers. My own recollection of the city is a blur of shanties, pestilential markets, and deafening traffic noises. To be poor and living in Chimbote is a desperate existence.

My companion told me of his daughter's first marriage to a man who frequently beat her and finally abandoned her and their two children. She had moved back into the family's house, but was soon pregnant again, this time by the man who had accompanied them as far as Huanchaco. They were married and her new husband had joined the crowded household. Just a week earlier, for no discernible reason, she began to show the symptoms of her present ailment. They had not taken her to any medical post because in his words, "The doctors don't understand these diseases."

About mid-afternoon, José called the father and daughter into his consultation room. Through the window in the door I could see him performing a ritual cleansing with a live guinea pig. As he rubbed the animal over the young woman, she began to scream and fight against the restraining arm of her father. José would usually end such a cleansing by cutting the animal open with the patient present to show the disease-affected organs, but the daughter had worked herself into such a frenzy that José had her father take her from the room. She collapsed in a corner and sobbed.

Patients kept José busy the rest of the afternoon. When he finally emerged from his consultation room, he seemed unconcerned with the young woman still huddled in the corner, and merely passed the time with a friend who had come by to share a few beers. I was struck by the extreme deference the patient's father showed to José; he listened closely to the conversation but did not seem to feel free to participate.

At dinnertime, José instructed the woman who cooks for him to take the young woman with her to buy some more drinks. While they were away, I asked José what he had diagnosed. He told me it was *daño por brebaje* ("harm by a poisoned drink") and that it was easily cured; he had cured more cases than he cared to remember. He asked if I had not noticed her quieting down after nothing more than the guinea pig cleansing.

During dinner, the young woman remained seated on the floor, but, at José's insistence, she accepted some food. After the meal, José invited her to sit next to him and share his beer. I watched as he gently coaxed her up from the floor, all the while repeating in a joking manner how we could hardly tell she had been screaming just a few hours earlier. Reluctant at first, she slowly surrendered to José's engaging style and took on the expression of an angry child trying not to smile.

When I awoke the next morning, the patient was sweeping the floor of the waiting room, where she and her father had slept. The terror of the previous day seemed to have been replaced by a listless acceptance of the situation. The day passed without much change in her mood, until the time for the healing ritual drew near. As other patients arrived and were taken by car to the site of the night session, she again became anxious and incoherent. She had to be forced into the car when her turn came.

The session began just after 11:00 P.M. We were in an open field with nothing but the moon for light; a cold breeze and an abundance of mosquitoes were making us all uncomfortable. In the course of the next six hours all present participated in José's carefully orchestrated ritual, which included ingesting the San Pedro and tobacco mixtures. The young woman struggled and fought each time she was called upon to swallow the remedy or to perform a ritual act. She was by far the most unruly of the twenty patients present.

By morning she was exhausted. Her father had to carry her to the car for the short ride back to José's house, where she immediately was put to bed. She was awakened at 11:00 A.M. and given some food, which she meekly accepted. José gave her father a bag of herbs for her to take and then disappeared into his own room to sleep.

Father and daughter left for Chimbote, a six-hour trip, that afternoon. They returned to Huanchaco the following two Thursdays to participate in the additional rituals that José had prescribed. I saw them both times and was startled by the marked improvement in the woman's appearance and comportment. She was still a little shy, but more communicative than before; she was less pale, and did not seem anxious or tearful. Her father praised José for having cured his daughter, who was once again caring for her children and behaving almost normally.

José told me that the woman's first husband had been responsible for the poisoning, but that he had done it in retaliation for her having cursed him with the help of a local sorcerer, or *brujo*. José had learned this from his visions during the first ritual, and had communicated his discovery to his patient and her father. He described the case as "very normal," and passed it off as an easy cure.

The last time I saw the father I asked about the cost of the treatment. At my request, he calculated all the expenses he had incurred. Indirect expenses (bus, taxi, food, hotel, et cetera) for the three trips from Chimbote totaled the equivalent of $34. José charged an additional $40, which he split with his two ritual assistants. The total bill, then, was almost $75. A full-time manual laborer in Peru at that time was earning about $2.50 per day; the woman's family therefore invested more than a month's full-time wages in her cure.

Daño: Escape Valve?

This case, the first experience of a patient I recorded, indicates the great importance of the illness *daño* (harm caused by sorcery) to the work of curanderos. The suspicion of *daño* is the primary reason individuals seek curanderos; reversing its effects is the objective toward which the curandero directs the powers of his curing altar. *Daño* is the most frequent diagnosis made by coastal curanderos and, as such, constitutes the axis around which the relationship between shaman and patient forms.

Glass-Coffin (1991:38) has provided a concise definition of this illness:

> *Daño*, in its many forms, is always a purposeful attack on another individual's physical, economic, or social health. *Daño*, in its most dangerous aspect, involves the evil intent of a human enemy (at least an acquaintance of the victim and often a family member) who, because of jealousy, envy, or revenge contacts a wizard (*brujo*) in order to intentionally hurt or kill the chosen victim. Through magical means involving the use of spirit familiars, the *brujo* effects the *daño* through capture of the victim's spirit or shadow.

A *brujo* (I prefer "sorcerer" to "wizard") may accomplish his/her attack by means of poisons (*daño por brebaje*) or through the air (*daño por aire*) by contagious magic. In the latter case, the sorcerer manipulates an article of the victim's clothing or some other representation of the victim (e.g., a photograph, a lock of hair, fingernails, et cetera) to capture or "tie-up" his/her soul. One curandero in the study, Nilo Plasencia, indicated that *brujos* make voodoo-like dolls (*muñecos*) of a victim and bury these in cemeteries. Whatever the means by which the attack is accomplished, the effect on a victim may include physical symptoms, psychological disturbances, and even unusually bad luck in everything from business to love. The connection seen in the above case between *daño* and male/female conflicts is especially common, as the following chapters demonstrate.

The powers of the curandero's mesa, especially those concentrated on the left side (see Part I), enable him to identify the person(s) who contracted for the sorcery, the motivation behind the act, and the means by which the attack was effected. The curative right side of the mesa permits the curandero to discover the appropriate remedy. Frequently, a cure includes a counterattack on the part of the curandero against the sorcerer's client. This is called the *volteada*, or "turning around," whereby the curandero employs the powers of sorcery on behalf of his client (see Chapter 17).

Those who have written about this "sorcery syndrome" have offered a psycho-functional interpretation of its societal impact (Chiappe 1969; Sharon 1978:23–29; Chiappe, Lemlíj and Millones 1985). They argue that in Peru's highly stratified society, where opportunities are limited by rigid class boundaries, individuals are frustrated by social inequities but are denied direct expression of their envy and hostility because they are forced to depend on those who are above them on the economic ladder. As a result, they employ sorcery as a covert outlet for their aggression. This has a positive social function in that it allows for the release of aggressive impulses without any serious threat to the social fabric.[1] As Sharon (1978:28) puts it, sorcery provides "an escape valve, permitting aggression resulting from frustration to express itself without attacking fundamental institutions" (see also Glass-Coffin 1991).

As I began to interview patients in earnest for the present study, I started to question how well this functional interpretation explained the impact of *daño*. In the actual context of individual lives, *daño* seemed less a harmless release of frustrations than an instrumental force in the politics of everyday life. The stories told by informants showed that the acts of sorcery behind *daño* are effective weapons in social relationships, not just emotional pacifiers. In the view of *daño* sufferers, sorcery has significant disruptive effects, both as a suspicion that alienates one from others and as an actual source of physical, emotional, and economic harm. Whatever emotional relief the "aggressor" may experience for having initiated an act of sorcery, the impact of that act, even if it is merely suspected, extends deeply into the network of social relations.[2]

Even the therapeutic work of curanderos, far from dissipating social tensions, can engender or intensify existing hostilities by confirming patients' suspicions that their suffering is the result of sorcery. In fact, many curanderos blur the line between curer and sorcerer by initiating assaults against the party or parties responsible for their patient's sickness. This vengeful element in the curandero's practice is especially evident in Nilo Plasencia's rituals, but it is also an implicit element in the work of many shamans.

If it is not an escape valve for social structural tensions, what role does the sorcery/curing complex play in Peruvian society? It seemed essential to me that the question be posed first at the level of individuals, who are caught up in the web of suspicion and suffering that constitutes the actual experience of *daño* and that structures the relationship between the curandero and his clients. An ethnography of patients' experiences would situate sorcery and curing in the context of actual social relations. It would also permit an elaboration of the cultural model of *daño*, as well as an estimation of the degree to which curanderos and their clients share the same conceptualizations of the illness.

With this patient-focused ethnography as a foundation, an extension of the analysis to the societal level would be possible. Not only would we know more about the therapeutic dynamics of curandero/client relations, but also we would be on firmer ground in judging the social impact of sorcery and curing. These were the objectives behind the patient-focused research upon which I report in the following chapters.

Documenting Patient Cases

The research team consisted of four Americans (Sharon, Joralemon, and UCLA anthropology doctoral candidates, Bonnie Glass-Coffin and Donald Skillman) and two Peruvians (Rafael Vásquez Guerrero, an anthropology student at the University of Trujillo, and Nancy Peña Pusma, a nurse based in Chiclayo). Our informants were drawn from the clientele of four curanderos: Víctor Flores, Nilo Plasencia, Eduardo Calderón, and Jorge Merino. Subjects were interviewed at least twice, once as they arrived for their consultations with the curanderos and a second time at least one month later.[3] A subsample of subjects was interviewed a third time.

We tried to approach every first-time patient, excluding only those whose homes were too far away to permit easy follow-ups. However, circumstances made it difficult to realize this ideal. The time required to gain sufficient confidence from the patients to encourage their participation, combined with the short interval between the patients' arrival at the curandero's home and the group's departure for the ritual site, often resulted in less than a hundred-percent success rate. Nevertheless, refusals were very rare for the initial interviews.

The patient sample (n = 129) is summarized in Table 2. The most striking features are the representation of women at sixty-two

TABLE 2

PATIENT SAMPLE

	TOTAL	VF	NP	EC	JM
CASES					
Male	49	10	10	13	16
Female	80	25	24	4	27
Total:	129	35	34	17	43
AGES					
Low/High:	6–84	17–60	6–72	21–53	10–84
Means:					
Male	36.7	32.2	34.4	35.2	42.1
Female	36.2	33.8	36.0	32.8	39.3
Total:	36.4	33.3	35.5	34.6	41.0
EDUCATION (Years in School)					
Low/High:	0–16	0–15	0–15	5–15	0–16
Means:					
Male	8.0	8.4	6.7	10.7	6.2
Female	6.2	7.6	6.6	13.0	3.5
Total:	6.8	7.8	6.6	11.2	4.5

percent of the total, and the consistent age centering of each patient group at around thirty-five years of age (the Merino sample is skewed by two eighty-four-year-old clients). The educational level is quite variable across the patient groups (Calderón's patients are the best educated, Merino's the least); however, at almost seven years of schooling, the mean for the total sample is very close to census-reported averages for the country as a whole (INE 1984:15). A majority of patients (fifty-five percent) are married or cohabiting.

Our Peruvian research assistant, Rafael Vásquez Guerrero, carried out an extensive investigation of the socioeconomic status of the Trujillo-based portion of the patient sample, using occupation, salary/income, residential location, house type, and schooling as measures of social classes. He found it difficult to delineate clear class boundaries but concluded that a tripartite classification adequately differentiated the sample: lower class (fifty-seven percent of the total sample), middle class (thirty-nine percent), higher class (four percent of curandero clientele).[4] His full analysis is included in a thesis submitted to the University of Trujillo (Vásquez 1988a).

While I discuss in greater detail below the nature of complaints brought to curanderos, I would make two general observations at this point. First, in the two core samples (Flores and Plasencia) almost two-thirds (sixty-three percent) of the curandero's patients had previously consulted with a biomedical specialist about their condition. Second, in the same two groups, more than seventy percent (seventy-one and seventy-eight percent, respectively) had suffered for more than three months from the problem for which they sought treatment. Thus, multiple resort and high chronicity are basic elements in the majority of the cases seen by these curanderos.

The subsample of patients (n = 20) chosen for long-term follow-up came in equal numbers from the clients of Flores and Plasencia. We made no attempt to randomize their selection, but we did try to keep a corresponding proportion of males to females. Individuals were included for several reasons: something was unclear or contradictory in the individual's first two interviews, the subject was unusually forthcoming, the case was still very much "in process" at the time of the second interview, et cetera.

The first interview consisted of three parts. First, we elicited basic sociodemographic background information (age, sex, civil status, number of children, education, profession, birth, and migration history). Second, we administered orally a standardized self-report questionnaire, the "Brief Symptom Inventory" (Derogatis and Spencer 1982).[5] Third, we asked a series of open-ended questions concerning the history of the individual's sickness: symptoms, prior resort, perceptions of cause. This last part was tape-recorded and subsequently transcribed. In most cases, the first interview lasted from ten to fifteen minutes.

The next part of case documentation took place during the ritual itself. Whenever the curandero directed observations, questions or specific treatments to one of our subjects, we tape-recorded the interaction and later had it transcribed. The degree of personal interaction between curandero and patient varied greatly according to the practitioner—from most to least time spent with individual patients during rituals: Merino, Plasencia, Calderón, and Flores.

The third segment of each case was an interview carried out after the end of treatment. These follow-ups, which took the same form as the first interviews, were exceedingly difficult to regulate. One reason is that, while we wanted these interviews to come after therapy was over, it is not easy to establish when curandero treatment has "ended." Patients may stop attending rituals for any number of reasons (e.g., the therapy is finished, inability to pay, difficulty scheduling time away from families, work-related travel), but, at the same time, often indicate that they intend to return for more sessions. In many cases, treatment for one complaint blurs into therapy for another in what becomes almost an avocational attendance at ritual performances. Finding informants at home was also an intensely frustrating undertaking, frequently involving repeat visits to diverse parts of the city and/or surrounding communities. It was because of these complications, as well as many others, that the "time to follow-up" is variable. For example, the mean elapsed time between the first and second interviews for the thirty-five patients of Víctor Flores is thirty-nine days; however, the range is from 7 to 126 days. For patients of Nilo Plasencia, the mean to follow-up is sixty days, with cases ranging from 12 to 143. While we were unable to find a practical way to standardize follow-up scheduling, we did maintain a minimum of thirty days between our first and second interviews in eighty-six percent of the Flores cases and in seventy-nine percent of Plasencia's. Any shorter term to follow-up might result in an overestimation of the impact of therapy by confounding temporary and more long-lasting effects.

The research team found that second interviews tended to be far longer and more open, probably the result of gained confidence and a more familiar setting. Patients frequently went into great depth about very personal issues during the open-ended section of the interview. This experience encouraged us to pursue an additional twenty third interviews. The format of these long-term follow-ups, carried out several months later, was informal and did not involve repetition of the "Brief Symptom Inventory." Rather, interviewers took this opportunity to explore in even more depth the life experiences of the patients as well as their perceptions of the curanderos who sought to help them.

Several circumstances over which we had little or no control affected the quality of the interviews with the patients. For example, it was not always possible to interview in private, often because the patient preferred to have a family member or friend present. Also, since the first interview was completed in the short time that the patient waited for her/his consultation or for the night's ritual to begin, there was little opportunity to develop rapport and to diminish the awkwardness of the first encounter.

Related to the difficulties of the initial interview situation, we found that patients were not always clear at first about who we

were and why we were asking so many questions. Especially unclear in their minds was the relationship between the researchers
and the curandero. Some saw us as collaborators with the curers,
seeking to confirm therapeutic success for the purpose of increasing the curer's clientele. This view, in fact, was promoted by one
curer, Víctor Flores, whose flamboyant introductions of the research team at the start of rituals must have confirmed in his patients' minds that we were in league with the healer.

The relationship between the research team and the patients developed over time, however, and an increasing level of rapport and
understanding of the purpose of the investigation is evidenced in
second interviews. Many patients came to treat one or more of the
researchers as confidants after they had participated side by side in
rituals and talked informally during breaks in the performances
and in the early morning hours after the rituals were finished. For
one of our Peruvian research assistants this level of trust resulted
in subsequent phone calls from patients, as well as exchanges on
the streets of Trujillo, during which his advice was sought and
more personal information was revealed to him. While this evolution in the researcher/informant relationships probably created an
imbalance in the depths of the first and second interviews, it also
yielded the rich narrative accounts from patients on which my
analysis depends.

Preview

In the following three chapters I present summaries of patient
cases which employ as many of our informants' own words as possible. To avoid the temptation to use only those cases with especially dramatic content or unusually clear and extensive informant
testimony, I begin with ten patient cases drawn at random from the
clients of Víctor Flores and Nilo Plasencia (five cases each). The
only selective criteria were gender and age, applied so as to include
men and women at roughly their proportions in the sample as a
whole, and to likewise represent the overall distribution of ages.[6]
Following this, however, I include additional material drawn from
some of the more remarkable interviews of the project, including
cases from the clients of Eduardo Calderón and Jorge Merino.
Thus, it is hoped that the general character of the client interviews
is portrayed without sacrificing the more exceptional cases.

The rituals in which these patients participated were described in general terms in Part I. In the next chapters, only the verbal interactions (if any occurred) between the curandero and the patient during rituals are described. In the case of the clients of Víctor Flores, such exchanges are rare since the curer has little nonformulaic interchange during sessions. On the other hand, Nilo Plasencia's cases almost always include dialogues between curer and patient during rituals; these are actually scripted into the performance as a part of Plasencia's *rastreo* or diagnostic tracking. Similarly, both Calderón and Merino engage in direct conversations with patients as the ritual progresses.

After I have presented the individual case summaries, I turn to an analysis of the shared interpretive frameworks by which patients make sense of their illnesses, using the transciptions of interviews as "collective utterances not individual texts" (Crain 1991: 68). I focus on the metaphors that patients repeatedly draw upon to describe their sicknesses and on the curative mechanisms of curandero therapy in the belief that metaphors provide insight into the conceptual system by which everyday realities are understood (Lakoff and Johnson 1980; Lakoff 1987). I show that patients use a core set of metaphors in a systematic fashion and that this metaphorical structure constitutes the cultural model of *daño* that both patients and curanderos share.

Both the individual patient interviews and the collective story they tell about *daño* implicate social relationships as the ultimate source of suffering for curanderos' clients. My final discussion asks the questions: What social-structural forces create the tensions between people that are manifested in sorcery acts, and what impact does the work of curanderos have on the social world of their patients? I argue that for most patients it is a gender-based hierarchy, supported by capitalist relations of production and a cultural ethos of male superiority (*machismo*), that lies at the heart of their suffering. I see the recourse of patients to sorcerers and curanderos as an example of what James Scott (1986) calls "everyday forms of resistance." I contrast this interpretation with the "escape valve" explanation reviewed above, and I point out that curanderos, most of whom are male, simultaneously challenge and promote the system of male privilege that conditions the lives of their patients.

16
Patients of Víctor Flores

Curer and Patients: General Observations

The description of Víctor Flores's ritual in Chapter 9 shows that Víctor delegates much of the actual ritual therapy to his assistants. While they do the tobacco raisings, Víctor walks around the circle of patients playing his rattle and sometimes singing. Only occasionally does he sing a diagnosis for a specific patient, or directly minister to individuals. His ritual is also less physically taxing for patients than are those of other curanderos, both because of the protected nature of the site (the *"Fortaleza"*) and because Víctor does not require that patients imbibe the tobacco liquid — this is entirely voluntary in his sessions. As our Peruvian research assistant put it, Víctor performs a good "show," meaning not only that his ritual is theatrical but that it also involves less aggressive therapy on the part of the curandero than is the case with other curers.

It is also important to note that Víctor strives to establish and maintain an exceedingly warm and polite relationship with his clients, despite the relative lack of individual attention he pays to them during his rituals. He speaks to them with deference and paternal concern and is never harsh or demanding. Víctor's cordiality impresses many patients, as in the case of one forty-eight-year-old man who preferred Flores to a curandero he had gone to previously: "It's that, how can I put it, the *señor* [Víctor] has more patience, more patience to treat people. The other, [*don* X], is a little angry . . . tough."[1]

The affable demeanor Víctor adopts with his clients is apparently successful. He has a loyal following of patients who routinely come for a check-up and ritual cleansing. This relationship can extend over long periods of time, as in the case of Dora, a sixty-year-old woman who had used Víctor as her "family curandero" for twenty-five years, bringing each family member to him as the need arose. Some of the most positive comments about curanderos in our entire study were made by Víctor's patients. The evaluation of Rosa, a forty-three-year-old woman, is typical:

> Q: Tell me, after your experience with *don* Víctor, what do you think of him as a curandero?
>
> A: I think that he is a *señor* who cures, who doesn't deceive people, who has cured me as well as my sister—and she is well to this day. . . . I'd say that, yes, he knows how to cure; because he has cured me!

One client's positive opinion of Víctor, however, does not necessarily lead to the conclusion that his treatment is entirely effective for all. For a variety of reasons, including the patient's failure to return for the prescribed number of rituals, many individuals judged Víctor's therapy either inconclusive or ineffective. One particularly striking case was that of Felicita, a thirty-one-year-old married woman with four children whose husband left her "like a mad man" for another woman. She suffered from menstrual bleeding that would not stop, even with a physician's attention, and came to Víctor on the advice of a neighbor. Víctor identified *daño*, and he explained that the husband's mistress was responsible for both Felicita's sickness and for her husband's behavior. Felicita attended five sessions, but afterwards she judged Víctor "insufficiently forceful" to have countered the sorcery entrapping her husband. Her spouse had moved to another town, taken up residence with the other woman, and had written to ask Felicita not to send his children for visits. She had begun legal proceedings against him.

Flores's Patients

Ana (VF2) This twenty-one-year-old, unmarried woman had resided in Trujillo since birth. Her mother worked at home and her father was a professional house painter. After completing secondary school, she began studying medicine at the University of Trujillo and had finished her first year at the time she was interviewed. She explained her reasons for seeking the help of Víctor Flores while she was simultaneously continuing with biomedical care:

> Well, six months ago they operated on me, here, on my breast, and, well, up until today we continue going back for exams, no? The treatment continues, but the truth is that there isn't [any] improvement. I don't feel that I'm better, and this discomfort [*malestar*] that

I had has diminished, no?, but not completely. This is the reason
that we have come.

An initial diagnosis, on the basis of a guinea pig cleansing (*limpia
de cuy*), suggested the possibility that "an evil person had, out of
envy, inflicted me with a bad air" (*me había puesto un mal aire*).[2]
When asked if there was anyone she suspected, she said that it
might have been some high school girlfriends, and invoked the
proverb: Faces are seen, and not hearts" (*Se ven las caras y no los
corazones*). She thought that the continuous competition for the
best grades, essential for those who wish to beat the astounding
odds against entrance into the university, might have caused them
to envy her success. "Our friendship has continued, but there is
something different, no? With one person, it isn't the same friendship; we speak out of a sense of duty."

At the second interview, thirty-six days later, Ana declared that
after attending three ritual sessions, "Well, I really feel better." The
surgical wound on her breast had healed "thanks to God and *don*
Víctor." Although she did not believe in Víctor's treatment at first,
and was even nervous at the initial ritual, her experience had convinced her that "folkloric medicine has a substantial influence on
us, and of course the *señor* has put in a lot of work himself; he has
helped me a great deal."

One year later (August 1988), Ana consented to a third interview, in which she modified her earlier evaluation of the part
played by Víctor in her cure. She still credited the curandero with
having cured her "in some way," but she now added that "a change
of doctor [had been] necessary." Her new physician explained that
her surgical wound had failed to heal because of a bacterial infection. Ana noted that the wound had started to heal before she went
to the new doctor (i.e., after Víctor's treatment), closing from a
width of five or six centimeters to just four, but that it did not close
completely until she received fourteen injections from the physician. Víctor started the healing process and made her feel more
tranquil; he contributed to her "psychological cure"; however, it
was the doctor's treatment that closed the wound in her opinion.

Interestingly, Ana maintained her belief that evil (*maldad*) exists
and that "there are people who dedicate themselves exclusively to
daño, be it for envy or for other feelings." She spoke eloquently of
the terrible competition between young people who want to gain
admission into the university, and of the understandable resent-

ment her friends must have felt when she got in and they did not, even though they had almost the same grades. She excused them for their hard feelings and claimed that they were now back on good terms with each other.

The interviewer also asked Ana to predict how, when she becomes a doctor, she would react to patients who wish to seek the help of a curandero. She admitted some hesitancy about her own willingness to work with curanderos, but she also expressed the view that doctor and curer can work together: "The two can go hand in hand; one doesn't hinder the other and the two are complementary." She qualified her generally positive view of curanderos by stressing the need for a way to evaluate the credentials of specific curers ("because some do evil things, no?"), and by restricting her judgment to the curer's knowledge of herbal medicinals (i.e., not to their ritual practices). She added that most of her fellow students, along with the majority of the medical faculty at the university, are convinced that progress in biomedicine will eventually make obsolete even the herbal side of curandero healing.

There was irony in the third interview with Ana. When asked if she had told her new doctor that she had been under the care of a curandero, she confessed that she had not because, "I didn't know how he would take it." She hesitated to reveal her participation in a curandero's ritual despite the fact that she had seen her physician leading a recent congress in Trujillo on the subject of traditional medicine. The doctor in question has been the contact person at the University of Trujillo School of Medicine for our research projects on curanderismo and has long supported the need for better understanding of Peru's ethnomedical traditions.

Emerita (VF4) At thirty-nine years of age, Emerita had three children and was separated from her husband, a truck driver. She was born in the sierra, inland from Trujillo, and had finished the fifth grade of schooling. She worked as a *comerciante*, a catch-all word which includes a wide variety of small-scale merchants, from traveling street vendors (*ambulantes*) to persons who own stalls at established public markets. Emerita's first interview was extensive and revealed very personal material about the conflict between herself and her husband; the follow-up was evasive and abbreviated. The gender of the interviewer, female in the first encounter and male in the second, might in part account for this difference.[3]

Emerita related her problem to difficulties she had with her in-laws, and to the affair her husband had started with her niece, whom Emerita had raised from the age of two. When her mother-in-law fell sick three years earlier, the woman's children had taken her to see a curandero, and "they told her it was *mal daño* and they blamed me, saying that I had arranged to do *mal daño*." Emerita did not know if her husband believed his siblings, but she noticed a change:

> He was distant with me, *doctora* [the interviewer], so I told him, "There can't be a home without affection. It's OK that we suffer from being poor, but there always ought to be tenderness." He told me, "I'm sick with bad kidneys," and I believed him.[4]

Subsequently, her mother-in-law died of liver cancer. When Emerita tried to go to the wake, her niece told her it would be better if she didn't attend because, "the gossip was that I had done *mal daño* and that by my hands she had died." Emerita confronted her husband, they argued, and she told him that if he sided with his family he'd better leave. She returned to her natal village in the sierra, but she later learned from her own children that her husband was having an affair with her niece.

Emerita's lack of responsiveness in the second interview (thirty days later) is well illustrated by the following exchange:

> Q: After Víctor's treatment, do you feel better?
> A: Yes, *doctor.*
> Q: Yes?
> A: Yes.
> Q: Has your condition changed?
> A: My condition has changed, yes, a lot.
> Q: What do you feel?
> A: Improvement in everything.
> Q: In everything?
> A: Yes.
> Q: And when you had your consultation with him [Víctor Flores], what did he tell you about your case?
> A: He told me to have patience, that he was going to resolve it.

Despite the interviewer's efforts, Emerita would not go into any detail about her condition after Víctor's therapy. However, Emerita's story is important in two regards: first, it shows the significant point of tension that exists between wives and their in-laws (especially mothers-in-law); second, it demonstrates that a curandero's attribution of problems to *daño* can further intensify, rather than reduce, existing hostilities. The role of spousal infidelity in Emerita's case is an additional factor of importance; it figures centrally in the problems brought to curanderos by many clients.

Hilda (VF11) This mother of eight was born and raised in Trujillo and had a fifth grade education. She was fifty-five when interviewed, worked in a food business, and had a husband whose occupation she identified simply as *comerciante*. In her first interview, Hilda described the following symptoms: headaches, leg and body pains, dizziness, heart pain, vision problems, "weakening" (*decaimiento*) of the body, loss of appetite and weight, and a lack of interest in work. She had begun to experience these symptoms five months earlier. Before coming to Víctor on the advice of a friend, she had gone to a doctor in Lima who told her that a vision problem was causing her headaches. He gave her eyeglasses.

Neither during the first nor second interview (forty-four days later) did Hilda identify a cause for her suffering; however, at the second interview she did describe her experience during the ritual session:

> Arriving there, he gave me the water of San Pedro, this little water he has prepared, and with that and nothing more, huh, and the little staff he has that one cleanses with. Just at early dawn, I felt, well, I felt a little of the . . . that I was clearing (*despejando*), no? After I took the *remedio* and, at about dawn, I rubbed myself with the little staff. I felt the pain, here in my head, and when it hurt more, well, it seemed that the sickness was there, because when I continued rubbing, it made me feel like throwing-up; but I didn't vomit. So, later the feeling passed . . . and, well, the next day I woke up feeling a little more tranquil.

Hilda judged the treatment she had received incomplete because she only had been able to attend two of the three recommended ritual sessions. She did say that she felt better and that many of the earlier symptoms had either disappeared or diminished. Her case illustrates the difficulty mentioned in the previous chapter of determining the end point of curandero treatment for the purposes of an "after" interview.

Augusto (VF18) Augusto, a fifty-two-year-old electrician, had lived in Trujillo all his life. He had six children from his first wife (who was deceased), and maintained a relationship with a *conviviente*, a woman to whom he was not married. He had a third-grade education.

Five years before our interview with Augusto, he had suffered injuries from a fall while working on an electrical pole. He rejected a doctor's advice to put his ankle in a plaster cast because the X rays had not shown any break. However, when pain continued for three months, a friend suggested that sorcery could be involved: "He said, couldn't it be that they have played one on you?" (*que te la hayan jugado*).[5] On his friend's advice, Augusto sought the help of Víctor, who treated the injured ankle with massage and had Augusto participate in rituals. Satisfied with the positive results, Augusto had returned repeatedly ever since, either for specific problems or simply for a "check-up" (*un chequeo*).

On this particular occasion, Augusto had come for two reasons: a general cleansing for himself to improve his luck, and a diagnosis in absentia for his sick sister, to be based on a *rastreo* or divinatory diagnosis of an article of her clothing. In the latter case, if the diagnosis so indicated, Víctor would do a *levantada*, or ritual raising, with the clothing vicariously standing in for Augusto's sister.

Thirty-two days later, at the second interview, Augusto declared that he felt much better, "My whole mind cleared, my body as well." Víctor had told him that he was a little "mistreated" (*maltratado*), "crushed" (*chancado*), and that he needed an "unbolting" (*destrancada*) and "flowering" (*florecida*). His sister had also improved. She had returned home from the hospital after fifteen days and, while not completely well, was more encouraged and spirited (*alentada*).

One year later, Augusto answered more questions for us. In the previous month he had attended three sessions with Flores because of a problem in his bronchial tubes:

> I have gone to a doctor, to a Dr. [G. Z.]. He told me that I had to have some X rays, that he had to give me some injections and various things, even though I already had at least three prescriptions from him for bronchitis that hadn't done any good. With the drink of *don* Víctor . . . now it has gotten rid of it. . . . Right now I have a little, a small cough.

Despite Augusto's obvious confidence in Víctor's ability to heal, when asked if he would go first to Flores or to a doctor when next sick, he said, "Well, before anything, I would go to a doctor, no?" Still, Augusto maintained a constant relationship with Víctor and compared him favorably to the one other curandero he had once consulted.

Segundo (VF35) The last of Víctor's clients to be discussed here was a twenty-two-year-old married man who was born in the mountain city of Cajamarca and had resided in the Trujillo area for only the past three years. He had an elementary-school education and, until just before the interview, had been working as a fare collector on a privately owned bus which ran between the city of Trujillo and an outlying community. Segundo had two children, one a newborn son. His wife worked at home.

> I have come here to the curandero because I feel very bad in my work, bored, preoccupied, bad dreams, anger against my family, with my friends, arguments with friends at work, with my closest companions. For a month and a half I have felt distressed because the money I get (I earn money every day) doesn't last; I have to spend it on something. I want to go out on the street, I don't want to be with my family. I feel ashamed. It seems strange, [because] I used to get along well with my family—I took my wife out for walks—but now it's to the point where I get angry if anything happens. And I wish he [Flores] would tell me what's going on and if he can cure me or give me some medicine. I think that it could be *maldad* from a girl who used to be my *enamorada* [girlfriend, mistress]. She took my photograph and threatened to make me go crazy. This was a year ago. I had a child by her, but it died. She took me to the police and made me spend a lot of money to get out of this. She is still threatening me, and now she has gone to the mountains and I haven't seen her.

Segundo said that previous visits to medical doctors had not revealed anything. His wife and friends had urged him to go to Víctor, guaranteeing that "he could cure me if it is related to *maldad*."

It was very difficult to locate Segundo for a second interview, but just over four months later (137 days) a follow-up interview was carried out. He related that Víctor, on the basis of a divinatory card reading, had identified his problem as "a sickness, a little peculiar, not a sickness of God, no? He told me I was envied (*estaba envidiado*)[6] at my work and that a woman had done a *maldad* on me earlier." This had confirmed his suspicion about his previous girlfriend and increased his faith in Víctor's abilities. However, despite an initial calming effect from his ritual participation, he remained troubled, especially by his lack of patience and his propensity to anger. "He [Flores] didn't cut [off] the sickness well for me" (*no me cortó bien la enfermedad*).

A third interview with Segundo was conducted nine months

later. He had not been back to Víctor, nor had he gone to any other curandero. Although his situation with his family had improved and he felt more tranquil, his economic problems had gotten worse as a result of his having been fired from his job on the bus. He related his employment difficulties to a conflict he had had with a drunken passenger, a young male alcoholic whose mother runs a small store/restaurant from her home along the bus route. When the drunk grabbed for the money that Segundo had collected in fares, Segundo pushed him out of the moving bus, causing the man to fall and hurt himself. Unfortunately for Segundo, the drunk's mother was rumored to be a *bruja* (sorceress):

> When I went to buy bread for breakfast she threatened me. She was sweeping there in her doorway and she told me, "Now," she said, "these problems you have, just wait, you'll see if all the time your job is going to last won't pass fifteen days." So, I think the woman has done *daño*, but for me alone, so that my family would hate me.

Not long after, following a massive set of government-ordered price increases on state-controlled products (September 1988), Segundo asked for a raise beyond the salary adjustment he had been given. He believed his request to be fair, given that the increase he had received wasn't sufficient to feed his family with the newly inflated prices, and also because other fare collectors were earning more. His boss, accusing Segundo of stealing money from the fares, fired him. Segundo attributed his job loss to the sorcery of the drunk's mother.

Segundo spoke at length of the effects of envy on his life. Passengers on the bus envied him and expected that he would extend favors on the basis of acquaintanceship (e.g., not charge them extra for bringing aboard several loaded baskets). Even friends envied him for having a job, and would ask his boss to hire them in his place. According to Segundo, the driver of the bus on which he worked is similarly affected by envy:

> The driver has the same problems as me: bored with his family, the money doesn't last. He thinks it's envy also, and since he has children in the street [i.e., from a mistress] he figures it must be that the other woman is *viva* [deceitful; i.e., harming him by sorcery].

Segundo had advised this friend to go to Víctor, whom he continued to hold in high esteem. This is clear from Segundo's final observation:

Now, with this problem that I have, without work, I don't know
what to do with myself. But I have hopes of finding work and being
a little more tranquil all my life. But for this I have to go to *don*
Víctor Flores so that he can give me a little cleansing (*una limpiadita*).

Segundo's case, which I have reviewed in some depth, illustrates
the degree to which fear of the envy and aggression of others can
shape an individual's life. It also shows the direct linkage between
envy and sorcery, be it related to adulterous affairs or economic
insecurities. Segundo's sense of vulnerability to the hostility of others and his apprehension that he could lose what little he had, is an
example of a regular motif in the testimony of curandero clients. It
is shared even by those in better economic situations. Segundo's
former employer, for example, owned several buses but felt sufficiently insecure that he hired a curandero to come to his home to
do ritual cleansings for the protection of his vehicles.

Conclusion

In addition to the insights Víctor's cases give to his therapeutic
style and the nature of the relationships he fosters with his clients,
they also reveal the degree of vulnerability patients experience in
their private and public lives. It was the potential aggression of
others, including family and friends, to which our informants felt
vulnerable. At risk was not only physical health, but also the fidelity
of a spouse, the security of a job, and even a general sense of being
safe from the vagaries of ill fortune. In this latter context, it was
not just the individual who was vulnerable, but his or her possessions as well. In one memorable case, Víctor and his assistants performed a luck ritual for a car used as a taxi, raising shells of tobacco at each of the four wheels. Similarly, several patients
recounted Víctor's visits to their homes for ritual cleansings of
their dwellings and belongings.

This experience of vulnerability, of being in harm's way, crosses
class boundaries. One need only travel through the middle- and
upper-class neighborhoods of Trujillo, past houses with barbed
wire on their walls and with private security patrols, to realize that
Peru's precarious economic situation introduces insecurity and risk
even into the lives of the affluent. Wealthy individuals, among
them the owner of a major bus company, turned to Víctor for protection from covert aggression born of envy, as well as from the

unpredictable misfortune that can mean the difference between success and failure in any endeavor.

All Peruvians, rich and poor alike, must adjust to a social reality that can cast classmates, in-laws, business clients, friends, and lovers as potential enemies. However, it is already clear in these initial patient cases that conflict between men and women is seen as the source of trouble and sickness for a significant number of curandero patients. In the Flores sample as a whole, nearly thirty percent of the patients attributed their suffering either exclusively or primarily to strains in their relationships with spouses or lovers.[7] This is also clear in the stories told by Nilo Plasencia's patients, which I present in the next chapter. In addition to deriving a general model of *daño* from the testimony of our informants, it is essential to show how *daño*, both as a sickness and as a threat of suffering, operates in the social arena of gender conflict.

17
Patients of Nilo Plasencia

Curer and Patients: General Observations

In many respects, the therapeutic style of Víctor Flores differs from that adopted by Nilo Plasencia. Two specific contrasts are worth noting before presenting Nilo's cases. First, unlike Víctor, Nilo interacts extensively with his clients during ritual sessions. Also, while Víctor delegates to his ritual assistants the responsibility for most individual curing acts, Nilo ministers personally to each patient. This is especially evident during a segment of the ritual that he calls his "game" (see Chapter 10). Transcribed material from these shamanic psychodramas is included in the following cases.

The second contrast concerns the physical demands placed on patients during rituals. Nilo's sessions are far more taxing than are Víctor's. He expects everyone to imbibe both the San Pedro brew and the tobacco liquid—which often results in nausea and vomiting for even the experienced, since Nilo prepares especially strong concoctions. Víctor permits all levels of participation, from mere observation to full involvement; ingesting the tobacco is purely voluntary. Nilo's ritual site, in an open area behind a small farmhouse, is also slightly more rustic than Víctor's special facility; patients therefore may find a night-long session with Nilo uncomfortable as well as exhausting.

For patients, the significance of these contrasting styles lies in the degree of personal engagement in the ritual process that each curandero requires. Víctor's patients can play a largely passive role in rituals since the "script" demands only a minimum of therapy directed expressly to the individual; and even that which does take place is essentially standardized. Nilo's patients, on the other hand, actively participate in a series of one-on-one encounters with the curer. Much individual attention from the curer and a greater degree of physical discomfort make a passive approach to Nilo's rituals impossible. It is precisely these differences between curanderos that individuals consider when they select and later evaluate a curer.

The relationship between Nilo and his patients is well illustrated in the following cases, especially in his interaction with them during rituals. He mixes an ingratiating warmth with a youthful jocularity as he shifts back and forth between endearing diminutives and tough street language. For example, Nilo addressed forty-one-year-old Andrés as "little brother" (*hermanito*) and "little companion" (*compañerito*), but during his *rastreo* exclaimed, "whoremother" (*puta madre*), "shit, damn" (*mierda, carajo*). Although Nilo uses slightly stronger language with males, his ritual speech with both men and women is laced with expletives directed at visions of sorcerers and enemies.

Like other comparatively young curanderos, Nilo is aware of the general preference for older curanderos among potential clients. He strives hard to create the bonds of faith and respect that curers like Víctor Flores, twenty-two years Nilo's elder, seem to win almost automatically from their patients. Nilo does not, however, permit his concern with attracting clients to stop him from being very frank and at times even critical of his patients. To a married couple (NP32) he inquired, "Why are you two fighting? Why are you growing apart? Isn't it the feelings that made you fall in love, that made you want each other, that we have come here for?" For two men (NP11, 14), Nilo bluntly asked if they were impotent, in one case asking, "You aren't the tiger you used to be, little brother?" In several cases, when patients either did not cooperate or when he sensed they doubted him, he grew very stern and challenged them to take him seriously.

Plasencia's Patients

Sabina (NP4) The importance of research interviewers slowly developing rapport with patient informants is demonstrated by this case of a forty-six-year-old woman from a small community in the sierra east of Trujillo, a town from which Nilo draws many clients. Sabina had no formal schooling and lived and worked at home with two children, running a small restaurant. In the first interview she claimed that she was a widow; in the second she admitted her husband had deserted her. She initially said that she had not gone to either a doctor or any other curandero for her problem; however, during the follow-up, she described visits to both an M.D. and another curer. The greater openness at the second encounter is probably related to the fact that the interview team had driven five long, hard hours up mountain roads to find Sabina and had shared lunch in her establishment before the interview.

The following is a sample from Sabina's first interview:

Q: Tell me, *señora*, why have you come to the curandero? What is your [health] problem?
A: I am sick.
Q: From what? What do you have?
A: In my stomach.
Q: What do you feel in your stomach?
A: It hurts.
Q: Does it hurt a lot?
A: Yes.
Q: And do you know how it happened, in what way?
A: No.

Little more was elicited from Sabina in the first conversation, except that she had suffered from her stomach problem for one month. More interesting information emerged, however, during the ritual as Nilo performed his diagnostic "game." It began by Nilo naming Sabina and calling on his "pretty remedy," "pretty San Pedro," to go looking for what had happened to her. Next, Nilo gave Sabina assurances that the researcher who was taping their conversation would not gossip about her, that he worked with a group from the United States which was there to determine "if I [Nilo] am good or bad." He asked her to answer the interviewer's questions honestly and without fear. Then the diagnostic work started:

N: We go raising, we go suspending, in your name, for your shadow, what did you say? Sabina, what?
S: X X [last names].
N: X X. Be calm pretty little mama,¹ in your womb, in your stomach. When I go on talking, pretty little mama, do me a favor, don't get ahead of me, OK?
S: OK.
N: Please, OK? After I finish your *rastreo*, then you tell me frankly, tell me all your little problems. You just tell me your secrets, OK? OK, little mama?
S: OK.

N: [Aspiration] Wait, don't get ahead of me. Get up, *cholo*, damn it, mmmmm, shit, [aspiration], get up, damn it, raise your womb [vomit sound], raise your stomach [vomiting]. What is this? [Vocalizations] Get down, handsome old Saint Cyprian. Don't you weaken, spirited herbs. [Snorting] Ah, *señora*, ah, *señora*, ah, little *señor*, little handsome father. So, you will also be filled with winds, whirlwinds of gases, no, little mama? Your belly? Speak, little mama, yes or no?

S: Yes.

N: Let's get it out, or no?

S: Yes.

The interchange continued in this style, with Nilo alternatively calling on his herbs, on saints, and on the San Pedro, as well as naming parts of Sabina's body that were uncomfortable (her head, belly, kidneys, hips, and legs). Then Nilo began his "game":

N: Come accounting, come naming, come invoking, to see if this lady, mmmmm, if this pretty gentlewoman, is screwed-up, is named, is invoked, at this auspicious time. Are you watching me, little mama?

S: Yes.

N: Yes? Let's see, mmmmm, [sniffing], who is the person who has screwed you, who named you, who summoned you, who invoked you, at this auspicious time? Go ahead herb, go ahead remedy, go ahead San Pedro, where we are looking at each other, face to face, eye to eye. Auspicious hours of J. [Sabina's town], well within, Sabina X, what more, my love? Sabina X, what?

S: X [second last name].

N: X, pull, call, carry, show, [aspiration]. Do you see me?

S: Yes.

N: The same [as before]?

S: No.

N: Like who?

S: A little like the father of my children.

N: The father of your children, he's sort of white, wouldn't you say?

S: More brown.

N: Mmmmm, he isn't, he isn't a little whitish?

S: No.

N: So, what's going on herb, damn it? Look at it, look at it, look at it. There, no more, my love. Don't look for me too hard, the thing is [to be] calm, that's all. Mmmmm, do you recognize me?

S: I see it [Nilo's face] the same, a man.

N: A man. Who?

S: The father of my children.

N: Father of your children, a *señor* who thinks he's very important, this gentleman is very conceited, no? [Aspiration], very conceited is this gentleman, no?

S: Yes.

N: [Aspirations], promises and promises, only promises, damn it, or no?

S: Yes.

N: [Aspiration], shit, [aspiration], very imperial, very powerful, damn it. [Aspirations], that's your beloved, wouldn't you say?

S: Yes.

N: Mmmmm, and promises, and promises, and years and years that were going by, no, *señora*?

S: Yes.

N: And? At the end of the journey, he goes on forgetting everything. You feel something like inflammations in your [body] parts, no, little mama?

S: Yes.

N: [Aspirations], and it makes you dizzy.

S: Mmmmm.

N: It makes you feel drunk, yes or no?

S: Yes.

N: Little mama? [Aspirations], we return to the tranquility, to the lightness, to the focal point. Pretty herb, [aspiration] come accounting, come naming, come invoking. Look, *señora*: you are screwed-over, you're named, you're invoked, and apart from that, you are also *enmuñecada*,[2] because your place of J. [Sabina's town], within, of the town of J. and all around J., these mountain folk often play with spiritism, in making filthy things of dolls, pretty little mama. And, so that you understand real clearly, you also have lost an article of clothing, intimate clothing, my love. You understand?

S: Yes.

N: OK, and in that clothing, they've got you.

Our second interview with Sabina was delayed because she lived a long way from Trujillo; but some four months later (109 days) she answered our interviewer's questions again. She said that her stomach problems had been cured, although she was presently sick with a number of other symptoms. Nilo told her, she explained, "that they had done a *soplón*" (blowing) against her, that she had *daño por la boca* caused by her absent husband. She recalled a day when a bug flew into her mouth, and interpreted the insect as the medium of a sorcerer's attack. She vividly recalled the "transformation"

Nilo's face had undergone during the ritual and again identified the image she saw as the father of her children, who "wanted to cause me [to suffer] *mal daño*."

Two other pieces of information emerged in this second interview. First, she had gone to another curandero before seeing Nilo, and also had previously been operated on by an M.D. for a hernia. Second, she confirmed an observation Nilo made during the ritual, that she had a terrible smell about her, "like a dead dog." She related this to the putrefying effect of the sorcery performed against her. I return to this olfactory feature of sorcery later (Chapter 19).

Mirta (NP10) Mirta was thirty-one years old when interviewed; she had one daughter and a husband who worked for a government export agency. Mirta had finished high school and had additional training in computer skills; she worked as a secretary. She was born in San Pedro de Lloc, and lived in Lima and Cajamarca before moving to Trujillo. On the advice of a Tarot card reader, she came to Nilo for problems with her husband, from whom she was "essentially separated."

> Q: How did it happen?
> A: This is what is so strange to me, because we had been happy and then, from one day to the next, he got restless, and then I found out that he was seeing another girl. When he decided to go, he wanted to leave me and I assumed the thing was serious. Because, like any man, I tell you, he can have [an affair], no? Whatever, no? But don't ever hurt me or let me realize it, no? . . .
>
> I spoke to him and he said to give it time. But time has passed. I have waited, quietly, no? [I was] hopeful that he would return, but, nothing! And I have seen that things have gotten worse, because they have even told me that the girl is pregnant.

Nilo's *rastreo* failed to elicit a response from Mirta during the game. Despite prompting from the curandero, Mirta simply did not recognize anyone in Nilo's facial changes. However, Mirta had brought along a photograph of her husband and Nilo used this to "track" him. Nilo characterized the spouse as a ladykiller, a cigarette smoker, a heavy drinker, and one who starts fights for no reason. Then Nilo added, "But you also have a strong character, little mama. Pardon me, [but] you have . . . you can also be strong willed. You weren't like a gentlewoman who just listens. You also take your stand, no, little mama?"

As the *rastreo* continued, Nilo concluded that Mirta's husband had been *"jalado"* (his spirit captured), "named," "invoked," so that he would grow apart from her: "Damn, they have given [it] by the mouth to this little gentleman, little mama. Damn, they have given [it] to him by the mouth." Advising Mirta "not to let them walk all over you," Nilo also warned:

> But now they've defeated you [*te ganaron*]. And that's how the adversaries, the enemies [feminine] win, how at times they dominate the will of gentlemen, the same as of gentlewomen.[3] So, first it's necessary to give you a raising [*levantada*], a "pulling" [*jalada*], and next "pull" this gentleman and dominate with tobacco and turn it around [*voltearlo*] on the opponent, the enemy. Because [aspirations] they are pulling this gentleman, they are pulling him, they are pulling him, they are pulling him, and they have him well tied up [*amarrado*], well bound up [*atado*], little mama.

Nilo's counterattack, or *volteada*, against Mirta's enemies followed. This merits extended translation as it conveys with dramatic force the vengeful element in curandero therapy. Nilo began by declaring that they (he and Mirta) were going to return "blow for blow" the interference of the mistress, whom Mirta named and Nilo invoked:

N: Daisy X X [last names], your name, your shadow, your face, your spirit, your body, your soul, with these pretty tobaccos, I am accounting, I am naming strong at this auspicious time, with this handsome bull.[4] Daisy X X, your name I am invoking, I am naming you, I am invoking you. . . . Deep within I go turning, further in I go accounting, so that hatred and loathing will struggle with the love of this great gentleman, by the name of?

M: Carlos Y Y [last names].

N: Easy, no more, little mama.

M: Carlos Y Y [last names].

N: Of Carlos Y Y with Daisy?

M: X X [last names].

N: X X, fight it out hatred, fight it out loathing, from night to morning, damn. I hit the mark, I hit the target. Pull, bull; call, bull; stop it, bull. Daisy . . . ?

M: X X [last names].

N: X X. Fight it out, hatred and loathing, with this handsome gentleman, what's his name, little mama?

M: Carlos Y Y [last names].

N: Carlos Y Y, remember it, damn it. Spirited herb, cover his mouth, damn it. I account for you, I name you, I defy you at this auspicious time, with this handsome bull. I am accounting, I am playing, I am invoking, my *banco*, damn it. Daisy X Z [mistaken second last name], . . . pardon!

M: Daisy X X.

N: Daisy X X! Your name, damn it! Those secrets, *señora*, what they have done to you! It's from a coca-using *brujo*. Daisy X X, damn it, you're supposed to leave [*te has de apartar*]. Battle it out, hatred and loathing; like dogs, they will fight all night. Pull, tobacco, damn it; stop his shouting. Oh, get him all confused, damn it, damn it. . . . [Sound of tobacco snorting.] Oh, so that's it, damn it, you're going to end up like a ragged bum, [aspirations], all embittered, damn it. Have faith, my love.

M: OK.

N: Have faith, have faith, that this is how the "art" works, how the little thing is [*sic*].

M: Sure.

N: [Aspiration.] That's how these things are, *señora*. This is how we pass the night.

M: Yes.

N: So, we are singing, so we are naming, Daisy X X, your name, damn it, so that you [plural] go separating [from each other], from night to morning, damn it, from night to morning . . . with . . . ?

M: Carlos Y Y.

N: Carlos Y Y, damn it, you're going to find her in the arms of another man. . . . Stop, damn it. Like black, a black skull, damn; come pulling it. I raise you with these pretty tobaccos. I'm making her drunk, I'm confusing him . . . damn it . . . shit . . . damn! So, in the gossip, damn it, let the story come out, damn it. [Sounds of Nilo blowing and vomiting.] Owls of the *huaca*, damn. [Sounds of Nilo vomiting.] So, damn it, you'll have belly cramps, in the stomach, in the abdomen, damn it. You're supposed to fall, well accounted, well named, well invoked, Daisy . . . ?

M: Daisy X X.

N: X X, your name, your shadow, your spirits, [sounds of Nilo blowing liquid into the air], walk over there, and don't come back. [Pause.] OK?

M: OK.[5]

When Mirta was interviewed a second time, fifty-two days later, she said that she felt calmer, and that the problem with her husband had improved, although not completely. Nilo had instructed her to return for another session. He advised that she would have "to call" to her husband "with love" on her own part (i.e., not just depend on her husband's effort). When asked whether she saw any conflict between her Catholic faith and the fact that she had resorted to curanderos, Mirta answered that since Nilo "works with herbs and not with evil" it was acceptable to seek his help. Interestingly, despite the aggressive tone of the *volteada*, Mirta insisted that she did not want to "harm" her husband's mistress, the source of the problem, but only to get her husband back.

One year later, Mirta consented to a third interview, but only over the telephone. She reported that her husband had returned eight months earlier and that their marriage was saved. She credited Nilo's treatment.

Alejandrina (NP28) This thirty-five-year-old mother of five was born and, when interviewed, was living in the Trujillo area; she also had lived in one of the villages in the foothills of the Andes. She had completed two years of secondary school and worked at home. Her husband was a *comerciante*.

In her first interview Alejandrina described a series of physical problems which included headaches, stomachaches (like colics), back pains, and dizziness. A doctor had diagnosed a "kidney defect"; but the medication he prescribed did not diminish the pains. From this, and from a consultation with her curandero godfather, she had concluded that "it can't be a sickness of God, but from *mal daño*." She came to Nilo on a female cousin's advice.

During the *rastreo*, Nilo asked if she didn't feel "an agitation, like desperation, like restlessness, like you want to run out of your house, far away, very far. *Señora*, to shout and have no one listen. Now you can't stand it anymore: your grief, your suffering, the fights in your house, your home, no, little mama?" Mixing in references to her physical symptoms, Nilo focused on Alejandrina's husband, whom he described as a lazy, pretentious, egotistical drunk who got into fights. Although Alejandrina did not identify anyone in Nilo's face during the game, he asked her about a woman with a gold tooth who appeared in his visualization:

N: Who is this woman with a gold tooth?
A: I have an aunt, no one else.
N: [Aspirations.] Take care with the salad, little mama, be careful of the mackerel salad. Do you understand me, or no?
A: Yes.
N: Be careful, because they have given [it] to you by your mouth, little mama. Do you understand, or no? You know where you eat

these mackerel salads? It's obvious, my love, [aspirations], or no?
Salads. Be careful, little mama, with these women, be careful
with these *comadres* who call you. Or am I speaking nonsense, my
love?

A: It's true.

Nilo finished his *rastreo* by telling Alejandrina that this *daño por
boca* had "screwed her," that she was "named," and "invoked." In
subsequent conversations neither Nilo nor Alejandrina further
specified the person(s) responsible for her sickness.

At her second interview, fifty-three days later, Alejandrina insisted that Nilo had cured her of all her previous symptoms, although she had begun to suffer from earaches and liver problems.
"He got rid of all that desperation I had." Even the problems she
had experienced with her husband had diminished. She had not
been able to return for a third session and so had yet to receive her
seguro, or good-luck charm.

After three more months, Alejandrina was interviewed a third
time. She repeated that Nilo had cured her, but said that she had
still been unable to identify the woman with the gold tooth who
poisoned her with the salad. On the other hand, she was taking
herbs prescribed by a Trujillo-based herbalist for continuing kidney pains and would soon be operated on for her ear problem. She
had not gone back to Nilo for her final session and for the prom-
ised good-luck charm. The interviewer probed for a reason. Alejandrina explained, initially in a roundabout and vague fashion,
that she was afraid of Nilo because of things her friend had told
her and because of her own experience with Nilo during the ritual.
Her friend accused Nilo of having made sexually aggressive ad-
vances. Alejandrina said that although this had not happened to
her, she had been very frightened when Nilo had her take her skirt
off. She added, philosophically, "Otherwise, clearly, the way he
cures in the session, everything is magnificent, everything is very
nice. The only thing is that he does personal [things] that he
shouldn't."

It is difficult to know what to make of this accusation, especially
since Alejandrina was the only person in our study to have reported any impropriety on Nilo's part.[6] None of the research team
witnessed such behavior. Whether factual or not, however, the fear
Alejandrina expressed is certainly related to the reluctance of
many female clients to come to curandero rituals unaccompanied,

and to their initial uneasiness with the degree of intimacy many curanderos seek to establish with their clients. The sense of vulnerability to men conveyed in Alejandrina's testimony also underscores the paradoxical position Peruvian women face when they come to male curanderos for relief from the abusive treatment of men. (I return to this dimension of client/curandero relationships in Chapter 20.)

José (NP21) José, a forty-seven-year-old married man with four grown children, was born and resided in Sausál, where he worked for a medical doctor; his wife worked both at home and as a *comerciante.* José had finished the third year of secondary school. His answers to our questions were long, rambling, and confusing. This is the clearest reconstruction of his story possible.

A year before the interview, José's brother-in-law had taken a photograph of José to Nilo for a *rastreo* (José's work hours prohibited him from personally attending the session). Nilo concluded that someone had buried *paquetes* (voodoo-like packets, dolls, or other likenesses) to harm José. José did not act on this information until he began to suffer from a burning in his stomach as well as liver pains, which his physician-employer had been unable to treat. The night before the interview he had finally taken Nilo's advice, traveling to the town of Barranca to contact one of Nilo's colleagues. This specialist, Martín, produced two *paquetes* for José, which impressed José sufficiently to encourage him to come to Nilo for a follow-up session, to see if there were more *paquetes* to be uncovered.

Nilo's *rastreo* included an especially clear explanation of how the game works:

> N: Look, just as I was telling you, this game goes like this: we are both "with herbs" [i.e., under the effects of the San Pedro], we are going to look at each other, face to face, and at the moment the "illumination" [i.e., vision] comes, [notice] the image, the change, the transformation. Then you go on talking to me and also, if you wish, I'll help you, OK?

Nilo suggested that the image looked like a diabolical carnival mask with a Chinese-looking face and a large nose. José, on the other hand, responded minimally, merely repeating Nilo's characterizations. The same thing occurred later in the *rastreo*, when Nilo asked José directly, "And this *caballero*, balder than you, who is it? [He's] fat. Who is it? . . . Don't you remember?" José was unable to identify the vision.

Two other parts of Nilo's monologue should be mentioned. At one point he declared, "I am the remedy, I am the San Pedro, I am the curandero, I am the plants, I am the spear, I am the sword." This expresses the sense of identification that the curer feels with the plants and artifacts of his mesa. Nilo asserted a similar identification with his patient when he ended his *rastreo* with these words of assurance:

> N: I'm going to pull your spirit, I'm going to raise your soul and I'm going to cleanse you and suck with my tobacco, and I'm going to vomit all of your ailments. [Sound of Nilo spitting.] This bitterness you have in your mouth, you're going to see how it goes away. You, yourself, will feel it, brother.

Finally, José's *rastreo* included the repeated use of expletives, some even stronger than those quoted above. This type of expression was not characteristic of most curanderos with whom we worked, and may have resulted from Nilo's apprenticeship with an especially aggressive sorcerer (see Chapter 10). In any case, employing strong language in ritual encounters with both male and female patients intensifies the sense that real hostile forces are being confronted.

When interviewed a second time, fifty-two days later, José said that he felt ninety-nine percent better, although some pains had begun to trouble him again two weeks after his last session with Nilo. Nilo gave José three good-luck charms, one to attract money and the other two to counteract pain, and recommended another trip to see Martín to recover yet another *paquete*. José planned to do that in the coming months. When asked what he felt during Nilo's ritual, José elaborated on his general opinion of curanderos:

> Well, I attended other sessions before, many years ago, but, to be sincere, I haven't had much . . . faith, you'd call it, my own interest, no? But having seen those *paquetes* with Martín, depicting my likeness in the little doll, and the series of things that have been put into those dolls . . . well, all that has caused me to believe, for my health. . . . And in the sessions I've been in with him, well, I have felt this . . . with profound faith . . . a believer, we'd say.

José's positive assessment of Nilo's treatment notwithstanding, he also reported having gone to another medical doctor after the rituals. He was diagnosed with gastritis and had been taking medication while awaiting further test results. He said that he had not told this second doctor of his treatment by a curandero, but that the first physician, his employer and friend, not only knew but approved. It seems that this doctor had also been successfully treated by a curandero!

Ernesto (NP26) Ernesto had lived and worked in Nilo's hometown for the past three years. At twenty-three, he was single, had completed high school, and was employed at a fish-processing plant. He was born in the Department of Ancash, in the north central highlands. He had come to see Nilo on the advice of his cousin, who was also a patient of Nilo. In his first interview he was a little evasive, but he revealed that he had come because he suspected he was suffering from *mal daño*, manifested in bad luck at work and in a general inability to make progress.

> Q: Do you think someone has done *daño* to you?
> A: Well, it could be, no? As you know, it isn't just one's own will that rules here, but the envy of others as well.

There was no *rastreo* for Ernesto, because Nilo had too many patients to attend to that night. Ernesto's second interview, 177 days later, was also brief. He said that Nilo had found no evidence of *daño* and had merely worked to raise his luck. However, he had recently experienced several failures, both economic and romantic, and so he was not convinced that the treatment had worked. He had not been to any curandero previously and when asked what he thought of Nilo, he replied, "Magnificent. It's practically like he's your father; he guides you well, he talks about everything. . . . He has helped me a lot."

The Game

Nilo's game is one of the most complex aspects of his interaction with patients. The cases reviewed so far give a sense of the dynamic Nilo seeks to create, but none of them illustrate a fully successful response on the patient's part.[7] A brief interchange from a very dramatic case provides a better understanding of how the game ideally should work. Edilberta, a twenty-seven-year-old mother of five, described a wide range of social, psychological, and physical problems, which she attributed to the machinations of her husband's mistress (who was also her cousin). During the ritual, at about 3:00 A.M., Nilo took her aside for a *rastreo*. He talked about her problems with her spouse and invoked the powers of Catholic saints to counter the presumed sorcery that her enemy, the mistress, had used to harm her. Drawing close to Edilberta and making facial gestures in the shadows, Nilo asked her to look at his face:

N: Who do you see? Her? [i.e., the cousin]
E: Yes!
N: Go after her!
E: She is looking at me and laughing.
N: Talk to her, tell her whatever you feel like. Don't be afraid of anything.
E: By denouncing her?
N: Whatever you feel. Tell her off; you have the right to!
E: [As if to her cousin] What do you want? Get out of my house, leave my husband alone, leave the father of my children alone— I'm going to see you beaten, bitch! You thought you'd harm us, but now I'm going to beat you, you wretch, bitch. Leave my husband, leave my house, my home, as we've always lived. Leave it alone, bitch, miserable thing. You're screwed, get out, get out!

A number of other patients, ten in all, were able to identify an adversary in Nilo's face without his direct prompting. A husband's lover, or the wayward spouse himself, was the person most frequently named (five cases), but a neighbor, a stepfather, a mother-in-law, and friends were also mentioned. A majority of clients, men and women, either accepted Nilo's prompting or failed to see anyone else's features in Nilo's face. Most often it was a female client, rather than a male, who did not wait for Nilo's prompting to identify an opponent in his transformed face.

There are several additional features of Nilo's game that merit attention. First, Nilo's speech assumes the presence of more than his patient and him; he directly addresses his herbs, sorcerers, saints, and other parties visible only to him. Second, Nilo makes constant use of tag questions (e.g., "yes or no?"; "no, little mama?") to check on the accuracy of his vision as he converses with each patient. When he suggests a physical feature of a person known to the patient and is told he is incorrect, as in the quoted passage from Sabina's *rastreo*, he shifts his conversational partners to ask his herbs why they have deceived him. This would seem to relieve Nilo of responsibility for mistaken interpretations.

Finally, and perhaps most interesting, is Nilo's shifting use of the subject and tense in his speech. Sometimes he is the subject of the verb, but at other times Nilo speaks as the San Pedro brew (see José's case summary) or from the point of view of the patient. A good example of this comes from the *rastreo* of Florencio (NP14), a thirty-nine-year-old father of two who was in the process of divorcing his wife. Nilo asked:

N: You separated [from her]?
F: Like a divorce.
N: Like a divorce, so that's it, *compañero*, so that's it, that explains it, [aspirations] that's why I've suffered, and that's why today I regret having grown apart, having caused a rift. . . . [Aspirations] Yes or no, *compañero*?
F: Yes, that's how it is.
N: At times you regret it, as if to say, I'm going to go on suffering. That's why I'll be that way, no? Why did I leave? Why did I separate, no? I regret it, damn it, but I have my reasons. And you come to a standstill, or no?
F: Yes, yes!

In most cases the outcome of Nilo's *rastreo* is the discovery that the patient is *enmuñecado*, that someone has buried a likeness of her/him so as to cause suffering. No other curandero represented in our project included this idea in his practice. Nilo, however, has integrated it into his therapy to the point of contracting with another specialist to whom he can send patients to have the *paquetes* removed. It is worth quoting two patients' descriptions of these "dolls" or "packets." First, forty-two-year-old Danilo (NP33), who traveled to Barranca to have two dolls unearthed:

Q: You have seen the dolls?
A: Yes, I've seen [them]. . . . It was a clay doll with a black face. It had, what do you call it, plastic extremities, both above and below [i.e., arms and legs]. It had something in its belly [that looked] like a Chiclets chewing gum, no?
Q: And have you felt something?
A: Yes, I felt, what do you say, that, for example, my body was constipated. I couldn't go [to the bathroom] for one, two, three days. And later, when I did, it was often difficult and blood came out. The other doll was wrapped up in old money, notes of a thousand *soles*, and [it had] a beer bottle cap on its head, really stuck in. Maybe that's why I had, what do you say, a pain in the head that at times [made it so] I couldn't sleep.
Q: And why a beer bottle cap? Didn't you ask?
A: This was so that I would only want to drink.

Q: You've been drinking a lot?
A: Yes, I have been drinking when I have money, and recently, how do you say it . . .
Q: You've spent a lot?
A: As I told you, I've [even] sold some of my possessions. . . .

A second patient, thirty-year-old Pilar (NP25), went to Chimbote on Nilo's advice to have her *paquetes* removed. She reported that her terrible vaginal pains stopped when the doll was destroyed, but they came back several days later because an unspecified couple was "still playing me" (i.e., practicing sorcery against her). She became a regular at Nilo's sessions and prided herself on having been invited to take Nilo's place behind the mesa while he attended to other patients. She described her doll in detail:

Q: And what was the packet like?
A: It was a kind of clay made into a doll, but a very old clay, and nails were pushed into this clay, in the shoulders, in the legs, in the extremities. All over the body there were these nails, and they were really rusty; he [Nilo's partner] grabbed the nails with his sword and pulled them out like this, and they were really rusted, they were really old.
Q: But, what did you think of the packet? When you saw the doll with the nails, what did he tell you? Did he tell you who had made the doll, the burial [*entierro*]? Or, did you think that it was related to your pains? What did you think? What did you feel?
A: No, look, when he took out the packet, when he took out the nails, I hurt here . . . yes, my uterus hurt, and then I said to him, "*Señor*, don't pull it [out] because it really hurts." "I have to take it out; you bear up," he told me. "Close your mouth, clench your jaw, grab the staff really hard, and swear." That's what he told me. Well, I began to swear . . . whatever came to my mind. Then I began to swear at the person who has [*sic*] done me harm. "I haven't done anything bad to you," I said. Then he said, "Go on, go on," and went ahead taking them out, until I was in a cold sweat, cold. I don't know if it was from nerves or as a result of the way he was taking them out. Then he said to me, "You have more."
Q: More packets?
A: Yes, he told me, "You have more packets and you have to do something about them soon because you're going to continue fighting with your husband."
Q: In other words, because of the packets, of those packets, you were fighting with your husband?
A: Yes, we had problems at home, there wasn't any peace there. We were always arguing.

Pilar's case not only provides information on the nature of the packets to which Nilo often traced his patients' suffering, but also illustrates once again the link between curandero therapy and gender-based discord. Among Nilo's patients, a majority (fifty-nine percent) attributed their suffering to conflicts with spouses or lovers. As the case material has shown, Nilo can be sympathetic to the position of women and critical of macho behavior on the part of men. When he described husbands in unflattering terms, when he took Mirta's side in her conflict with her husband and his lover, and when he encouraged Edilberta to verbally abuse the woman who had occupied her spouse's attention—in all of these cases—Nilo appeared willing to adopt the female point of view on the injustices of male behavior toward women.

On the other hand, Nilo repeatedly relieved men of responsibility for their extramarital affairs. Instead, he blamed the women with whom they became involved for having trapped them with sorcery. He also encouraged female patients to forgive their husbands' abuses, as when he instructed Mirta to approach her philandering spouse "with love." Also, consider Nilo's closing advice to Edilberta, offered immediately after he had directed her through her verbal assault of her husband's lover (quoted above):

> N: A love, a life of twelve years can't be destroyed overnight, my dear *señora*. A man can be very much a man, a man can be very proud. But his blood flows in his children. You, as a mother, suffer a lot; I do also, and that's why I dare to do your "work." Otherwise, I wouldn't risk doing some dirty trick—if it weren't that your man truly loves you, that he has made your house, your home, by his sacrifice and with the sweat of his brow (despite that you also work).

Conclusion

The stories of Víctor Flores's patients made clear their perceptions of vulnerability that underlie the symptomatic expressions of *daño*. With Nilo's patients, we begin to see that the therapy of curanderos aims not just to alleviate symptoms but to address this core experience of being at risk. Nilo's ritual, especially the avenging *volteada*, defines the curandero's role as therapist-combatant, and transforms the patient from the aggrieved to the aggressor. Nilo does not just provide his patients with a benign opportunity to release pent-up anger and frustration, as the "escape-valve" argument would have it (see Chapter 15); rather, he enters directly into the conflict-laden social world of his patients and initiates redressive actions, both through the powers concentrated on his mesa and by his advice and admonition.

As with Víctor's patients, it is the social arena of male/female relationships that is often implicated in the suffering of Nilo's clients. The centrality of gender conflict to the curandero's practice will lead me to focus on women as *daño* sufferers in a subsequent chapter (Chapter 20). I show there that the sorcery/curing complex of northern Peru provides women with a strategic means by which to hold men morally accountable for abusive behavior. This interpretation situates *daño* in the context of gender politics, and permits an analysis that accommodates the dynamic contribution of the curandero as "combatant."

First, however, I add comparative material from the patients of two curanderos whose clients and therapeutic styles contrast in significant ways with those of Flores and Plasencia. This provides the basis for a synthetic view of how patients conceptualize *daño* and assess curandero treatment.

18

Comparative Cases: Patients of Jorge Merino and Eduardo Calderón

Contrasting Curanderos

In the preceding chapters I have noted significant contrasts between Víctor Flores and Nilo Plasencia in the way each relates to patients, both generally and in the specific context of ritual performances. When the patients of Jorge Merino and Eduardo Calderón are added to the analysis, further contrasts in therapeutic styles may be seen. I begin by identifying some of the features that set these two additional curanderos apart from each other and from the two already covered, and I then present selected case material to show how these differentiating characteristics help shape the patients' experiences.

At least at this point in their respective careers, Jorge Merino and Eduardo Calderón represent two distinct approaches to Peruvian shamanic healing. Jorge is committed to intensive, long-term treatment with herbal medicinals; the extended duration of his therapy also enables him to acquire in-depth knowledge of his patients' lives. Even more than most curanderos, Jorge structures his rituals in a fashion consistent with his devout Catholic faith. His clients are almost exclusively persons from the small, rural communities near his home, in contrast to the more urban-based clientele of Eduardo, Víctor, and Nilo.

Eduardo's relationship with his clients is shaped to a great degree by his high-profile reputation. As a result of the publicity he has received in newspapers, magazines, and documentary films, Eduardo draws clients from throughout Peru, as well as from other nations. In addition, promotions by a tour agency in Lima and by New Age travel organizations in the United States and Europe have brought Eduardo into contact with many foreigners, some of whom seek his therapeutic help.[1] This national and international fame is reflected in our patient sample by the inclusion of three persons from other countries (Italy, Spain, and Germany), as well as five from distant parts of Peru (e.g., Iquitos, Ica, and Cuzco).

Eduardo's current travel schedule keeps him away from the Trujillo area for months at a time. This means that potential clients cannot be sure of finding him at home and are not able to count on a regular schedule of ritual sessions. His frequent absences also prevent Eduardo from managing extended treatments; consequently, he leaves his patients with therapy that rarely extends beyond a single night's ritual, and he limits the individual attention they receive.[2] Eduardo's very public profile, his frequent traveling, and his willingness to draw inspiration from non-Peruvian healing traditions combine to create a ritual dynamic between shaman and patient that is different from that of any other curandero in our project.

Merino and His Patients

Jorge's patients were, on average, older and had fewer years of formal schooling (see Table 2) than the clients of the other three curanderos in our study. As indicated above, most were from small, rural communities. These factors contributed to a reticence in interviews that our research assistant, who was less experienced than were the two in Trujillo, was unable to overcome. Fortunately, many of the noteworthy elements in Jorge's practice are discernible in the diagnostic orations he offered patients during his sessions, which we were permitted to tape-record.

Almost sermonlike in tone, these discourses were entirely unlike Nilo's theatrical *rastreos*. They were formal, respectful recitations in which patients were addressed with the polite *Usted*, and no expletives were uttered. Jorge included many religious references in his speech, as in his effort to persuade a thirty-seven-year-old man (JM20) suffering from a venereal disease not to commit suicide:

> Here you have to be strong; you have to be brave and not think about killing yourself. . . . This won't do, by no means is it worth that. Instead, you have to beg the *Señor* Jesus Christ with love, with passion, and with resolution so that he can help us at any moment. So, you shouldn't think, "I'm going to end my life," or anything of the sort. We don't have any reason to take that right away from God. God and Jesus Christ Divine, they have to look out for us. . . . You

have to make yourself strong, you have to remember that you are a son of God, like us all, and stand strong.

While Nilo encouraged patients to identify the person(s) responsible for their troubles, and even performed ritual counterassaults, Jorge hesitated to name names. Many times he indicated in general terms that sorcery had been practiced against a patient, but refused to specify the guilty party, saying, "It's not in my interest to tell you who." Even when Jorge named a sorcerer, as he did in the case below, his language was far more tame than was Nilo's:

> There is this worthless old lady [the sorceress], excuse the phrase and I hope all of you will forgive me for, well, stepping out of line, but it makes me angry to see the tremendous sickness they've caused, the nuisance so enormous that you have to tolerate day and night. . . . It makes me angry, and maybe I am insulting this woman who I neither know nor care to know personally. This person shouldn't exist, for all practical purposes. She should be outside the human community, outside our human congregation. This lady should be outside, and these people, these little merchants who have done this *daño* against you, who ordered it to be done, should also be outside, they should be removed, nothing less, I say, nothing less.

Jorge's diagnoses were more specific regarding physiology than were Nilo's, and the range of ailments he identified was greater. Nilo used formulaic recitations of physical pains, and they sometimes sounded like an inventory of organs in distress. They were repeated in similar form for each client. Almost invariably, he concluded that the patient suffered from *daño*. On the other hand, Jorge's descriptions of symptoms were detailed and individualized. Far more frequently than either Nilo or Víctor, Jorge diagnosed conditions other than *daño*, most notably the culture-bound syndrome *susto* (fright or soul loss), a condition resulting from an unexpected shock, usually the result of a natural phenomenon such as a strong wind or lightning.[3]

The case of seventy-year-old Mercedes (JM16) is illustrative. A widow with four grown children, Mercedes had no formal education. She fell ill while visiting relatives near Lima for a marriage of a nephew. She experienced head pains, general body discomfort, and had some weight loss. She consulted various physicians, but found the medications they prescribed ineffective. Jorge attributed her condition to a fright caused by a cold wind that struck her somewhere near an irrigation ditch, not far from a pre-Hispanic ruin. He described her symptoms: head pains that made her feel

dizzy, weakness due to anemia, and pain in the knee joints. Referring to her physicians, he commented:

> I don't deny that doctors know what they're talking about; they study
> a lot more then we do—at least I don't have any [formal]
> education—but what they have been able to understand as an al-
> lergy, in fact, is not. It's due to the *susto* that I told you about.

In another case, an early childhood experience of *susto* was identified as the original cause of epileptiform seizures. Adelina (JM1),
thirty-one years old and single, was three when her brother found
her prostrate under a tree, her face contorted. Infrequent and
mild in years past, the "dizzy spells" increasingly became more severe and regular, finally occurring at least once a month. This condition led her siblings to insist on her contacting Jorge. Jorge
prides himself on his ability to cure epilepsy, but he cautioned
Adelina that her cure would take time because the sickness was
"old," that is, of long duration. She attended three sessions and,
when interviewed for the second time twenty-one days after the
third session, said: "Now I am tranquil, neither my head nor my
brain hurts. The dizzy spells are diminishing little by little. Before
they came all the time, but not now; now they come only rarely."

Despite cases like those above, attributions of sorcery do play an
integral role in Jorge's therapeutic system. *Daño* was Jorge's most
frequent diagnosis (41% of his documented cases), and although
he was reluctant to name the person(s) responsible, he sometimes
did provide details about the nature of the sorcery. In one particularly elaborate case, Jorge attributed a patient's sickness to the efforts of a sorcerer who was trying to deliver a soul to the devil.
Mariano (JM28), a sixty-four-year-old married man with four children, was an electrician. His sickness began with his skin developing a scale-like quality—"like a snake"—and then large blisters
formed, especially under the arms. The blisters made his whole
body feel inflamed. As he explained, a team of doctors had dis-
agreed about whether an operation was required:

> One of them wanted to operate, but another called me aside secretly
> and told me not to allow the operation because they hadn't found
> anything, because [i.e., although] they had done all the tests; and
> this one [doctor] wanted to open me out of whim! So, I did what he
> told me and I left for the countryside, to have a session done for me.

The person Mariano initially sought out for help was more sorcerer than curandero, as he learned from the second curer he consulted. Describing the first specialist in some detail, this second curandero explained to Mariano that he was being "pursued" by a "*brujo compactado*" and that he would have to find a third healer because "I can't cure you." This notion of being "*compactado*" implies a bargain with the devil: your soul in return for power. According to Jorge's analysis, the sorcerer plaguing Mariano was endeavoring to substitute the souls of others because he was not yet ready to give up his own:

> It wasn't because of some whim that this *señor* delivered it [Mariano's soul], but because the pact required him to deliver himself [i.e., his own soul]. In other words, his time had come, and, not wanting to surrender himself, he was obligated to turn over someone else. And he has done it not just with you.

Jorge explained that the other specialists involved in Mariano's sickness had complicated the original sorcery-related ailment (scales and blisters) and that it would take some time to cure him. He noted that some people think a quick cleansing is all there is to a cure, but that it would take patience and repeated treatment to heal Mariano. He added:

> At the beginning you had a terrible odor about you. I tell you this not because it was your fault or because you had acquired it on purpose, but [it occurred] because of the very same pact; [it derives] from the same situation that this guy created. So, this was the cause of the very foul odor, the stench.

This recalls the comment of Nilo's client, Sabina, about the putrid smell that emanated from her during a session. Jorge explained that a curer's vision is not just visual, but includes sounds, smells, and even perceptions of taste. The synesthetic effect of hallucinogens, by which a stimulus in one sense modality produces a sensation in another, may be at work here. It would also be interesting to investigate how body chemistry under conditions of sickness changes the odors of a person. In the present context, it is worth remembering that the rituals performed by curanderos include olfactory stimuli and imagery such as perfumed waters, the idea of *florecimiento*, et cetera. In the later discussion of the basic metaphorical structure of curandero therapy (Chapter 19), I will return to this logic of smells.

Calderón and His Patients

Eduardo's travel commitments had severely reduced his curing activities at home. His irregular schedule also made it difficult to document as many cases as was possible with the other three curanderos in the study. Also, it is not appropriate, at this point in Eduardo's career, to speak of a regular curing practice with an identifiable client population. Thus, generalizations based on our seventeen cases are of limited comparative utility. There are several features of the sample, however, which appear to be representative of Eduardo's practice and which distinguish his patients from the clients of other curanderos: his patients had more formal schooling, he treated a higher proportion of males, and many of his clients learned of him through the mass media (newspapers, magazines, television) rather than by word of mouth.

One other general characteristic of Eduardo's client pool deserves special mention and separate discussion. While Víctor and Nilo have, on rare occasions, treated non-Peruvians, Eduardo's sessions frequently included foreigners, many of whom came to the Trujillo area expressly for the purpose of meeting Eduardo. Some were spiritual seekers accustomed to traveling great distances for consciousness-raising experiences; others, like the three in our sample, sought help for specific sicknesses. Often, Eduardo's international clients stayed at the small hostel he has built to accommodate visitors.

Two foreign patients, a forty-seven-year-old Italian and a twenty-three-year-old Spaniard (both men), came because of complications related to hepatitis. The former, Giovanni (EC17), explained that the disease had damaged his liver and that the medical treatments he had received had caused numerous secondary problems, including hair loss and swelling of his hands. The failure of doctors to cure him convinced him that "official medicine can't do anything." He inquired at a Lima travel agency about traditional healers and was referred to Eduardo, whose ritual diagnosis was brief. Eduardo said that Giovanni had enemies who would try to obstruct his every move. At the follow-up interview, conducted in the Sheraton Hotel in Lima just eleven days later, Giovanni expressed some skepticism about Eduardo's "theater" and the general nature of his diagnosis, but indicated he intended to take the thirty-day herbal remedy Eduardo had prescribed.

The Spanish patient (EC7) explained that in addition to a case of hepatitis, which resulted from heroin use, he had experienced difficulty concentrating on his university studies and was frustrated with the course of his life. He had begun to turn things around on his own, but had also sought the help of a physician and of an herbalist in Spain. A magazine article about an Amazonian shaman who successfully treated hepatitis with the hallucinogenic vine *ayahuasca* (*Banisteriopsis caapi*) convinced him to come to Peru. A friend had suggested that he see Eduardo in order to try San Pedro. The *rastreo* for this patient is worth quoting to give a sense of how Eduardo adjusted his diagnosis for a non-Peruvian.

> Your search comes from many years ago. . . . You have the ability to understand many things; your third eye is well developed. With a little exercise you can perfect it. You will be capable of developing many things; you are going to achieve insight, prepare yourself. Prepare yourself a little bit. There are things you still haven't understood that are basic. . . . You are always searching, searching, but if you're going to achieve [insight], prepare a little. Life teaches, experience teaches; books are only to consult, nothing more. Learn from life, practice, and afterward go to the book and there verify the things [you've learned].

Two weeks later, the Spaniard reported no improvement in his condition. Although he had been impressed by the evidence of Eduardo's clairvoyance in the treatment of another patient, he judged the shaman incapable of treating "organic diseases." He seemed unimpressed by the "little hallucination" he experienced during the session and he said, "The results didn't convince me." He still planned his trip to the Amazon for treatment with *ayahuasca*.

The third international patient was a thirty-six-year-old German woman, Christina (EC6), who had spent the last eight years living in Peru. Her symptoms (nervousness, headaches, and stomach upset) had begun five years earlier, but no physician had been able to find an "organic cause." Eduardo did not address her during the two sessions she attended; however, in a consultation he advised her "to take decisions calmly and serenely," and that she "ought to be strong willed." At the follow-up interview she indicated she was taking the prescribed herbs from time to time, and that she felt relief from her headaches. Commenting on Eduardo's treatment, she said:

> Well, above all it has helped me to talk about my problems with this *Señor* Eduardo. . . . Not in the sessions, because I have my own opinion about that, but in conversations. His advice, his way of viewing

things and analyzing them, forcing one to think and decide—this is what has helped me.

Eduardo's general approach to international patients was to serve as a counselor, giving them advice about how to live in terms that made sense to them. Most striking was the absence of references to *daño*, or any other sorcery-related idea. Even when Eduardo told Giovanni that his enemies were "screwing" him, there was no effort to frame this in an idiom related to sorcery. Eduardo simply told his Spanish patient to "learn from life"; and, apparently, he gave Christina similar general counsel. When we turn to Eduardo's Peruvian patients, however, we see clearly that he was able to shift back into the cultural code of sorcery when treating "insiders."

Twenty-three-year-old Jorge (EC4), an accountant who is native to the Trujillo area, was suffering from the abrupt end of a three-year relationship. His former girlfriend, now dating other men, mocked him and told him she didn't love him; but he still wanted her back desperately. He was unable to work and had lost all hope. He suspected that he was under the influence of a sorcerer from a community to the north, a man whom his girlfriend had visited with her parents:

> I don't know if it's true or not, but my grandfather is a friend of a friend of my father-in-law [sic] and this friend told my grandmother that this same *señor*, my father-in-law, had told him that he had gone to see the *señor* Hermogenes [the sorcerer] with his daughter so that we would split up.

Eduardo's *rastreo* for Jorge was extensive and complex. He explained that he was visualizing four people talking with one another and pointing at Jorge. He asked, "They are pursuing you in your dreams, no?" Rather than placing blame on the girlfriend's father, as Jorge seemed to have done in our first interview, Eduardo identified her mother as the responsible party:

> E: It's her mother who's the wicked one. She doesn't want to have anything to do with you. They took you to a mesa, no? To a session? You tasted something strange in the drink they gave you, a flavor?
> J: They gave me a drink, but I didn't take it.
> E: But you didn't drink any? You didn't taste anything?
> J: Yes, a little bit.

E: It had a strange taste, no? She had her socks washed in your cup. They wanted to reassure you, but the sorcerer had very different intentions about you. He didn't do the job as it should have been [done]. . . . He screwed you. Now they laugh at you. The *señora* is looking for something better for her daughter. They all repudiate you. Smell? [Sound of sniffing.] The smell of a sock. They wanted to tie you up but the sorcerer did the opposite. See? [Sound of sniffing.] These people are very dirty; smell, smell the socks also. Damn! They're in league with the sorcerer.[4]

Continuing, Eduardo described Jorge's girlfriend as a "complete idiot," all "tangled up" in the sorcerer's web. He asked Jorge how he felt:

J: I feel a little, ahh, outside of myself.
E: Ah, you are walking there, you are going down by some mountain stream, wishing you could forget her. You are going to wake up, don't worry. . . . Her voice? No? You hear her voice, but very distant?
J: Distant, yes.

Eduardo then guided Jorge through a ritual cleansing, pausing at one point to tell him to go ahead and weep if he had to "because it isn't a crime for a man to cry for a woman." Invoking the love and faith of Solomon, as well as the Ten Commandments, Eduardo declared: "I come arousing all evil, all contempt, all dirty tricks, evil hour . . . and in the kindness of King Solomon, his wisdom, his perspicuity, intelligence, and his great heart . . . there [is] my account."

When Jorge was interviewed about six weeks later (forty-four days), he said he was much better after two sessions. He had accepted Eduardo's determination that *daño* "by mouth" caused by his girlfriend's family was the source of the trouble. Looking back, he commented:

What I was doing was stupid, how I worried. I was thinking that I would never be rid of the problem. But, although one doesn't completely forget, now I don't feel the same as before, so worried, so desperate. How can I put it? Now I worry about other things, I have other diversions to turn to. I take it normally and now the previous problem doesn't affect me much.

A second case of *daño* shows that Eduardo not only used the idiom of sorcery to account for the fact that one was suffering but also shared with other curanderos a male perspective on the gender conflict that was frequently the source of his Peruvian clients' troubles. Maria (EC2) was a twenty-one-year-old student whose *conviviente*, a bus driver, had left her and no longer gave her money. She complained that he had turned into a drunk and a womanizer, carrying on relationships with three other women. A Tarot card reader had supplied Maria with a *muñeco* or doll of her lover and a special powder to put in his bed and in his food so that he would return to her. She attributed both his behavior and an unexplainable wound on her own leg to the machinations of his other women. Adding to Maria's troubles was a long-standing conflict she had with her lover's mother, who believed Maria's university-level education put her son to shame. An uncle of Maria's, a curandero, had been treating her, but she had seen no results. She came to Eduardo for help.[5]

In a short *rastreo*, Eduardo referred to Maria's lover as a "real flatterer" and indicated that he was being "pursued" by a woman who carried his photograph in the heel of her left shoe. He also admonished Maria to recover a memento that she had given to her lover. Eduardo then told Maria how to recapture her lover (recall Nilo's advice to Mirta):

> You go on making him love you, calling him sweetly, with lots of tenderness, OK? No bitterness, or you'll break all the spell (*el sortilegio*), [which is so] well prepared. You are going to do it mentally. Now, soften him, call him, flatter him, pull [attract] him, because the other [woman] has him tied up, well bound up. Nothing dirty, filthy. With the permission of Jesus, with the most holy power.

In her second interview, fifty-six days later, Maria said she felt better even though the problem with her lover was "getting worse every day." At least the wound on her leg had healed. She had been able to participate in only one session with Eduardo because he had left on a trip, but she had attended a total of fifteen sessions with Eduardo's son. Comparing father to son, Maria indicated that she had more confidence in Eduardo and was waiting for him to return.

At a third interview, five months later, Maria stated even more bluntly her dissatisfaction with Eduardo's son: "He didn't do anything." She and her lover were separated, but she remained uncertain when asked if her experience had shaken her faith in curanderos. Perhaps, she reasoned, the lack of results was due to Eduardo's unfinished work: "My only hope was the *señor* [Eduardo] and not his son." She remained resolute in her determination to regain her lover's affection, even though he had started an affair with Eduardo's niece. Maria worried that Eduardo would favor his relative, a suspected preference which Maria thought explained why the woman was so confident when they met. Maria recalled the other's words: "If you'd like, we'll bet; but keep in mind, your husband stays with me!"

Clearly, Eduardo is able to work within the rhetorical framework of sorcery when treating those patients for whom it provides a meaningful way of conceptualizing suffering. Since his *rastreos* are based on the visions related to patients that he experiences, it is perfectly reasonable that he seeks to interpret his perceptions in terms intelligible to each individual. To put it in overly simple terms, saints and sorcerers make more sense to his Peruvian patients than would observations about developed third eyes. It may also be the case that the visions themselves are quite different when Eduardo focuses his mind on non-Peruvians. To the degree that hallucinations are culturally conditioned (Furst 1976:15–16), Eduardo's international experiences and exposure to different cultures may well affect the content of his visions as he shifts attention between foreigner and compatriot.

Eduardo's reputation and his ability to employ culturally meaningful explanations for suffering does not necessarily result in uncritical evaluations from his clients. In fact, his fame may well have increased the expectations of those who still seek his help despite his irregular schedule. Some, like Maria, seemed willing to excuse poor results on the basis of Eduardo's frequent absences and consequent inability to follow through on treatments. In several cases, however, clients made unambiguous critical judgments of Eduardo's therapeutic efforts.

An example of this latter is found in the case of Norman (EC16), a twenty-seven-year-old day laborer, born in the Peruvian Amazon but a six-year resident of Trujillo. He complained of skin eruptions on his legs, which doctors had diagnosed as an allergy but had been unable to treat effectively. His suspicion of sorcery was confirmed by a Tarot card reader, who sent him to Eduardo. At our second interview, Norman recalled feeling "completely exhausted" the morning after Eduardo's session: "Damn, I went to bed and instead of feeling relief, damn, [I felt] worse. I went to bed, and I couldn't even get up." The "infection" spread and he was unable to stand due to the swelling in his legs. Disappointed in Eduardo, he had sought the help of a spiritist healer, who prescribed for him a long and expensive treatment with herbs and injections. As a result of this therapy he declared himself cured, but he repeatedly indicated that Eduardo had misdiagnosed the problem.

In another case, a negative judgment of Eduardo's treatment was made by one of the more exceptional individuals in the study. Thirty-five-year-old Oswaldo (EC12), a university-educated office worker, had lived in Trujillo for twenty years. For about a year he suffered from nervousness, insomnia, and emotional sensitivity. He suspected that two tenants of his whom he had taken to court might have harmed him by sorcery: "They did a job on me psychologically." Although many patients may seek help from several other types of curing sources both before and during curandero treatment, Oswaldo could well set the standard for "multiple resort": he had been to a variety of physicians, a psychiatrist, a naturalist, two religious cults (Mahikari and Jehovah's Witnesses), *and* he had also participated in curandero rituals with Nilo Plasencia. About Nilo's ritual, he commented that its "extravagant" style made him feel even more nervous: "I don't like his method."

Eduardo diagnosed an endocrine problem, but he found nothing related to sorcery. When interviewed a second time, forty-two days later, Oswaldo said he felt "just about the same," and described Eduardo's *rastreo* as shallow and his treatment "superficial" because he had not prescribed an herbal remedy. He referred to himself as a "boat without a sail." The following dialogue shows that Oswaldo had clear expectations that were unmet:

Q: You had gone to other curanderos before?
A: Yes, I've gone.
Q: On the basis of that, did you believe in curanderos?
A: Well, I have gone with the hope that they were going to tell me everything, "Such and such person has done this to you. I always had this in mind."
Q: And now, these two curanderos, you could say, haven't satisfied your anxiety?
A: Yes, that's right.

Conclusion

The patient case material I have presented in this and the previous two chapters has taken the brief, abstract discussion of *daño* with which I introduced my analysis (Chapter 15) to an intimate, biographical level. I have shown how in the context of individual lives this illness category of *daño* is used to interpret the source and significance of a wide range of physical symptoms and other misfortunes. In the interviews and in the transcriptions from rituals *daño* emerges as the pivotal concept by which both patients and curanderos link personal suffering to the "harmfulness of others" (Kiev 1968:116).

The material also demonstrates that when our informants, both patients and shamans, use the concept of *daño* they are doing more than giving a clinical name to a person's pain and misfortune. They are also calling forth a complex network of metaphoric associations to which the term is meaningfully connected. The following chapter sets out to explore this "semantic network" (Good 1977) on its own terms, detached from the particulars of individual life experiences. To do this, I treat the entire body of taped interviews and ritual exchanges as though it were a collective conversation about suffering that reveals, in addition to the specifics of personal crises, a common framework of understanding, a cultural model of sickness and healing, shared by patients and curanderos. It is this same model, I argue, that is materially represented by the symbolic artifacts of the curandero's mesa and that is played out or enacted in ritual songs and ministrations.

19
Metaphors of Mistrust and Suspicion

The Metaphors of Illness

For [the sake of] my health, for [the sake of] my happiness, with these exquisite [servings of] tobacco I am recovering, I am getting stronger. Up with my name! Up with my shadow [soul]! Up with my luck! I go on raising, I go on suspending. For my name, for my shadow [soul], [patient's name], turning around my misfortunes, turning around my contagions, turning around my hexes, turning around evil spells, turning around obstacles. Up with my name! Up with my shadow [soul], and down with my misfortunes! Down with the contrary party! Down with the enemy party [adversary]! Raise up, now![1]

This invocation, which Nilo Plasencia requires that his patients recite as they drink their doses of the San Pedro remedy, draws upon a set of metaphors according to which sickness and misfortune are "down," while health and luck are "up." These up/down tropes are part of a larger metaphorical structure within which curanderos and their patients talk about the effects of *daño* and the processes of healing. In the following discussion I analyze the metaphors that recur in the testimony of patients, compare them to the metaphors found in the ritual speech of curanderos, and show that, taken together, they constitute a shared conceptualization of *daño*.

To derive a conceptualization of *daño* from the metaphors that patients and curanderos employ is to assign to these "figures of speech" more of a role in cognition than some would accept. George Lakoff and Mark Johnson (1980:3) note that "metaphor is typically viewed as characteristic of language alone, a matter of words rather than thought or action." When they subjected this assumption to careful scrutiny, however, they discovered that metaphor plays a far more significant role in human experience:

We have found, on the contrary, that metaphor is pervasive in everyday life, not just in language but in thought and action. Our ordinary conceptual system, in terms of which we both think and act, is fundamentally metaphorical in nature . . . the way we think, what we experience, and what we do every day is very much a matter of metaphor (ibid.).

Lakoff and Johnson's ground-breaking research also demonstrated that metaphors are systematically related to one another, as when one metaphor structures others (e.g., "time is money," so time can be wasted, spent, saved, et cetera), or when one metaphorical concept "organizes a system of concepts with respect to each other" (ibid.:14). They cite as an example of the latter the metaphorical concept that "health and life are up; sickness and death are down." In English this "orientational metaphor" organizes a system of other concepts (e.g., "peak of health," "down on one's luck," "to fall ill"). My analysis of the metaphors of *daño* shows that the same up/down metaphor, evident in the above invocation of Nilo Placencia, is linked to several other core metaphorical concepts.

In medical anthropology several scholars have made use of metaphorical analyses that draw, either explicitly or implicity, on Lakoff and Johnson's work.[2] For example, Emily Martin (1987, 1990) argues that the metaphors of biomedicine (e.g., reproduction is production, disease is warfare) mirror and provide support for socioeconomic hierarchies defined by race, class, and gender. Like Lakoff and Johnson, Martin insists that metaphors are not innocent figures of speech, but should instead be viewed as key parts of ideologies that shape perceptions and influence behavior. Her concern for the sociopolitical force of metaphors is also found in Libbet Crandon-Malamud's (1991) study of medical pluralism in Bolivia, although in the latter analysis medical metaphors are viewed less as supports for the status quo than as means by which the established order may be criticized and challenged. I have found Crandon-Malamud's interpretation useful in establishing the linkage between the metaphors of *daño* and the social impact of the curing/sorcery complex (see below and Chapter 20).

The "cultural hermeneutic" model championed by Byron Good and Mary-Jo Delvecchio Good (Good 1977; Good and Good 1980, 1981, 1982) relies in part on an analysis of metaphor to derive a group's conception of particular sicknesses.

An illness or a symptom condenses a network of meanings for the
sufferer: personal trauma, life stresses, fears and expectations about
the illness, social reactions of friends and authorities, and therapeutic experiences. The meaning of illness for an individual is
grounded in—though not reducible to—the network of meanings
an illness has in a particular culture: the metaphors associated with
a disease, the ethnomedical theories, the basic values and conceptual forms, and the care patterns that shape the experience of the
illness and the social reactions to the sufferer in a given society
(Good and Good 1980:176).

The task for the ethnographer according to this "meaning-
centered approach" (ibid.:166) to illness realities is to unravel the
network of associations that are condensed into sickness terms, be
it "heart distress" in Iran (Good 1977) or, as in the present case,
daño in Peru. The metaphors used in discourse related to a sickness
episode help to delineate the "semantic illness network" (ibid.:180)
that a given sickness term brings into operation as individuals seek
to construct meaning out of their experience.

The idea that illness realities are fundamentally semantic (Good
and Good 1980:167) has inspired other scholars to conceive of
healing, especially in a ritual context, as a process by which a transformation in the sufferer's self-understanding is accomplished. As
Csordas (1983:360) puts it, "The net effect of therapy is to redirect
the patient's attention to various aspects of his life in such a way as
to create a new meaning for that life, and a transformed sense of
himself as a whole and well person." Csordas (ibid.) explores the
persuasive power of healing metaphors in this "rhetoric of transformation" in the case of Catholic Pentecostal rituals in the United
States. A focus on healing metaphors has also been central to interpretations of the therapeutic force of Anasternaria fire-walking
rituals in Greece (Danforth 1989), spiritist healing in Brazil
(Greenfield 1992), and, closer to home, of biomedical treatment
(Moerman 1979).

Since we are accustomed to think of metaphor strictly as a liter-
ary trope, it is hard to grant it the kind of power that these analysts
suggest it has. After all, isn't it "just a matter of semantics"? It is
only when we remember that in humans vital physiological systems
directly respond to mental states (e.g., stress and disease; see
Dressler 1990) that the error of this popular view is made clear. To
paraphrase Moerman (1983:165), "meaning matters" and "metaphors mend." As I turn from the metaphors that patients use in

talking about *daño* to those that occur in ritual discourse it will become evident how much of the power of the curandero's treatment derives from the rhetorical force of curing metaphors.

Metaphors in Patients' Speech

Patients in our sample expressed their suffering with metaphors of contamination and entrapment. Informants spoke of someone having "played dirty" against them (*jugado sucio*), often of having buried some personal object of theirs (e.g., hair, underwear, socks) with a voodoo-like doll, an *enterrado*. They frequently used the following words to describe their condition: *cochinado* (made filthy, pig-like), *podrido* (rotten), *apestado* (pestilential), *jodido* ("screwed"). Expressing the idea of entrapment, patients referred to being *agarrado* (caught, seized), *amarrado* (tied up), *jalado* (pulled in), *trancado* (bolted in).[3]

Patients also drew upon metaphors of spiritual demoralization and disquietude; indeed, the words *demoralizado* (demoralized) and *inquieto* (uneasy) occurred often in the patients' general descriptions of their conditions. According to the metaphorical logic of our patients' symptomatic reports, to be demoralized is to be down and heavy, as in the frequently appearing adjectives they used: *decaido* (fallen, declined), *chancado* (crushed), *pesado* (heavy), *desfallecido* (faint, weak), *deprimido* (depressed), *desanimado* (downhearted). Inquietude (*inquietud*) was expressed as *agitación* (agitation), *nerviosismo* (nervousness), *trastornado* (upset), *desorientado* (disoriented), and *fregado* (pestered), *molestado* (molested), *fastidiado* (bothered).

Those patients who indicated satisfaction with their treatment when interviewed a second time used metaphors of purification and liberation to describe their transformed condition. To be healed of *daño*, in their words, is to be *limpiado* (cleansed), *despejado* (cleared), *refrescado* (refreshed), *suelto* (loosed, untied), *libre* (free), *desamarrado* (untied), or *destrancado* (unbolted). Cleansing is accomplished by having the sickness *botado* (thrown away), and the sorcerer's influence *quitado* (taken away, removed).

In addition to these healing metaphors were others of spiritual restoration and tranquility. The former, in general terms described as being *animado* (enlivened) or *restablecido* (reestablished), was also expressed via upward directional metaphors, as in patient references to being *levantado* (raised), *parado* (stood up), *elevado* (elevated) or *alzado* (lifted), or *liviano* (light). Very frequently, patients described themselves in follow-up interviews as *tranquilo* (tranquil), *calmado* (calm), *contento* (content), and *relajado* (relaxed).

In sum, patients talk about the suffering associated with *daño* and the healing process in terms of a metaphorical transformation from contaminated to cleansed, entrapped to liberated, demoralized to enheartened, and from agitated to tranquil. A comprehensive directional metaphor, from down to up, is layered on top of these other associations. Of the most common metaphors in our patients' testimony, this final trope was the only one which occurs regularly in sickness discourse unrelated to sorcery (e.g, *caer enfermo*, to "fall sick"). The others appear to be specific to the semantics of *daño*.

Metaphors in Ritual Discourse

Many of the same metaphors used by patients are also found in curanderos' invocations and *rastreos*, as is evident in the transcripts quoted in the previous chapters. They are also central to the power songs, or *tarjos*, performed by curanderos to activate the forces on which healing depends.[4] The lyrics equate healing with cleansing, throwing away, raising, standing up, clearing, untying, unbolting, et cetera—the same metaphorical concepts patients draw upon to describe their condition when they have been healed of *daño*.

The use of metaphor in the shamans' *tarjos* is not only significant because of its correspondence with the concepts that patients use to describe their conditions, but also because the metaphors take a different grammatical form in the songs. The simple adjectival construction common in the patients' symptomatic descriptions (the verb *estar*, "to be," combined with an adjective or a past participle serving as an adjective) is replaced in the *tarjos* by the repetitive use of the first person (plural or singular), present progressive tense. Furthermore, rather than using the construction of the present progressive in which the verb "to be" (*estar*) is combined with the present participle (e.g., *estamos levantando*, "we are raising"), shamans employ the alternative form, which uses the verb "to go" (*ir*) with the gerund: *vamos levantando* ("we go on raising"), *voy suspendiendo* ("I go on suspending"), *voy contando* ("I go on accounting"), et cetera.

I see this as an example of a linguistic feature known as "performativity" (see Tambiah 1981). The English expressions "I promise" or "We pledge" are examples of performativity; to say the words is to accomplish the thing to which the words refer. The present progressive form that shamans use in their songs (and invocations) is meant to have the same effect. They are not merely describing a state of being, as is the case with the patients' testimony, nor are they simply indicating that a progressive action is in process; instead, they are actually making a process (i.e., healing) *happen* as they name it. When they use the first person plural, they are also drawing all those listening into the performative act.

It is important to keep in mind that the metaphors used in the *tarjos* (and invocations) are simultaneously experienced by the listener aurally and physically; the patient hears the curandero singing as he/she ingests and reacts to the San Pedro and the tobacco, feels the massage of a staff, and so on through the ritual acts described in Part I. The performativity of the shaman's metaphorical expressions has a corporeal quality; they are literally "transacted" (Dow 1986) on the patient's body as they are communicated verbally through ritual song. This same physicality is evident in other aspects of the curandero's use of metaphor, as I show below.

Not all of the metaphors of curanderos' songs are represented in patients' interviews. Curanderos refer to patients as being "named" (*nombrado*) or "accounted" (*contado*) to indicate that the patient's spirit is under the control of a sorcerer; they add the adverb "well" to these words to convey the idea that the spirit is released in the act of healing (e.g., *bien contado, bien nombrado*).[5] While curers use these metaphors frequently in songs and invocations, patients employ them rarely, if at all. Given that patients and shamans otherwise draw from a common pool of *daño*-related metaphors, it is not clear why there should be these exceptions.

Metaphors in Relation to Mesa Symbolism and Healing Acts

In Chapter 14 Sharon builds on Giese's (1989:152) argument that the associations by which mesa artifacts are organized—left/sorcery/pagan/downward *versus* right/curing/Catholic/upward—are replicated in the healing actions of curanderos, with cleansing rituals linked to the left (down) side and "raising" rituals to the right (up) side.[6] I want to elaborate on this point and add a third set of associations between mesa symbolism and ritual actions, those related to the metaphor of the *volteada*, or "turning around."

Many of the therapeutic actions of curanderos are directed at cleansing their patients of the effects of sorcery (associated with the left). As Giese (ibid.) points out, this is described by curanderos as "throwing away" (*botando*) the negative, dark, "dirty" forces that cause sickness; it is accomplished by ritual acts (e.g., the *limpia de cuy*, massages or rubbings with mesa artifacts) that follow a downward movement, moving from the patient's head to his/her feet. The ingestion of the San Pedro brew, as well as the nasal imbibing of the tobacco mixture, are also represented by curers as *limpias*, cleansings, both figuratively and physically (i.e., as spiritual and physiological purgatives). In rare cases, the curandero will also perform a shamanic sucking-out of the harmful substance or force which is causing the patient's illness.

Giese (ibid.) notes that in addition to "cleansing," a number of healing actions (associated with the right) aim to "raise" the patient. During the *levantada*, or "raising," the curer and/or his assistant(s) position themselves next to the patient and lift shells filled with the tobacco liquid from the ground upward, touching the shell to the patient's body at the feet, knees, waist, chest, and finally the top of the head. The person is "*parado*," or "put on his/her feet" (ibid). As shown in previous chapters, the patient's belongings (e.g., trucks, houses, cattle) may also be "raised."[7] In all these cases, it is not only health but also luck and fortune that are elevated by this ritual.

Curanderos also talk about raising in reference to the logic of smells to which I have referred at several points in the previous chapters. Sorcery smells bad, perhaps, as Polia (1989:220) suggests, because of its relation to the putrefaction of death (e.g., sorcery artifacts which come from cemeteries and archaeological ruins, *enterrados* [objects buried in graves to cause *daño*]). In contrast, the sweet smells of the perfumed waters used in the final phases of rituals, during the *florecimiento* ("the flowering"), symbolize life, health, and well-being. It would seem an easy step to connect these olfactory metaphors with Giese's (ibid.) observation that sorcery is down and dark, while curing is up and light. I would simply add fetid and "flowering," respectively, to these assocations.

The purgative and emetic effects of the ritual's medicinals, the tactile sensations of downward-directed diagnostic and curing rubbings, and the olfactory experience of perfumed sprays all relate to the metaphors of cleansing and raising. Here again, therapeutic metaphors are translated into direct physical sensations, and the performative power of the ritual's rhetoric is enhanced.

This analysis of the links between metaphors, ritual acts, and mesa symbolism would be incomplete without reference to the ritual segment which expresses the vengeful element in curing, the *volteada* (the "turning around"; see Chapter 17). Curers describe their rituals as contests which pit their powers against those of their adversaries. The objective is to dominate (*dominar*) the sorcerer responsible for the patient's affliction, not only by removing the sickness or misfortune but also, for some curanderos (e.g., Plasencia, Rojas), by sending it back to its source.

The concept of a "turning around" is clearly linked to the left side of mesas. For example, the forces used by Nilo Plasencia to send back the effects of sorcery come from the Ganadero or left mesa field, and the *volteada* ritual is performed in front and to the left of the altar (in contrast to the *rastreo*, which is done to the right). I should add, however, that curanderos distinguish on moral grounds their use of sorcery from the sorcery acts which caused their patient's affliction in the first place. For those curanderos who include this ritual in their sessions, it is seen as an integral part of curing, even though it draws upon the powers of sorcery.

The metaphors of *daño* are summarized in Figure 20.[8] Following the above analysis, I distinguish the use of metaphor in the referential speech of patients and shamans ("referential metaphors") from their performative use in ritual discourse ("performative metaphors"). The latter are intended to transform patients' self-understanding, and presumably physical condition as well, from "harmed" to "healed," as these states are metaphorically conceived and described. The right/left and up/down orientation of the chart represents the isomorphism between mesa symbolism and metaphorical structures; were it possible to present the chart in three dimensions, it would match well with the symbolic and cosmologic organization of mesas (see Chapter 14).

The Social and Economic Context of Daño

The patient cases reviewed in the previous chapters show that when Peruvians report feeling "entrapped," "heavy," "fallen," and "dispirited" they are not merely describing clinical symptoms. They are invoking an analysis of suffering, condensed in the concept of *daño*, that links individual distress to a social world where mistrust and suspicion are an integral part of relationships, even

Referential Metaphors   Performative Metaphors   Referential Metaphors

--- --- --- --- --- --- --- --- --- --- --- --- --- --- --- --- ---

HEALED (CURADO)

Cleansed
Liberated
Enheartened
Tranquil
Up

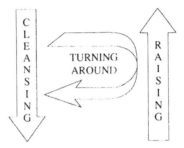

HARMED (DAÑADO)

Contaminated
Entrapped
Demoralized
Agitated
Down

Figure 20 Metaphors of Daño

between close friends and relatives. To understand why such an analysis makes sense to the patients of curanderos it is essential to look at the broader social reality to which the metaphors of *daño* ultimately relate.

In the Introduction, the principal political and economic factors that shaped Peruvian life during the 1980s were summarized. Natural disasters, political and economic chaos, violence associated with revolutionary organizations and cocaine trafficking—that decade tested the survival skills of every Peruvian. In particular, an increasingly precarious economic situation introduced uncertainties into the lives of persons from every social class. The merchant began to hoard his goods in anticipation of price increases, quickly converted earnings to dollars on an irrepressible black market, and took steps to protect personal property against the ever more likely risk of theft. Strikes disrupted the activities of professionals of all types, from university professors to bank tellers, and many found that they had to moonlight at other jobs as daily price increases outstripped their salaries. Multiple jobs at substandard wages was also the pattern for the unskilled sector of the labor force, many of whose families suffered from a range of poverty-related health problems, including malnutrition. By one estimate, sixty percent of all Peruvian children under the age of five were malnourished (Reid 1985:98).

One response to the deepening crisis was an expansion of the informal economy, the functioning of which is described in the landmark study, *The Other Path*, by Hernando de Soto (1989 [1986]). This extralegal economy has long been an essential source of work for the huge population of un- or underemployed, but in recent years it has also come to provide for a large part of the sub- sistence, transportation, and consumer needs of all but the wealth- iest, since the formal economy is either unequal to the task or sim- ply too expensive for the majority of the inhabitants of the country. In the absence of legal protections and state administrative con- trols, the informal economy works on networks of personal rela- tionships between worker and employer, as well as on those be- tween buyer and seller. At the same time, the intense competition and riskiness of the informal economy threatens those very rela- tionships, as individuals often are forced to choose self-interest over cooperation and reciprocal obligation.

The centrality of personal networks in this economic context, and the difficult mix of dependence and risk that accompanies re- lationships so essential to survival, is just one expression of a per- sonalistic ethos that is more broadly a part of Peruvian (if not Latin American) culture (see Gillin 1955; Rotondo 1970). The effort to establish relationships of *confianza*, or trust, is a basic means by which Peruvians seek both security and opportunity in a world of uncertainty and frustration. The correlate of "trust," after all, is the expectation of help and favors. The highly charged nature of close interpersonal relationships, enmeshed as they are with eco- nomic interests, contributes to the paradox that trusted persons are not always trustworthy (see Glass-Coffin 1991).

This is the social context that makes it perfectly reasonable to attribute one's own suffering and misfortune to the surreptitious aggression of others. *Daño* encapsulates a well-grounded appraisal of the risks of social intimacy within the existing conditions of economic uncertainties and structural inequalities. The rich metaphorical language associated with the concept gives voice to the desperation of persons who sense that their trust has been abused, that the face of a friend or lover may disguise betrayal.

If the analysis were left at this point, *daño* would be little more than a metaphorically rich concept used by individuals to comment on the social injustices they have suffered, and the rituals of curanderos would be no more than forums for complaint. In effect, this is the conclusion of the "safety valve" interpretation I reviewed earlier (Chapter 15). In the concluding chapter I argue, however, that *daño* is not just a culturally meaningful construction of suffering but also the focus of remedial and redressive action. I find evidence that the work of curanderos has a social impact beyond that of providing an arena for patient catharsis.

20

The Work of Curanderos

The Goal of Curandero Therapy

At the end of Part I Douglas Sharon described the dialectical symbolism of curandero rituals as a "code for the problem-solving entailed in curing." The patient case material I have presented in the previous chapters indicates that the central "problem" curanderos are most often engaged in solving is encompassed by the concept of *daño*. My analysis of the metaphors of *daño* demonstrates that this term articulates the lived experience of patients and their suffering with the dialectical symbolism of curandero rituals. The ritual encounter between curandero and patient can be viewed as a dialogue about *daño* in which the shaman uses a persuasive rhetoric (in song and speech) in conjunction with powerful physical sensations to transform his client's self-understanding (Csordas 1983; see also Frank 1973).

Of course, neither curanderos nor their patients would limit the potential impact of ritual to changes in self-perception. Both expect that the powers unleashed by the ritual will have a discernible effect on the social lives of clients, that they not only will feel better (i.e., symptoms will be reduced or eliminated) but that the personal relations implicated by the diagnosis of *daño* will change. Ana (VF2) hoped to have her surgical wound heal as well as to see a renewal of her relationships with school friends. Segundo (VF35) wanted to feel less anxious and angry, but he linked this outcome to being freed from the effects of jealousy (of his former girlfriend) and of envy (from bus riders and friends). Sabina (NP4), Mirta (NP10), and Alejandrina (NP28) sought relief from a variety of physical symptoms, rectification of their relationships with husbands, and revenge on those responsible for the sorcery that caused them harm.

The interpretive analysis of ritual process and outcome presented

in the last chapter can be linked with the concrete expectations that
patients have of therapy results when it is recognized that the dialogue about *daño* occurs in a social space not restricted to the time
and place of rituals nor to the patient/healer dyad. Family and
friends often know, or at least suspect, when an individual consults
with a sorcerer or a curandero and some of them may even accompany him/her to the ritual(s). The person who contracts for a sorcery attack may reveal that fact to allies, who subsequently pass the
news along a network that eventually leads to the intended target.
Similarly, the curandero's analysis of the source of a patient's suffering is often a topic of subsequent conversation between social
intimates of the client; this is also true of the countermeasures
(e.g., the *volteada*) undertaken by the shaman.

The implication of all this is that the transformative rhetoric of
curandero rituals is merely one dramatic component of an ongoing dialogue that embraces, directly or indirectly, all those whom
the sufferer either suspects of harboring malicious intentions or
trusts as social confidants. The manner in which the sufferer and
other interested parties talk about and interpret symptoms, and
the therapy choices made throughout the course of a sickness episode, carry significance beyond the physical and psychological condition of a single individual:

> Medical dialogue is potent as a mechanism for empowering individ-
> uals, creating alliances, and instigating change because its subject is
> overtly and concretely the individual, while the real object of the di-
> alogue is covertly and abstractly social relations. . . . Through the id-
> iom of medicine as a primary resource, people communicate infor-
> mation about themselves, their relationships to others, and their
> intentions, in order to obtain secondary resources, restructure social
> relations, and create social change (Crandon-Malamud 1991:208).

A "medical dialogue" that makes reference to sorcery acts is especially potent in a society like that of Peru where personal relationships are crucial to economic survival and where the powers of
the sorcerer and the curandero are assumed to have empirically
verifiable effects. *Daño*, as a threat or as an accepted diagnosis of
suffering, can have serious social repercussions no matter how
skeptical outsiders to the tradition might be about the forces that
sorcerers claim to control. It is with this in mind that I analyze in
the following sections the broad social impact of curanderos' rituals. I focus on the suffering of women—this is because women are

the majority of curandero clients and because no other single category of *daño* cases is as common as that which includes problems
attributed in part or entirely to conflicts between men and women.

The Context of Gender Asymmetry in Peru

Recent scholarship on the position of women in Peru has stressed
the contrast between traditional Andean patterns of gender complementarity and the subordination of women under Spanish custom and law (Allen 1988:78–85; Andreas 1985:54; Glass-Coffin
1992:76–81; Rasnake 1988:66, 81, 205; Silverblatt 1978, 1987).[1]
During the colonial period isolated mountain hamlets enjoyed sufficient cultural autonomy to maintain a definition of gender roles
that gave each sex authority in separate economic and social
spheres while promoting balanced decision making in arenas of
shared responsibility. Even where the expansion of the colonial
commercial system brought native communities under the influence of European patriarchal values, defiance was common (Silverblatt 1987:213; Spalding 1984:299–300). Andean men and women
fought Spanish practices that ran counter to their traditional patterns through the colonial court system, in open rebellions, and
through more subtle "everyday forms of resistance," that is,
through "foot dragging, dissimulation, desertion, false compli-
ance, pilfering, feigned ignorance, slander, arson, sabotage, and so
on" (Scott 1985:xvi).

After independence was gained in 1821, the penetration of capitalist enterprises (first British and then American) gradually accomplished what centuries of Spanish rule had failed to achieve,
the progressive disintegration of Andean agricultural communities
and their indigenous cultural patterns. Granted that contemporary ethnography continues to demonstrate the retention of native
languages and customs, it is nevertheless clear that wage labor and
market integration have caused unprecedented changes in basic
social and economic relations in even the most remote regions of
the country. This is especially apparent in changing sex roles, as
capitalism combines with Spanish custom to privilege men in law,
politics, and economics (Andreas 1985).

> The dependent capitalist economic ideology and social structure
> of a developing country like Peru is supported by the traditional
> Catholic family system and by the Spanish cultural heritage which

spawned the ideology of *machismo*. *Machismo* involves a system of beliefs and attitudes that espouses the superiority and social and economic value of one gender over another: masculine over feminine.
Capitalism, sexism, and age-grading become inextricably intertwined and perpetuate one another through family and society at
large in the posture of cultural patterns, values, and attitudes that
regiment relationships between the sexes and, at the same time, establish and extol the dominance of the husband over the wife. She
as well as her children are completely subordinate to the authoritar-
ian male head of the family (Bunster and Chaney 1985:185).

In the specific context of northern Peru, intensive capitalistic
development came after the War of the Pacific (1879–1883) in the
form of investment in large-scale sugar plantations in the fertile
coastal valleys of the region. An expanding network of railroads
and port facilities (Dobyns and Doughty 1976:191–94) supported
an increasing concentration of sugar production on a limited number of immense north coast plantations (e.g., Casa Grande, Roma,
Cartavio, and Chiclín; see Klarén 1976). The northern departments of La Libertad and Lambayeque were producing seventy-
one percent of Peru's sugar exports by 1911; sugar accounted for
as much as forty-two percent of Peru's export earnings by 1920
(Deere 1990:23).

The labor requirements of sugar production were met by labor
recruiters, who offered peasants in highland communities an ad-
vance for temporary work contracts (two to three months) on specific coastal plantations (see Deere 1990:44–50). The system, called
the *enganche* ("the hook"), initiated a migration pattern that involved increasing numbers of highland laborers, more men than
women, who remained on the coast for increasingly longer periods of
time. The wealth generated by the sugar industry also improved urban environments and created new opportunities there in an expanding regional market. This, in turn, stimulated further highland-
to-coast migration. The city of Trujillo, for example, experienced an
average annual growth rate of 2.1 percent between 1876 and 1923,
reaching a population of 23,000 by the latter date (ibid.:41–42).

Migration to coastal cities substantially increased after 1950, as
industrialization supported by foreign capital created even greater
demands for labor. One of the more remarkable cases is the city of
Chimbote, whose population grew from about 5,000 in 1940 to
159,000 in 1972 as a result of employment created by the construction of anchovy and tuna processing plants and a steel mill (made

possible by a hydroelectric dam and railroad links to Andean mineral deposits; see Dobyns and Doughty 1976:226). Trujillo, which had no peripheral squatter settlements or suburban districts prior to 1957, had a population of 424,844 in 1984 (INE 1984:5), and was ringed by a series of satellite communities (*areas integradas*) reaching far out into the surrounding desert.

There is general agreement that this pattern of migration worked to the disadvantage of women (Andreas 1985:9; Bourque and Warren 1981:204; Deere 1990:142, 310–11). Feudal haciendas in mountain regions had already begun the process of replacing indigenous complementary gender roles with patriarchal relations, most significantly by abandoning the traditional system of bilateral inheritance of land (i.e., both sexes inherit rights to property) in favor of rental agreements exclusively between landlords and male household heads (Deere 1990:110).[2] Coastal migration greatly intensified and accelerated this transition to living in accordance to a Hispanic definition of male privilege and female responsibility. Wage-earning opportunities were disproportionately available to male migrants; therefore, women either remained behind, shouldering the added burden caused by the migrant's absence, or accompanied their mates only to find that nothing but the most degrading kinds of jobs were available to them (e.g., domestic service, low-wage piecework at home, street sweeping, prostitution). Men who spent time on the coast alone, even if only for short periods, were exposed to new cultural patterns, including the values associated with *machismo*, and often resisted traditional customs when they returned to the sierra. It also was common for a male migrant to estabish a second family on the coast and eventually to abandon his original wife and children (ibid.:310).

Machismo, together with the idealization of women as spiritually superior to men,[3] constitutes the ideological foundation for the combination of sexual inequality and economic stratification that leaves Peruvian women in a more precarious economic position than men. The "double exploitation" (Babb 1989:56) women suffer has consequences in every aspect of their lives. They are far more likely than men to be illiterate; their economic activities are severely restricted, undervalued, and poorly compensated; and their health is often compromised by a series of unwanted pregnancies that may begin before the age of fifteen (see Figueroa and Anderson 1981:5–8). Even the household can be an arena of abuse— for the domestic servant who is raped by her male employer or for the woman who is repeatedly beaten by her husband (Andreas 1985:65–67; Bronstein 1982:164–74). The constraints of patriarchy are described in poignant terms in the following passage taken from a letter written to a women's publication on Mother's Day, 1981:

> For how long are men of all ages and social classes going to make victims of their mothers, wives, and sisters because of their frustrations, bad moods, and unfounded jealousies? . . . How long will it take you to realize that as women we get twice the trouble this oppressive society has to offer? Every day things cost more, and in order to get a little better price from the butcher, the milkman, the baker, or the vegetable man, we have to smile at his bad jokes and foul language, just so that we'll have something to give you and your children to eat. . . . In our workplaces we have to put up with insults from our bosses and fellow workers in order not to lose our jobs, in order to earn a little money to help you, and at the end of an exhausting day you start yelling at me and injuring me, without even caring if the children are listening or hurt. If you can't start changing the way you behave, please don't come around hypocritically offering me gifts on Mother's Day (quoted in Andreas 1985:105–6).

James Scott (1990:2) refers to the social and economic relations that result from and perpetuate hierarchical ideologies as the "public transcript," which he defines as the "open interaction between subordinates and those who dominate." He contrasts this with the "hidden transcript"—"the offstage speeches, gestures, and practices that confirm, contradict, or inflect what appears in the public transcript" (ibid.:4–5). He argues that however powerful the institutions and values are that support the public transcript, there are always social forms through which subordinates challenge the relations of domination. Sometimes this takes the form of social protest movements and other open struggles against tyranny. At other times, however, subordinate groups employ "low-profile forms of resistance" (ibid.:19) in order to "insinuate their resistance, in disguised forms, into the public transcript" (ibid.: 136).

The historical process by which male domination came to supplant gender complementarity as the public transcript of social relations in northern Peru did not cause the traditional cultural pattern of balanced relations between the sexes to disappear as circumstances favored the Hispanic patriarchal system. Rather, what was once a public transcript of complementarity became a hidden transcript of resistance to female subordination. At times, the resistance is "offstage," as when women communicate their anger and frustrations to other women; but at other times women find ways to confront the sources of their oppression. Women are by no means passive victims of male domination (Bourque and Warren 1981:214).

During the past several decades, Peruvian women have struggled against economic oppression through participation in labor unions (Andreas 1985:125–55), and they have fought against government neglect in mass mobilizations and community organization (e.g., mothers' clubs, the Municipal Milk Program [*Vaso de Leche*], and communal kitchens; see Fort 1988; Barrig 1989; and Anderson 1989). By means of a variety of strategies, they have forged economic roles for themselves beyond the household, especially in the small-scale commerce of the informal economy (Bourque and Warren 1981; Babb 1989; Bunster and Chaney 1985). Women who have found all of these measures insufficient have taken even more extreme steps, including armed struggle. By some accounts, women predominate in the revolutionary group Sendero Luminoso and occupy central leadership positions in that organization (Andreas 1985:178–87).

Still, however, Peruvian women's economic and political activities are ultimately constrained by a public transcript that subordinates females to males. This is experienced intensely in the context of the intimate unions which women establish with men, either formally (i.e., marriage) or informally (i.e., consensual unions). On the one hand, women must depend on men for access to economic and social resources not otherwise available to them because of the sexual division of labor and the patriarchal social system. On the other hand, the leverage they can exert in their relationships with men is limited by the freedom society grants males to enter and abandon unions with women virtually at will and with few consequences (especially if the unions are not legally constituted).[4]

Male prerogative in intimate relationships remains a cornerstone of Peru's public transcript of female subordination, comparatively unaffected by the kind of mass struggle that has marked women's political efforts in other arenas. This is not to say, however, that male authority in unions with women goes uncontested, for in addition to the more dramatic struggles against the public transcript there are a multitude of minor skirmishes, "low-profile

forms of resistance," that characterize the "infrapolitics of subordinate groups" (Scott 1990:19).

Among the "weapons of the weak," argues Scott (ibid.:143–44),
is magical aggression:

> The use of magic represents an attempt to move beyond gossip and
> turn "hard words" into an act of secret aggression that will bring di-
> rect harm to one's enemy, his family, his livestock, his crops. An ag-
> gressive wish to bring misfortune on someone becomes, through the
> performative act of magic, the agency of harm. . . . In a society that
> practices magic, those who perceive a lively resentment and envy di-
> rected at them from below will easily become convinced that any re-
> verses they suffer are the result of malevolent witchcraft.[5]

Scott's identification of magical aggression as a "weapon of the
weak" (Scott 1985) has clear relevance for the clients of sorcerers
and curanderos in Peru. Our interviews make it clear that women
use *daño* and love magic as instruments of resistance which challenge male privilege through disguised means of manipulation. At
the same time, the study material raises important questions about
the applicability of an interpretation of magical aggression which
associates it with forms of resistance on the part of subordinate
groups. First, how can we account for the fact that *daño* cases often
involve one woman combating another, as in several of Nilo
Plasencia's cases? What sort of resistance is this if it promotes division and conflict among those who are the victims of domination?
Also, how can a male curandero, presumably a beneficiary of the
public transcript, serve as a champion of the oppressed?

The Moralization of Social Injustice

According to Scott (1990:14), "the frontier between the public and
the hidden transcripts is a zone of constant struggle between dom-
inant and subordinate—not a solid wall." Curers and sorcerers work
in this contested zone, serving in many instances as agents of those
who suffer from the public transcript of male privilege. Their women
clients expect them to do more than offer an emotional outlet; they
expect concrete results in their conflicted relationships and consequent improvements in their economic circumstances.

Is this just wishful thinking? Are Peruvian women who seek the
help of curanderos deluding themselves into thinking that what is
just an opportunity to express their suffering can actually affect

their lives? Is shamanic ritual really a mystification of oppression, accommodation masquerading as pragmatic action? Does the curandero threaten or does he support the ideology of *machismo* that puts women in harm's way?[6]

On the one hand, the basic values of *machismo* which support gender-based hierarchies are very much in evidence in the discourse of *daño*. These values are explicit in curanderos' admonitions to women patients that they should live according to the submissive standards of male domination (e.g., Plasencia and Calderón), as well as in their lectures on the "nature" of masculinity (e.g., Plasencia). They are also implicit in the very common willingness of women and curanderos to relieve men of the responsibility for their philandering by assigning blame to the "other woman" and/or to interfering in-laws.

On the other hand, there are also challenges to patriarchy in the practice of curanderos. In earlier chapters repeated instances were found in which the curandero critiqued, sometimes with severe language, the behavior of men that caused their spouses/mates to suffer. A more general criticism of *machismo* was voiced by Claudius Giese's curandero informant, Don Ruperto:

> Here in Peru ninety percent of households are miserable. The man has at least two or three women, but he always ends up neglecting one. He has two or three children with the first, then leaves her for another. But he doesn't give anything [to the first]; he doesn't support the children. He has two or three children with the second, and then leaves her for a third, again giving nothing [for his children]. Neither to the first, nor to the second; now, everything is for the third. And his children grow up to be what signifies the seed of evil, the seed of the country's ruin. . . . Here, men are womanizers; that's how it is. They have three households, but don't support two (quoted in Giese 1989:133, our translation).

A curandero's moralizing about the abusive behavior of men would be a relatively empty gesture if it were offered only in the spirit of sympathy. For it to do more than console, the curandero's critique must convey some sense of accountability upon the male whose behavior is the focus of attention. This requires, first, that the message reach the man and, second, that it carry sufficient moral force to convey both a sense of responsibility and a motive to alter behavior.

The curandero's analysis of the social relations of his patients does go beyond the immediate ritual context in which it is formulated.

The curandero's words do travel beyond the patients' ears, as when men accompany their mates to the ritual and find themselves directly addressed by the curandero, or when a close relative or friend goes with the woman patient and is a party to the curandero's *rastreos*. Either the companion or the woman herself may convey the sense, if not the substance, of the curandero's narrative back to the man involved. In still other cases, it is enough for the man to suspect that his mate has sought the assistance of a curandero; a general perception of being held accountable can result.

The question of the moral force of a curandero's analysis, and the ritual therapy it inspires, is more complicated. Our own positivistic world view, which denies the existence of the kinds of powers which curanderos say they enlist, makes it more difficult to see the pragmatic force of symbolic action. We are therefore led to wonder how a Peruvian male's behavior could be constrained by the ritualistic ministrations of a curandero, or the magical assaults of a sorcerer. We can find psychosomatic value in the catharsis of a woman permitted an opportunity to express her suffering to a sympathetic person, but we would assume that any direct effects of the curandero's ritual would be restricted to the physiological impact on patients of the pharmacological substances employed.

Our own doubts notwithstanding, there is ample evidence in the testimony of patients that men as well as women in Peru credit curanderos and *brujos* with the ability to manipulate forces that can directly affect their lives. Recall, for example, the conviction of Víctor Flores's patient, Segundo, that his economic and emotional problems were attributable to the sorcery contracted by either a former girlfriend or the mother of a drunk whom Segundo had thrown from his bus. Segundo turned to Flores for help because he believed that curanderos master real forces in the world.[7] This is the context of understanding within which we must consider the question of the moral force of the work of curanderos and sorcerers.

From this perspective, the curanderismo complex (we must include both sorcery and curing in our evaluation of social effects) opposes male prerogatives by empowering women. Through the *brujo*, women gain access to powers that guarantee fidelity (e.g., love magic) and eliminate competition (e.g., *daño*). Even the apprehension that a woman might pursue this alternative can act as an effective sanction. The curandero, on the other hand, provides women with the means to redress wrongs and to hold men accountable for their actions.

The essential point regarding the accountability imposed on a man by the work of a curandero is that it both excuses and convicts. The account offered for a patient's suffering may implicate the "other woman," and may even construct the man as another victim, but it frames all this as the consequence of a man's unfaithfulness and irresponsibility. By partially displacing blame, the curandero's analysis gives the man the moral space to renew his commitment to the woman he had indirectly exposed to harm. They are fighting a common enemy. The man is not thereby required to call into question the basic assumptions of patriarchy, which are actually celebrated by the curandero; he must only recognize that patriarchy has moral boundaries, which women are free to enforce.

It is interesting to note that two recent ethnographies have offered similar gender-related interpretations in relationship to cultural forms which, like curanderismo, simultaneously express and confront ideologies of sexual inequality. Loring Danforth (1989) describes the spirit possession and fire-walking rituals of the Anastenaria of Greece:

> In androcentric communities like those of the Kostilides women are clearly subordinate to men and experience a variety of psychological and social conflicts that are often dealt with through involvement in spirit possession rituals like the Anastenaria. Through these rituals women seek to address the discrepancies that characterize the relationship between an official ideology of male dominance and a social reality in which women actually exercise a significant degree of power. Spirit possession, then, provides a context for the resolution of conflict often associated with gender roles and gender identity (ibid.:99).

Danforth points out that association with the possession rituals does empower participants, especially women and marginal men. "It provides them with access to the supernatural power of Saint Constantine, which enables them to participate in the dramatic public performance of the firewalk, to speak forcefully in public meetings dealing with ritual matters, and to restructure their important social relationships to their advantage" (ibid.:103). However, since possession entails women submitting to a male saint, the sexual hierarchy is replicated at the same time as it is challenged (ibid.).[8]

The second comparative case comes from the Bedouins of the western desert of Egypt. Here, young men and women, those who are most dependent and disadvantaged, recite formulaic poems, the *ghinnawas*, to express personal feelings of sadness, vulnerability, betrayal, and deep attachments. Lila Abu-Lughod (1986) points out that although these sentiments oppose the "discourse of ordinary life" and its ideals of honor and modesty, they are partially legitimized by the very conventionality of the poetic form: "poems, as part of a great cultural tradition, cannot represent rebellions against the values of society" (ibid.:240).

At the same time, Abu-Lughod argues that recitations of the poems are not intended merely to express feelings, but also "to move people and thus get them to act toward one in a particular way" (ibid.:242). Furthermore, this poetry is a "discourse of opposition to the system and of defiance [to] those who represent it; it is antistructure just as it is antimorality" (ibid.:251). The poems draw on ultimate Bedouin values, namely freedom and a refusal to be dominated, but when voiced by those "slighted in the system" these very same values constitute a "discourse of defiance" (ibid.:254).

In both these societies, and, as I have argued, for Peru as well, persons who are disadvantaged and/or marginalized by the social system draw on cultural forms that simultaneously articulate *and* redress the experience of domination. However, because these defiant discourses challenge the social system (the "public transcript," in Scott's terms) in culturally conventionalized forms (i.e., possession rituals and formulaic poetry), they draw on precisely those shared values that support the injustices to which they object. The defiance consists in extending to persons ordinarily disenfranchised by these values the power to use them instead to their own ends.

In the Peruvian case, it is important not to overstate the redressive power gained by women through the agency of curanderos. Many of the cases we documented were inconclusive; the ongoing suffering they indicate is evidence that women gain moral leverage, not control, by the intervention of a curandero. Still, in a social system that only minimally constrains the actions of men in regard to women, anything that provides pressure for moral accountability is a strategic resource.

Conclusion

In the Introduction, Sharon and I traced in brief outline the social and economic chaos that has shaped Peruvians' lives in the recent past, especially the period during which we interviewed curanderos and their patients. In Chapter 19 I argued that Peru's deepening crisis, together with the society's rigid social hierarchies, has made people increasingly depend on personal networks in order to survive. The resulting burden of economic self-interest loaded onto personal relationships has contributed to a social world in which mistrust inevitably accompanies interdependence. It should not be surprising, therefore, that social relations would be the assumed source of misfortune and suffering for Peruvians of the north coast. This contrasts with traditional Andean attributions of sickness to natural forces and supernatural transgressions.[9]

In this chapter I have shown that the historical forces that promoted a patriarchal public transcript also left women more vulnerable than men to the Janus-face of social intimacy. The "double exploitation" that women suffer as a result of the combination of sexual inequalities and economic stratification leaves them few open channels by means of which they can attempt to protect their own interests and those of their children. One avenue left to them, one means by which women "insinuate their resistance into the public transcript" (Scott 1990:136), is to find recourse in the practices of sorcerers and curanderos.[10]

It might well be argued, as other scholars have done for women's involvement in peripheral possession cults, that whatever gains women achieve through sorcery and curing are merely "rewards for colluding in their own oppression" (R. Gomm, in Lewis 1989:78). By this view, the work of curanderos and *brujos* could be credited with having more effect than merely serving as an emotional release for the oppressed (the "safety-valve" interpretation) without sacrificing the functionalist assumption that their rituals contribute to the maintenance of the status quo. In I. M. Lewis's (1989:78) words, "the tolerance by men of periodic, but always temporary, assaults on their authority by women appears as the price they have to pay to maintain their enviable position."

I would counter, following Scott (1990:192–97), that while male authority per se is not seriously challenged by the kind of resistance offered by curers and sorcerers, its limits are continually being tested by the threats and realities of magical aggression. By counterposing a public transcript of male domination against a hidden transcript of resistance we avoid an overly static view of gender relations. When we situate the work of curanderos and *brujos* in the contested frontier between the public and hidden transcripts, we acknowledge that these specialists help to keep the boundaries of male privilege in dispute.

Epilogue
Tinku

BY DONALD JORALEMON AND DOUGLAS SHARON

The commingling of opposites in ritual battles called *tinkus* is thought by many scholars to reflect a central conceptual category in traditional Andean culture (e.g., Hopkins 1982). Regina Harrison (1989:103) summarizes the key elements of the concept:

> It is a domain where two contrary or opposing forces or concepts co-exist and intermingle. This idea is apparent in González Holguín's gloss of *"la junta de las dos cosas"* (the coming together of two things) (1608). However, this co-existence, this meeting up of the two forces, is not without a sense of competition, too. The seventeenth-century dictionary gives one variant of the word as "to be opposites, to compete," with an underlying sense that this competition takes place between equals: "a pair of equal things such as gloves."

Tinku in traditional settings is said to address points of tension in various aspects of community life, especially those which stem from divisions within and between villages (Allen 1988:183–87, 206; Harrison 1989:52). The rituals are performed to promote and insure the regeneration of both the human community and the plants and animals on which it depends (Hopkins 1982).

Sharon (see Chapter 14) finds it useful to draw upon the notion of *tinku* in explaining how mesa symbols and rituals can simultaneously express opposition and mediation or balance. He argues that the syncretic combination of Hispanic and native Andean symbolism evidenced in the rituals of curanderos is itself a *tinku*-like competitive union, in which opposed forces are brought together in a temporary conjunction and applied to the task of healing (see also Bastien 1989). The curandero, Sharon explains, is employing philosophical and cosmological principles of great antiquity in the Andean region.[1]

Partial support for the *tinku*-like nature of curandero therapy can be found in the healers' terminology. For example, all of the shamans in our study refer to both the mesa and the healing ceremony as the "*juego*" (game). Joralemon (1984:7–10) has commented on the ludic and psychoanalytic implications of this word. We would simply amplify that interpretation here by noting an observation made by Hopkins (1982:182) in her survey of the literature on the *tinku*. She indicates that this ritual battle is frequently referred to as a "*juego*," probably translated from the Quechua *pukllay* (game, to battle), which is the term used in the southern highlands to designate the time of year (*Carnaval*) when such symbolic encounters take place.

Joralemon's analysis of the social impact of curanderos' rituals may also be related to the *tinku* notion of a competitive union. He shows the relationship between the suffering of the curanderos' patients, especially their women clients, and the "social truths and contradictions" (Lock and Scheper-Hughes 1990:71) of economic stratification and male domination. The work of curanderos, he argues, entails a balancing of these components of the public transcript with the opposed assumptions of reciprocity and complementarity of the hidden transcript. As is the case in the *tinku*, there is no question of any final resolution of these opposed definitions of social and economic reality. However, with the shaman acting at the "juncture of opposing forces" (Myerhoff 1976:102), there can be resistance offered and realignments of power in the context of individual lives.

The two parts of this book have also attempted what some might consider a *tinku*-like union: an ethnographic analysis that looks for the cultural roots of a curing tradition brought together with one that focuses on its application in the "here and now" of socioeconomic realities. We hope to have shown, however, that these are not opposed objectives. Each is contingent upon the testimony of individuals, both curanderos and their clients, whose thoughts and actions are conditioned by the forces of both cultural continuity and change.

Notes

Introduction

1 Gillin distinguished between *brujos curanderos*, who engaged in a benevolent form of sorcery (he preferred the Spanish word *brujeria*), from *maleros* or *hechiceros*, "bad *brujos*." He used the term *curandera* to refer to a woman herbal curer. In contemporary Peru, an herbalist is called *yerbatera*, or *herbolaria* and Gillin's contrast between a good and bad *brujo* is simply captured by *curandero* vs. *brujo*.

2 The widespread use of the word *ganadero*, literally "rancher, livestock herder," for the left side of the mesas of curanderos is difficult to explain, especially given the associations to sorcery and forces of the dead. However, several possibilities suggest themselves: 1) the name is incorrectly derived from the verb *ganar*, to win or dominate, and not from the noun or adjective *ganadero*; this yields the translation, "field of the one who wins or dominates" (Sharon's [1978:62] "Field of the Sly Dealer, Satan" was meant to be a poetic rendering encompassing the devil's guile in bargaining for domination of the souls of sorcerers and their victims [Glass-Coffin 1991:45]; 2) given the many animal and natural referents of the left side of the mesa, "herder" could be taken to indicate the ability of the curer to control or manage "animalistic" or subhuman forces; 3) the word *ganadero* during colonial times might have been associated with the Spanish who brought the cattle (*ganado*) and other European livestock to the New World, thus linking the power of the overlord to the forces of domination concentrated on the left side of the altar (see Ingham 1986:107–12); or 4) in contrast to the previous hypothesis, it might reflect the colonial association of pre-Hispanic fertility cults and artifacts (*huacos*, pre-Columbian ceramics, which predominate on the *ganadero* side) with Satan, symbolizing something not unlike the denigration of the pre-Christian religions of Europe. Whatever the case, it is striking that on the left side of a number of the mesas documented by Sharon and others there appear small figures, often in metal, of bulls. In highland folklore, silver bulls are associated with lagoons and the underworld Amaru serpent. See also note 5, below. See Glass-Coffin (1991:44–47, 51) for a "symbolic commodity" interpretation.

3 For just over one year (September 1978 to November 1979) Varvara Ferber, from the University of California, Los Angeles (UCLA) School of Education's graduate program, studied the transmission of herbal lore in Trujillo curanderismo. She apprenticed herself to two female herbalists (one of whom was Eduardo Calderón's mentor), earning her position as an assistant

by working as a vendor at her informants' herbal stands in a Trujillo market. Ferber (1992) has written a UCLA doctoral dissertation on her work with her second informant, Maria Vásquez.

In the early 1980s, Leonidas Cevallos (1983) participated in a session with a Chiclayo healer and discovered that the shaman associated the left side of his mesa with sorcery and the right with curing (ibid.:298).

From December 1983 to January 1984 the Peruvian scholar Carlos Molina (1984) studied a northern curandero from the town of Jequetepeque, located between Trujillo and Salas. His report offers verbatim interviews with the healer, concluding with a psychological analysis of his therapy. The documentation of the healer's mesa independently verifies the same balanced dualism expressed in other northern mesas.

Molina's informant applies an interesting variation of the dualistic formula for the spacing of mesa artifacts. For example, his mesa has a "defensive sector" running from the lower right corner, where stones from archaeological sites are positioned, to the upper left corner, where the healer places three flasks used to psychically visualize impending danger. A "curative sector" runs from the lower left-hand corner of the mesa, which contains two swords and a rattle, to the upper right-hand corner, where there are three flasks used to visualize curing remedies. At the intersection of the two sectors, in the middle of the mesa, there are no artifacts; instead, there is a cross stitched into the cloth on which the power objects rest at this center point. A "defensive axis" links the stitched cross to a defensive bottle, a candle, and a cross from the community of Motupe to the front and center of the mesa.

In the summer of 1984, another UCLA student began work on traditional healing in the suburbs of Trujillo. Bonnie Glass-Coffin (1984) completed an initial field survey on Peruvian attitudes to curanderismo, especially among the middle class. She has recently completed a doctoral dissertation (Glass-Coffin 1992) on women curers based on a year of fieldwork and archival research (October 1988 to September 1989).

In the late 1980s, Peruvian scholar Javier Macera (1989) studied traditional medicine in the communities of Mórrope and Salas, north of Chiclayo. His article provides a drawing of a mesa divided into two sides, designated as good and evil (ibid.:127, 135).

From 1984 to 1989, American anthropologist Donald Skillman (1990) has worked with four healers from Batan Grande, La Pescadera, and Salas. His 1990 publication documents the biography, mesa, and ritual of Salas healer Jorge Merino, whose patients are included in the outcome study related in Part II. Skillman's work with Merino is summarized in Chapter 12.

4 Peruvian anthropologist Lupe Camino (1992) has produced a thorough survey of traditional medicine in Huancabamba based upon ten field trips of about twenty days each, carried out from 1987 to 1989.

5 An interesting detail is provided by the healer's alternative designations of the three sections of the charted mesa. The left side is also called *mesa curandera* (curing), while the right is designated as *mesa criandera* (breeding). At first this would appear to be the opposite of Calderón's nomenclature. However, Giese (1989:101, 103, 148, 151) contends that curing, or at least the "cleansing" and "throwing away" aspects of curing, are left-hand functions, while "breeding" is a right-handed fertility function essential to the farming and herding people of the *sierra* where Polia works; fertility is also an aspect of good luck (*suertera*, luck-bringer)—a third designation provided for the right by Polia's

informant. The Moors (*moros*, or *moriscanos*) as well as the *gentiles* (ancient pre-Christian forefathers) are both unbaptized pagans and appear to have cure-facilitating and fertility/luck-bringing powers. This is shown by Polia's informant providing as second and third designations for his central *mesa mora* the terms *levantadora* ("raiser") and *paradora* ("stander"), both of which relate to the "raising" of tobacco, a major therapeutic action. A fourth designation for the middle sector, as Ganadero, may be based on the positive, fertility-enhancing functions associated with the literal translation of "rancher" in the highlands, while it carries the significance of "devil" on the coast (see Quispe 1969).

6 Women are also diviners (with Tarot cards) and specialists in a cleansing ritual performed with guinea pigs, the *limpia de cuy*. The focus on male curanderos in this text should not be taken as an indication of the relative contribution of males and females to curing in Peruvian culture. It simply reflects the fact that males clearly outnumber females in this specific curing role.

7 The male curers with whom we have worked whose rituals and curing philosophy are more influenced by Catholic liturgy and dogma also stress the importance of redemption through faith. In addition, we would note that several of Glass-Coffin's female informants perform rituals that are similar to those of our male informants, and that even the team whose ritual seems very different draws on the core notion that the sicknesses from which their patients suffer stem from acts of aggression (via sorcery).

Chapter 1

1 Fieldwork with Calderón was conducted during July and August, 1970; September and October, 1971; October and December, 1973; January to March, 1974; January, 1975; and February to September, 1977; as well as sporadically from March to May and from July to September, 1978. A preliminary case study of his patients was conducted from August to November of 1979. I also visited him briefly in June 1980, August 1981, and August 1985, as well as during six recent trips to Peru (1987 to 1991).

2 Joralemon (1990) has some provocative thoughts on the anthropologist as advisor and advocate—but not protector—of informants who become celebrities.

3 For the derivation of the word *tarjo*, see Giese (1989:319).

4 The ingredients are: liquified hallucinogenic San Pedro cactus, black tobacco juice, three perfumes (Tabu, *florida, cananga*), cane alcohol, sweet lime juice, lime, and sugar.

5 Power animals associated with the four cardinal directions is a concept partially traceable to the influence of psychologist Alberto Villoldo (Villoldo and Krippner 1986:92–97, 108, 142; Villoldo and Jendresen 1990:29, 248–50).

Chapter 2

1 Víctor's wife, Humildad, inherited his mesa and continued curing for two and a half years. During this time she literally wasted away out of grief, eventually dying in 1991. Her explanation before she died was that Víctor's

departed soul was calling her to accompany him in the afterlife, although on another occasion she suspected being a victim of sorcery.

Chapter 4

1 Motupe is famous throughout Peru for its August 5th religious festival, when a cross from Chalpón Mountain is brought down to the church on the main square. This cross is reputed to have been placed on the mountain in the mid-nineteenth century by the folk-saint Padre Guatemala, a hermit who inhabited a cave high on the heights above the town. This cave is now a pilgrimage site, where the faithful come to pray for miracles or to place tokens of gratitude for favors granted by the saint. Apparently, in an effort to eliminate the vestiges of pre-Columbian paganism, this semimythical personage placed four crosses on mountains which were sacred sites carried over from pre-Hispanic religion.

2 This sector of Guerrero's mesa is similar to the central *mesa mora* documented by Polia (1988a:149).

3 Longinus, according to tradition, was the Roman soldier who pierced Jesus with his lance.

Chapter 5

1 At the time that this book was in final revision, I received a letter from Peru informing me that Porfirio passed away in late 1991.

Chapter 9

1 Víctor subsequently changed his ritual site to the location in Moche described in this chapter, and, even more recently, to his home in Trujillo.

2 Víctor's hearing impairment is severe. He hears only when spoken to loudly and when there are no competing sounds in the room.

3 Despite the reduced patient load and less regular schedule, Víctor's clients are extremely dedicated and faithful, as is illustrated in Part II.

4 On the previous mesa these swords were placed at the far right.

5 Both of these seem incongruous with the symbolism of the Gloria section of the mesa.

6 When the group is large, the assistants must ingest substantial quantities of tobacco, which is vomited later in the night.

Chapter 11

1 Fieldwork in 1980–1981 was supported in part by a grant from the Organization of American States, as well as by travel funds from the Department of Anthropology of the University of California, Los Angeles.

Chapter 12

1 For a thorough ethnohistorical analysis of the *encanto* concept, see Giese (1989:158–74).

2 Giese (1989:171–72) notes that some northern healers tend not to differentiate between the powers of highland mountains and lagoons.

Chapter 13

1 For more on the enculturation of the curandero in Peru, see Sharon 1976b.

2 For a longer discussion of these issues, see Joralemon 1990.

Chapter 14

1 Giese seems to agree that our positions are not too far apart, as evidenced by his letter to me dated November 12, 1990: "I am glad about the solution you are giving about our discussion explaining the two points of view, showing that the differences are not so big and also mentioning that within the different healers there are differences. Likewise the quotations of Allen and Myerhoff fit well into this discussion."

2 The Ganadero's association with sorcery and pre-Columbian objects is complicated somewhat by the reference to Spaniards implied by the name "*ganadero*." See Note 2, Introduction.

3 The possibility of the mesa being used in Spanish folk medicine is being investigated by Claudius Giese (personal communication). If found there, the question arises as to whether the Latin American mesa is a cultural innovation borrowed from Spain or a syncretic blending of the two folk traditions. It would also be germane to investigate whether or not a shamanic Iberian substratum plays a role in popular Spanish Christianity.

4 Lionel Vallée (1982:114–19) maintains that Pachacuti's drawing also depicts the three vertical levels of the Inca cosmos, each with its own horizontal tripartite divisions of left, right, and center.

5 Claudius Giese (personal communication) points out that the shaman's body is also an axis linking three levels: feet (lower), trunk (middle), and head (upper).

Chapter 15

1 Trotter and Chavira (1981:167–68) also note the extensive use of this functional argument in the literature on Mexican-American curanderismo.

2 The real weakness of the psychofunctional model, in addition to its assumption of unproven psychological effects, is that it is built on a paradox. On the one hand, the model requires that a sorcerer's client believes that the act of aggression he/she contracts will have a real impact on its intended victim. Otherwise, there would be no psychological release of the frustrations that led the client to seek a sorcerer in the first place. On the other hand, the paradigm holds that, in fact, the sorcerer's aggression has no empirical effect; it

has only expressive or symbolic power and, even at that, only for the sorcerer's client. If sorcery had real, instrumental effects on others (i.e., the victims) then its social impact could well be negative, exacerbating already strained social relationships and leading to a cycle of attacks and counterattacks. Were this the case, it would be hard to maintain that sorcery contributes to a state of social equilibrium.

3 Most interviews were conducted by a single researcher, but circumstances sometimes resulted in a second team member being present. It was not feasible to regulate who did which interviews (e.g., same gender as the subject, randomized assignments).

4 Clients from upper-class backgrounds are underrepresented in the sample due to a consistent reluctance on their part to participate in the research. Ethnographic observation, however, indicates that they constitute a percentage of curandero clientele roughly equal to their numbers in the population at large. It should be noted that wealthier patients frequently contract for special, private rituals rather than taking part in regular performances. In one case, a curandero was brought to a prestigious hotel in Lima to perform a private healing ritual.

5 The BSI is a questionnaire "designed to reflect the psychological symptom patterns of psychiatric and medical patients as well as non-patient individuals" (Derogatis and Spencer 1982:6). In the present work I do not use the results from this part of the interviews because my primary concern here is not with the sorts of clinical questions (e.g., diagnosis, outcome) for which the instrument was designed.

6 Anthropologists have often used case material on patients in a highly selective fashion, using only those cases which contribute to a given argument and which include rich narrative detail. I cannot present all 129 of our cases, but this effort at randomizing those selected for presentation at least conveys a general sense of the range of persons who come to curanderos and of the quality of the interviews they provided us.

Chapter 16

1 This was the curer Nilo Plasencia originally assisted. It will be recalled that he is known for being very forceful, the perfect contrast to Víctor's style.

2 *Mal aire* is a culture-bound syndrome, usually seen as the result of exposure to naturally occurring forces associated with specific places (e.g., cemeteries). Here, the patient has described the sickness as the result of human intention. She may have meant something other than what is normally entailed by *mal aire*, since she referred to a hex or other sorcery related harm.

3 Since our female research assistant in Trujillo was American, while our male research assistant was Peruvian, it is difficult to determine whether gender or nationality played the greater role in the response of informants. Our Peruvian assistant elicited extensive and intimate answers from women and our American assistant completed similarly comprehensive interviews with men. My own experience doing these interviews, with or without one of our assistants present, confirms that the dynamics involved are far more complicated than would be suggested by the simplistic view that same-sex interviews are the ideal.

4 In Peruvian popular speech, to be *mal de los riñones* (sick from the kid-

neys) or *del hígado* (of the liver) can mean one is generally not well. The phrases are used to refer to any number of general abdominal complaints and/or digestive disorders.

5 The use of the verb *jugar*, to play, in this context refers to hexing, or ensorcelling. Elsewhere (Joralemon 1984a:7), I have discussed in greater detail the use of a ludic metaphor in curanderismo.

6 To be *envidiado* carries more significance in Peru than the English word "envied" conveys. Since envy is the operative emotion behind acts of sorcery, to be "envied" is to be at serious risk of being hurt by surreptitious aggression.

7 I suspect the percentage is actually higher since many of Flores's patients (32%) declined to specify the actual source of the *daño* from which they suffered.

Chapter 17

1 Nilo uses many diminutives in dialogues with patients during rituals, such as *mamita* (little mama), *caballerita* (little gentlewoman), *yerbitas* (little herbs), and *Diosito* (little God). He also mixes in expletives, neologisms, and onomatopoetic words/phrases. All of this makes translation very difficult. I have tried to maintain something of the flair of his speech, while also staying as close as possible to the Spanish.

2 To be *enmuñecado(a)* is to have had a voodoo-like doll made of you, with some article of your clothing on it, by a sorcerer. Nilo was the only one of the curanderos with whom we worked who included this idea in his curing, although Glass-Coffin (1992) reports on other shamans who refer to sorcery dolls.

3 The verb *ganar* is used here in several senses: to beat, to win, to dominate. It will be recalled (see Introduction, note 2) that the designation of the left side of mesas as the Ganadero might be derived from this verb, rather than from the noun.

4 Nilo's mesa has a brass bull on the left side used for counterattacks.

5 Nilo's speech during *rastreos* is frequently hard to follow, in part because it relates to visions to which only he is a party. Rather than clear up all the confusions, I have tried to stay as close to the Spanish transcription as possible.

6 The only other references to sexual misconduct on the part of a curandero were made by two patients recalling second-hand information about a curer in Iquitos. One other patient, a very troubled twenty-year-old who had been sexually assaulted by her stepfather, expressed a fear that Nilo would rape her.

7 The presence of a researcher taping the conversation between Nilo and his patient must have affected the interaction, even though Nilo tried to encourage his clients to speak freely. It is probable that patients are more responsive when no stranger is listening.

Chapter 18

1 See Joralemon (1990) for a discussion of Eduardo's involvement with New Age tours and its significance for his status as an anthropological informant.

2 In one of the cases we documented, Eduardo tried to shift responsibility

for continuing treatment to one of his sons, who has begun to perform rituals on his own, but the client was not entirely satisfied with this arrangement.

3 Mario Chiappe Costa (1979) noted the more frequent diagnosis of *susto* in rural, sierra communities. See Chapter 20 for further discussion of this contrast to the diagnosis of *daño* in urban settings.

4 Note that Eduardo's vision, like Jorge's and Nilo's, has olfactory content and that the metaphorical linkage between bad smells and sorcery is the same in all three cases.

5 Coincidentally, Maria's uncle was among those curanderos we had contacted earlier about participating in our study. We did not pursue this opportunity further because he was clearly not succeeding as a curer and had almost no patients.

Chapter 19

1 The Spanish is: "*Por mi salud, por mi felicidad, con estos lindos tabacos me voy convaleciendo, me voy fortaleciendo. ¡Arriba mi nombre! ¡Arriba mi sombra! ¡Arriba mi suerte! Voy levantando, voy suspendiendo. Por mi nombre, por mi sombra,* [patient name], *volteando mis males, volteando mis contagios, volteando mis hechizos, volteando maldades, volteando contrariedades. ¡Arriba mi nombre! ¡Arriba mi sombra y abajo mis males! ¡Abajo la parte contraria! ¡Abajo la parte enemiga! ¡Levanta, ya!*"

2 Susan Sontag's *Illness as Metaphor* (1977) analyzes what she takes to be the inappropriate use of sickness metaphors (e.g., of tuberculosis and cancer). Her argument, that we should eliminate metaphors from our language of disease, runs counter to Lakoff and Johnson's (1980) notion that even scientific concepts draw upon metaphor. The idea that our disease language is cleansed of metaphors when biological terms and concepts are used is refuted by the work of some medical anthropologists, including Emily Martin (1987, 1990).

3 It is striking that a similar analysis of the metaphorical structure of sickness and health done by Loring Danforth (1989) found "confinement" and "freedom" to be basic conceptualizations underlying the Anastenaria, the northern Greek fire-walking/possession ritual. In this case as well, women constitute the majority of the participants, and sociocultural gender inequalities are involved.

4 Curanderos vary according to the degree to which they compose songs specific to the situation of specific patients. For some, *tarjos* are essentially conventionalized; for others, a general formulaic structure is merely a point of departure for lyrics addressed to particular clients.

5 My suspicion is that the two metaphors are linked and that they relate to the accounting of sins on Judgment Day in the Roman Catholic tradition. The biblical reference (Rev. 3:5; 20:15) to the Book of Life, in which every person's sins are recorded, is included in the Catholic funeral mass. More importantly, in Peruvian folk Catholicism the idea is related to Satan as the record keeper. In ritual processions, for example, a costumed performer representing Satan carries an open book in which he writes the names of sinners. To be "accounted," then, is to have lost one's soul to Satan. Given the extensive associations in curandero philosophy between sorcery and the devil, the idea of being "named" or "accounted" is likely derived from this element in popular religion. Glass-Coffin (1991) offers an interesting alternative interpretation.

6 As Sharon noted, Giese's observations about the left/right associations

of curing acts builds on my earlier analysis (Joralemon 1983, 1984a), and on Hocquenghem's (1987) work on the Inca ceremonial calendar.

7 Allen (1988:149–50) reports that in communities near Cuzco ritual libations are performed for machines and animals on which households depend. Skillman found similar protective/luck rituals in the region near Salas (personal communication).

8 It is not possible to represent adequately the sensory/physical component of metaphors; the reader's empathy and imagination are required!

Chapter 20

1 Complementarity does not imply total equality between the sexes (Silverblatt 1987). However, relative to the situation that exists under Spanish custom and law, women were advantaged by traditional Andean social structure.

2 It would be a mistake to assume that complementary roles in independent communities assured stable marital unions; but access to land via bilateral inheritance at least gave women a "meaure of economic security and bargaining power not available to women on the haciendas" (Deere 1990:141).

3 Stevens (1973:91) calls this correlate to machismo "marianismo," "the cult of feminine spiritual superiority which teaches that women are semi-divine, morally superior to, and spiritually stronger than men." Because it supports the assumption that women are "naturally" altruistic and forgiving, marianismo denies women the opportunity to speak out against the abuses they suffer at the hands of men.

4 Even recent changes in the civil code designed to improve the rights of women in regards to receiving child support have proven ineffective because of a backlogged and corrupt legal system. In addition, legal costs often inhibit poor women from pursuing enforcement of their civil rights.

5 Scott's argument parallels I. M. Lewis's (1989:26–27) analysis of women's possession cults as an "oblique aggressive strategy" that can "protect women from the exactions of men, and offer an effective vehicle for manipulating husbands and male relatives."

6 Scott (1990:184–92) debates these questions in general, theoretical terms. He identifies the shortcomings of the "safety-valve" argument, which, as I reviewed it for the Peruvian case, sees a variety of forms of resistance on the part of subordinate groups as harmless releases of anger. He concludes that "the aggregation of thousands upon thousands of such 'petty' acts of resistance has dramatic economic and political effects" (ibid.:192).

7 Glass-Coffin (1992:186–87, 201, 253) reports on several cases that are similar to Segundo's, that is, in which women are suspected of causing harm to men.

8 Danforth's analysis represents a significant improvement over the argument of I. M. Lewis (1989) that possession rituals like these do nothing more than give women an approved channel for releasing frustrations and anger. Another challenge to Lewis's explanation is found in Holmberg (1983).

9 See Note 3, Chapter 18.

10 While I have focused on the clients of curanderos who link their afflictions to gender-related conflicts, the same line of analysis would apply as well to those who attribute their suffering to daño stemming from tensions or

NOTES TO PAGE 271

ruptures in other types of social relationships. All instances of *daño* are ultimately traceable to the effects of competition in a society where privilege,
whether defined by gender or class, burdens personal relationships with economic interests. Sorcerers and curanderos, in all cases, step into the contested
domain of interpersonal relations and fight to tip the scale in favor of those
whom the social system has disenfranchised or who fear the retribution of the
oppressed.

Epilogue

1 A 1988 symposium on Andean cosmologies held at Indiana University
explored the topics of persistence and emergence. These two themes are described by Robert Dover (1992:7) in the introduction to the resulting anthology as "different and complementary aspects of a process of Andean cosmological thinking."
   With regard to persistence or "structural continuity," Dover (ibid.:8) points
out that "Throughout the Andes, duality or some permutation of duality (bi-
partization, mediated tripartization, quadripartization, reciprocity, hierarchical opposition, balanced and non-hierarchical opposition, among others) in-
forms most . . . relationships . . . : people to people, people to supernatural,
people to nation-state, and Andean to non-Andean. . . . Andean peoples tend
to perceive or structure their personal and cultural relationships in dualistic
terms. How they do this varies according to circumstances."
   On the other hand, Dover (ibid.) shows that emergence or "processual continuity" results from "Andean peoples' facility for the incorporation of intra-
and intercultural systems into a specific Andean context. Transformation; ap-
propriation; reappropriation; invention; metaphoric, metonymic, and structural substitutions; repetition of coreferential structures and metaphoric cultural relations between cultural systems: these are the tools of cosmological
discourse by which Andean peoples contextualize preexisting cosmologies
and imposed social and political constraints and influences."

Glossary

afición: inclination
agua: water
agua florida: perfumed water
aire: air
aire de huaca: air of the pagan dead, associated with archaeological ruins
aire de muerto: air of the dead, associated with cemeteries
alzador: "raiser," shaman's ritual assistant
amarrar: to tie-up
ánimo: spirit, soul (popular speech), courage
antimonio de gentiles: a folk disease related to "airs" from ancient tombs
ara: altar
atar: to bind, fasten
banco: bank, bench, field, zone, area (syn. *campo*)
bejuco: reed, liana, branch
botar: to throw out, *botando*
brujo(a):   sorcerer (sorceress)
calavera: skull
calicanto: force of accumulated spirits; opposite of *encanto*
campo: field, zone, area (syn. *banco*)
cananga: red perfumed water
caracol: spiral seashell; conch shell
carbunco: supernatural guardian spirit
centro: center, middle
cerro: mountain
coca: *Erythroxylon coca*
compactado: contracted to the Devil
compacto: close, pact (as used in Peru), deal
compadrazgo: godparenthood
compadre: godfather
contar: to tell, to narrate, to count
contra: counter
conviviente: common-law spouse
cristal: crystal, cut-glass perfume bottle, quartz crystal
cuenta: story, narrative, "account"
curanderismo: shamanic healing
curandero(a):   curer, shaman (shamaness) (Peru)
cuy: guinea pig; *limpia de c.*:   guinea pig cleansing
chacra: agricultural field

cholo: half-breed, mestizo, dark-skinned
chonta: palmwood staff
chullo: Quechua cap
chupa: sucking-out
daño: harm caused by sorcery; *d. por boca*, harm . . . through the mouth; *d. por aire*, harm . . . through the air
defensa: defense
derecha: right (side)
despacho: dispatch; burnt offering (Peru)
despejarse: to clear one's mind, to become clear-sighted
destrancar: to unbolt, unchain
diamante: "diamond," quartz crystal, iron pyrites, cut-glass bottle
doga: large jungle snake, probably the anaconda
don: gift, talent
encantar: to enchant
encantos: charms, spells, enchantments
enguayanchero: specialist in love magic
enterrado: buried; a buried voodoo-like object (syn. *entierro*)
envidia: envy
envidiado: envied, vulnerable to sorcery
enyerbado: under the influence of San Pedro
espada: sword
espiritista: spiritualist medium
espíritu: spirit
florecimiento: flowering, fortune-enhancing
ganadero(a): livestock herder (see Introduction, Note 2)
genio: genie
gentiles: gentiles; pre-Hispanic peoples of Peru; pagan ancestors
gloria: heaven
golpe: blow; *golpeado*; *golpeando*; *golpear*
gringo: foreigner, of light complexion
guardián: guardian, custodian, watchman
guayanchero: specialist in love magic (syn. *enguayanchero*)
hacienda: agricultural estate
herbolario(a): herbalist
huaca: archaeological sites, ruins, shrines
huacos: archaeological artifacts
huaqueros: robbers of pre-Columbian graves
Huaringas: highland lagoons sacred to shamans
illas: fertility figurines, power objects (Aymara)
imán: magnet
incaychus: fertility figurines, power objects (Quechua)
izquierda: left (side)
jalar: to pull, capture
juego: game, set, "playing"; *j. de gloria*: playing or game of heaven
levantadora: the one who raises, ritual assistant
levantando: raising
levantar: to raise (up)
limpia: cleansing
llamar: to call
macho: masculine, tough

madriguero(a):   burrow, den, lair; of the dawn and herbs
maestro: teacher, wise person, *curandero*, shaman
mal: evil, bad
mal aire: evil wind (a culture-bound syndrome)
maldad: a hex; something evil or wicked
medio: middle, center
membrillo: quince tree
mesa: curer's altar; *m. blanca, negra, mora, curandera, criandera, ganadera, yerbatera, del astro, del imán, de afuera, contra m., de respaldo*
mestizo: mixed breed
minerales: minerals
misha: Datura
moriscano: of or pertaining to pagan Moors
moros: Moors
muñeco(a):   doll, used in sorcery *enmuñecado(a)*:   the victim of whom a sorcery-doll has been made
naipes: Tarot cards
palo: stick, staff
paquete: a likeness of a person used in sorcery; usually buried in a cemetery
parada de suerte: standing-up of luck
paradora: one who stands-up others, ritual assistant
parando: standing-up
prendas: article of clothing or photograph used in sorcery and/or curing
rastreo: tracking, diagnosis
rastrero(a):   one who tracks, diagnoses
rayar: to create lightning
refresco: refreshment; specifically, the mixture of cornmeal, holy water, white flowers, sugar, and sweet lime juice used at the end of rituals
remedio: the San Pedro mixture
remolinos: whirlwinds, whirlpools
respaldar: reinforce
santo: saint
seguro: good-luck charm
shapingos: spirits of the dead in general
sombra: shadow, shade, spirit
soplón: sorcery by blowing
sorber: to sip, suck, sniff, sniffle; to soak up, absorb
suerte: luck
suertera: luck-bringer, *mesa* field
susto: fright or soul loss resulting from a sudden shock caused by a variety of agents
tabaco: tobacco; specifically, the mixture of liquified tobacco, perfumes, lime juice, and cane alcohol used during rituals
tarjos: shamanic power songs
tartamudo: stutterer
telepatía: telepathy
traga luz: a place where light is sucked in or "swallowed"
Tucuricoc: "chief" (Quechua)
tumi: a Moche sacrificial knife
visión: vision, sight, insight

vista: sight, vision, insight
vista en virtud: sight in virtue, vision, insight
vivo(a): clever, tricky, deceitful, untrustworthy
volteando: turning around; *volteada*: ritual in which sorcery is reversed
yerba: herb
yerbatero(a): herbalist
yonque: sugarcane alcohol

References

Abu-Lughod, L.
  1986   *Veiled Sentiments: Honor and Poetry in a Bedouin Society.*
          Berkeley: University of California Press.
Allen, C. J.
  1988   *The Hold Life Has: Coca and Cultural Identity in an Andean
          Community.* Washington, D.C.: Smithsonian Institution.
Anderson, J.
  1989   Women's Community Service and Child Welfare in Urban
          Peru. In *Women, Work, and Child Welfare in the Third World.*
          American Association for the Advancement of Science
          Selected Symposium, No. 110. J. Leslie and M. Paolisso, eds.,
          pp. 237–55. Boulder, CO: Westview.
Andreas, C.
  1985   *When Women Rebel: The Rise of Popular Feminism in Peru.*
          Westport, CT: Lawrence Hill and Company.
Atkinson, J. M.
  1987   The Effectiveness of Shamans in an Indonesian Ritual.
          American Anthropologist 89:342–55.
Babb, F. E.
  1989   *Between Field and Cooking Pot: The Political Economy of
          Marketwomen in Peru.* Austin: University of Texas Press.
Barrig, M.
  1989   The Difficult Equilibrium between Bread and Roses: Women's
          Organizations and the Transition from Dictatorship to
          Democracy in Peru. In *The Women's Movement in Latin America:
          Feminism and the Transition to Democracy.* J. S. Jaquette, ed., pp.
          114–48. Boston: Unwin Hyman.
Bastien, J. W.
  1987   *Healers of the Andes: Kallawaya Herbalists and Their Medicinal
          Plants.* Salt Lake City: University of Utah Press.
  1989   A Shamanistic Curing Ritual of the Bolivian Aymara. *Journal
          of Latin American Lore* 15(1):73–94.
Bolton, R.
  1974   To Kill a Thief: A Kallawaya Sorcery Session in the Lake
          Titicaca Region of Peru. *Anthropos* 69:191–215.
Bonner, R.
  1988   A Reporter at Large: Peru's War. *Atlantic Monthly* 63
          (6):31–58.

Bourque, S., and K. B. Warren
1981   *Women of the Andes: Patriarchy and Social Change in Two Peruvian Towns.* Ann Arbor: University of Michigan Press.
Bronstein, A.
1982   *The Triple Struggle: Latin American Peasant Women.* Boston: South End Press.
Bunster, X., and E. M. Chaney
1985   *Sellers and Servants: Working Women in Lima, Peru.* South Hadley, MA: Bergin and Garvey.
Burger, R. L.
1992   The Sacred Center of Chavín de Huántar. In *The Ancient Americas: Art from Sacred Landscapes.* R. F. Townsend, ed., pp. 265–78. Chicago: The Art Institute of Chicago.
Calderón, E., R. Cowan, D. Sharon and F. K. Sharon
1982   *Eduardo, el Curandero: The Words of a Peruvian Healer.* Richmond, CA: North Atlantic Books.
Calderon, E., and D. Sharon
1978   *Terápia de la curanderia.* Trujillo: Edigraf.
Camino, Lupe
1992   *Cerros, plantas y lagunas poderosas: La medicina al norte del Perú.* Lima: Lluvia Editores.
Cevallos, L.
1983   En la mesa de don Gerardo Pizarro. *Anthropológica* 1:291–300.
Chiappe Costa, M.
1967   Alucinógenos nativos. *Revista del Viernes Médico* (Lima) 18(3):293–99.
1969   Psiquiatría folklórica peruana: El curanderismo en la costa norte del Perú. *Anales del Servicio de Psiquiatría,* Vol. 11, nos. 1–2. Lima: Hospital del Obrero, Sección de Psiquiatría.
1970a   El curanderismo con alucinógenos de la costa y la selva del Perú. In *Psiquiatría Peruana* (Primer Congreso Nacional de Psiquiatría). O. Valdivia P. and A. Péndola, eds., pp. 318–25. Lima: Imprenta Amauta.
1970b   El síndrome de "daño" y su tratamiento curanderil. In *Psiquiatría Peruana.* O. Valdivia P. and A. Péndola, eds., pp. 330–37. Lima: Imprenta Amauta.
1979   Nosografia de la curanderia. In *Psiquiatría folklórica.* C. A. Seguín, ed., pp. 76–92. Lima: Ediciones Ermar.
Chiappe Costa, M., M. Lemlíj and L. Millones
1985   *Alucinógenos y shamanismo en el Perú contemporáneo.* Lima: Ediciones El Virrey.
Cowan, R., and D. Sharon
1978   *Eduardo the Healer.* Distributed by Pennsylvania State University Audio-Visual Services, University Park, PA.
Crain, M. M.
1991   Poetics and Politics in the Ecuadorian Andes: Women's Narratives of Death and Devil Possession. *American Ethnologist* 18(1):67–89.
Crandon-Malamud, L.
1991   *From the Fat of Our Souls: Social Change, Political Process, and*

Medical Pluralism in Bolivia. Berkeley: University of California Press.

Cruz-Sánchez, G.
1948a   Farmacología de Opuntia cylíndrica. *Revista de Farmacología y Medicina Experimental* (Lima) 1:143–65.
1948b   Informe sobre las aplicaciones populares de la címora en el norte del Perú. *Revista de Farmacología y Medicina Experimental* 1:253–58.
1951   Estudio folklórico de algunas plantas medicamentosas y tóxicas de la región norte del Perú. *Revista de Medicina Experimental* (Lima) 9(1):159–66.

Csordas, T. J.
1983   The Rhetoric of Transformation in Ritual Healing. *Culture, Medicine and Psychiatry* 7:333–75.
1988   Elements of Charismatic Persuasion and Healing. *Medical Anthropology Quarterly* 2:121–42.

Dammert Bellido, J.
1974   Procesos por supersticiones en la provincia de Cajamarca en la segunda mitad del siglo xviii. *Allpanchis Phuturinqa* 9:179–200.
1984   Procesos por supersticiones en la provincia de Cajamarca en la segunda mitad del siglo xviii. *Allpanchis Phuturinqa* 20:177–82.

Danforth, L.
1989   *Firewalking and Religious Healing: The Anastenaria of Greece and the American Firewalking Movement.* Princeton: Princeton University Press.

Deere, C. D.
1990   *Household and Class Relations: Peasants and Landlords in Northern Peru.* Berkeley: University of California Press.

Derogatis, L. R., and P. M. Spencer
1982   *The Brief Symptom Inventory (BSI): Administration, Scoring and Procedures Manual.* Baltimore: Clinical Psychometric Research.

Dobkin de Rios, M.
1968   *Trichocereus pachanoi*: A Mescaline Cactus Used in Folk Healing in Peru. *Economic Botany* 22:191–94.
1968–69   Folk Curing with a Psychedelic Cactus in North Coast Peru. *International Journal of Social Psychiatry* 15:23–32.
1969a   Curanderismo psicodélico en el Perú: Continuidad y cambio. *Mesa Redonda de Ciencias Prehistóricas y Antropológicas* 1:139–49. Publicaciones del Instituto Riva-Aguero, No. 53A.
1969b   Fortune's Malice: Divination, Psychotherapy, and Folk Medicine in Peru. *Journal of American Folklore* 82:132–41.
1976   The Relationship between Witchcraft Beliefs and Psychosomatic Illness. In *Anthropology and Mental Health: Setting a New Course.* J. Westermeyer, ed. The Hague: Mouton.
1979   Curanderismo psicodélico en el Perú: Continuidad y cambio. In *Psiquiatría folklórica.* C. A. Seguín, ed., pp. 67–75. Lima: Editorial Imprenta Amauta.
1989   Power and Hallucinogenic States of Consciousness among the

Moche. In *Altered States of Consciousness and Mental Health: A Cross-Cultural Perspective*. C. A. Ward, ed., pp. 285–99. London: Sage.

Dobyns, H. E., and P. I. Doughty
1976   *Peru: A Cultural History*. New York: Oxford University Press.

Doore, G. (ed.)
1988   *Shaman's Path: Healing, Personal Growth and Empowerment*. Boston: Shambhala.

Dover, R., K. Seibold and J. McDowell, eds.
1992   *Andean Cosmologies through Time: Persistence and Emergence*. Bloomington: Indiana University Press.

Dow, J.
1986a   *The Shaman's Touch: Otomi Indian Symbolic Healing*. Salt Lake City: University of Utah Press.
1986b   Universal Aspects of Symbolic Healing: A Theoretical Synthesis. *American Anthropologist* 88:56–69.

Dragunsky, L.
1968   El curanderismo en la costa norte peruana. Unpublished manuscript.

Dressler, W. W.
1990   Culture, Stess, and Disease. In *Medical Anthropology: Contemporary Theory and Method*. T. M. Johnson and C. F. Sargent, eds., pp. 248–67. New York: Praeger.

Eliade, M.
1964   *Shamanism: Archaic Techniques of Ecstasy*. Princeton: Princeton University Press.

Ferber, V.
1992   The Magical and Medicinal Lore of Herbal Healing in Peru: Flowers from Maria. Ph.D. dissertation. Los Angeles: University of California.

Fernandez, J.
1971   Persuasions and Performances: Of the Beast in Every Body . . . And the Metaphors of Everyman. In *Myth, Symbol and Culture*. C. Geertz, ed., pp. 39–60. New York: W. W. Norton and Company.

Figueroa, B., and J. Anderson
1981   *Women in Peru*. London: Change International Reports, Women and Society, No. 5.

Finkler, K.
1985   *Spiritualist Healers in Mexico: Successes and Failures of Alternative Therapeutics*. South Hadley, MA: Bergin and Garvey.

Fort, A.
1988   La mujer en la política de servicios. In *De vecinas a ciudadanas: La mujer en el desarrollo urbano*. M. Barrig, ed., pp. 143–85. Lima: Grupo de Trabajo SUMBI.

Frank, J. D.
1973   *Persuasion and Healing: A Comparative Study of Psychotherapy*. New York: Schocken Books (first published, 1961).

Friedberg, C.
1959   Rapport sommaire sur une mission au Perou. *Journal d'Agriculture Tropicale et de Botanique Appliquée* 6:439–50.

1960   Utilisation d'un cactus a mescaline au nord du Perou. *6th
            International Congress of Anthropological and Ethnological Sciences*
            2:21–26.
1963   Mission au Perou—Mai 1961–Mars 1962. *Journal d'Agriculture
            Tropicale et de Botanique Appliquée* 10:33–52, 245–58, 344–86.
1979   L'imaginaire dans les therapeutiques populaires. *42nd
            International Congress of Americanists, Proceedings* 6:427–43.
            Paris.
Frisancho Pineda, D.
1986   *Curanderismo y brujería en la costa peruana.* Lima: Lytograf.
Furst, P. T.
1973–74   The Roots and Continuities of Shamanism. *Artscanada* 184–
            87:33–60.
1976   *Hallucinogens and Culture.* Novato, CA: Chandler and
            Sharp.
Gente Editores
1988   Secretos de curanderos. *Gente* (Lima) 653 (July 14):68–70.
Giese, C.
1983   Cerro Mulato Felsbilder eines "Encanto" im Norden Perus.
            Baessler-Archiv 31:299–312.
1988   Dualismo y tripartición. Paper presented at the 46th
            International Congress of Americanists. Amsterdam.
1989a   "Curanderos," Traditionelle Heiler in Nord-Peru (Küste und
            Hochland). *Münchner Beiträge zur Amerikanistik*, Band 20.
            Hohenschaftlarn: Klaus Renner Verlag.
1989b   Die Diagnosemethode eines nordperuanischen Heilers. *Curare*
            12:81–87.
Gillin, J. P.
1947   *Moche: A Peruvian Coastal Community.* Washington, D.C.:
            Smithsonian Institution, Institute of Social Anthropology, No.
            3.
1955   Ethos Components in Modern Latin American Culture.
            American Anthropologist 57:488–500.
Glass-Coffin, B.
1984   Health Care Decision Making among an Urban Middle Class
            Population: Trujillo, Peru. M.A. thesis. Los Angeles:
            University of California.
1988   El daño, el cuento, y el chisme: El poder de la palabra en la
            medicina tradicional de la costa norte del Perú. *2° Congreso
            Internacional de Medicinas Tradicionales*, pp. 157–62. Lima.
1991   Discourse, Daño and Healing in North Coastal Peru. *Medical
            Anthropology* 13(1–2):33–55.
1992   The Gift of Life: Female Healing and Experience in
            Northern Peru. Ph.D. dissertation. Los Angeles: University of
            California.
González Viaña, E.
1979   *Habla, San Pedro: Llama a los brujos.* Barcelona: Editorial Argos
            Vergara.
Good, B. J.
1977   The Heart of What's the Matter: The Semantics of Illness in
            Iran. *Culture, Medicine and Psychiatry* 1:25–58.

Good, B. J., and M. Delvecchio Good
  1980   The Meaning of Symptoms: A Cultural Hermeneutic Model
            for Clinical Practice. In *The Relevance of Social Science for
            Medicine*. L. Eisenberg and A. Kleinman, eds., pp. 165–96.
            Dordrecht, Holland: D. Reidel.
  1981   The Semantics of Medical Discourse. In *Sciences and Cultures,
            Sociology of the Sciences*, vol. 5. E. Mendelsohn and Y. Elkana,
            eds., pp. 177–212. Dordrecht, Holland: D. Reidel.
  1982   Toward a Meaning-Centered Analysis of Popular Illness
            Categories: "Fright Illness" and "Heart Distress" in Iran. In
            Cultural Conceptions of Mental Health and Therapy. A. J. Marsella
            and G. M. White, eds., pp. 141–66. Dordrecht, Holland: D.
            Reidel.
Greenfield, S. M.
  1992   Spirits and Spiritist Therapy in Southern Brazil: A Case
            Study of an Innovative, Syncretic Healing Group. *Culture,
            Medicine and Psychiatry* 16:23–51.
Gushiken, J.
  1977   *Tuno: El curandero*. Lima: Universidad Nacional Mayor de San
            Marcos.
Gutiérrez-Noriega, C.
  1950   Área de mescalinismo en el Perú. *América Indígena* 10:215–20.
Gutiérrez-Noriega, C., and G. Cruz Sánchez
  1947   Alteraciones mentales producidas por la Opuntia cylindrica.
            Revista de Neuro-Psiquiatría 10:422–68.
Harrison, R.
  1989   *Signs, Songs, and Memory in the Andes: Translating Quechua
            Language and Culture*. Austin: University of Texas Press.
Hocquenghem, A. M.
  1985   El Orden Andino: Materialien zur Lehre des Lateinamerika-
            Instituts der Freien Universität Berlin. Berlin.
  1987   *Iconografía mochica*. Lima: Pontificia Universidad Católica del
            Perú, Fondo Editorial.
Holmberg, D.
  1983   Shamanic Soundings: Femaleness in the Tamang Ritual
            Structure. *Signs* 9:40–58.
Hopkins, D.
  1982   Juego de enemigos. *Allpanchis Phuturinqa* 17(2):167–89.
Ingham, J. M.
  1986   *Mary, Michael, and Lucifer: Folk Catholicism in Central Mexico*.
            Austin: University of Texas Press.
Instituto Nacional de Estadística, Ministerio de Salud
  1984   *Encuesta nacional de nutrición y salud: Informe general*. Lima:
            Dirección General de Censos y Encuestas.
Isbell, W.
  1978   Cosmological Order Expressed in Prehistoric Ceremonial
            Centers. *42nd International Congress of Americanists, Proceedings*
            4:269–97. Paris.
Joralemon, D.
  1983   The Symbolism and Physiology of Ritual Healing in a
            Peruvian Coastal Community. Ph.D. dissertation. University of

California, Los Angeles. Ann Arbor, Mich.: University Microfilms.

1984a   Sacred Space and Ritual Time in a Peruvian Healing Ceremony. *San Diego Museum of Man Ethnic Technology Notes*, No. 19.

1984b   The Role of Hallucinogenic Drugs and Sensory Stimuli in Peruvian Ritual Healing. *Culture, Medicine and Psychiatry* 8:399–430.

1985   Altar Symbolism in Peruvian Ritual Healing. *Journal of Latin American Lore* 11:3–29.

1986   The Performing Patient in Ritual Healing. *Social Science and Medicine* 23:841–45.

1990   The Selling of the Shaman and the Problem of Informant Legitimacy. *Journal of Anthropological Research* 46(2):105–18.

Kennedy, J. G.

1967   Psychological and Social Explanations of Witchcraft. *Man* 2:216–25.

1969   Psychosocial Dynamics of Witchcraft Systems. *International Journal of Social Psychiatry* 15:165–78.

1974   Cultural Psychiatry. In *Handbook of Social and Cultural Anthropology*. J. J. Honigmann, ed., pp. 1119–98. Chicago: Rand McNally.

Kiev, A.

1968   *Curanderismo: Mexican-American Folk Psychiatry*. New York: Free Press.

Klarén, P.

1976   *Formación de las haciendas azucareras y origines de APRA*. Lima: Instituto de Estudios Peruanos.

Kleinman, A.

1980   *Patients and Healers in the Context of Culture: An Exploration of the Borderland between Anthropology, Medicine and Psychiatry*. Berkeley: University of California Press.

Kleinman, A., and J. L. Gale

1982   Patients Treated by Physicians and Folk Healers: A Comparative Outcome Study in Taiwan. *Culture, Medicine and Psychiatry* 6:405–23.

Kleinman, A., and L. H. Sung

1979   Why Do Indigenous Practitioners Successfully Heal? *Social Science and Medicine* 13B:7–26.

Kluckhohn, C.

1967   *Navaho Witchcraft*. Boston: Beacon (first published, 1946).

Lakoff, G.

1987   *Women, Fire, and Dangerous Things: What Categories Reveal about the Mind*. Chicago: University of Chicago Press.

Lakoff, G., and M. Johnson

1980   *Metaphors We Live By*. Chicago: University of Chicago Press.

Lastres, J. B.

1951   *Historia de la medicina peruana*. 3 vols. Lima: Imprenta Santa Maria.

Lathrap, D.

1971   Gifts of the Cayman: Some Thoughts on the Subsistence

Basis of Chavin. In *Variations in Anthropology*. D. Lathrap and
J. Douglas, eds., pp. 91–105. Urbana: Illinois Archaeological
Society.
1985   Jaws: The Control of Power in the Early Nuclear American
Ceremonial Center. In *Early Ceremonial Architecture in the Andes*.
C. B. Donnan, ed., pp. 241–67. Washington, D.C.: Dumbarton
Oaks Research Library and Collection.
Levi-Strauss, C.
1967   The Effectiveness of Symbols. In *Structural Anthropology*. New
York: Doubleday.
Lewis, I. M.
1989   *Ecstatic Religion: A Study of Shamanism and Spirit Possession*,
Second Edition. New York: Routledge.
Lock, M., and N. Scheper-Hughes
1990   A Critical-Interpretive Approach in Medical Anthropology:
Rituals and Routines of Discipline and Dissent. In *Medical
Anthropology: Contemporary Theory and Method*. T. M. Johnson
and C. F. Sargent, eds., pp. 47–72. New York: Praeger.
Lyon, P. J.
1979   Female Supernaturals in Ancient Peru. *Ñawpa Pacha* 16:
95–140.
MacLean y Estenós, R.
1942   *Sociologia peruana*. Lima: Gil.
Macera, J.
1989   Medicina tradicional y curanderismo en las comunidades
campesinas de Mórrope y Salas. *Alternativa* 11:117–35.
Martin, E.
1987   *The Woman in the Body: A Cultural Analysis of Reproduction*.
Boston: Beacon Press.
1990   Toward an Anthropology of Immunology: The Body as
Nation State. *Medical Anthropology Quarterly* 4(4):410–26.
Millones, L.
1981   Los hechizos del Perú: Continuidad y cambio en las religiones
andinas en los siglos xvi-xviii. *Cielo Abierto* 15:3–15.
1982   Brujerías de la costa/brujerías de la sierra: Estudio
comparativo de dos complejos religiosos en el área andina.
Senri Ethnological Studies, No. 10. El hombre y su ambiente en
los Andes Centrales. Osaka, Japan: National Museum of
Ethnology.
Moerman, D. E.
1979   Anthropology of Symbolic Healing. *Current Anthropology*
20:59–80.
1983   Physiology and Symbols: The Anthropological Implications of
the Placebo Effect. In *The Anthropology of Medicine: From
Culture to Method*. L. Romanucci-Ross, D. E. Moerman and L.
R. Tancred, eds., pp. 156–67. New York: Praeger.
Molina, C.
1984   Don Hermógenes Miranda: Un curandero llamado Pato
Pinto. *Anthropológica* 2:345–86.
Myerhoff, B.
1976   Shamanic Equilibrium: Balance and Mediation in Known and

Unknown Worlds. In *American Folk Medicine*. W. D. Hand, ed.,
pp. 99–108. Los Angeles: University of California Press.

1978   Peyote and the Mystic Vision. In *Art of the Huichol Indians*. K.
Berrin, ed., pp. 56–70. New York: Harry N. Abrams, Inc.

Ness, R.

1980   The Impact of Indigenous Healing Activity: An Empirical
Study of Two Fundamentalist Churches. *Social Science and
Medicine* 14B:147–80.

Nichter, M.

1982   Idioms of Distress: Alternatives in the Expression of
Psychosocial Distress: A Case Study from South India. *Culture,
Medicine and Psychiatry* 5:379–408.

Peters, L., and D. Price-Williams

1980   Towards an Experiential Analysis of Shamanism. *American
Ethnologist* 7:398–418.

Polia Meconi, M.

1988a   *Las lagunas de los encantos: Medicina tradicional andina del Perú
septentrional*. Lima: Gráfica Bellido.

1988b   Glosario del curanderismo andino en el Departamento de
Piura, Perú. *Anthropológica* 6:179–238.

1989   "Contagio" y "perdida de la sombra" en la teoría y práctica
del curanderismo andino del Perú septentrional: Provincias
de Ayabaca y Huancabamba. *Anthropológica* 7:197–231.

1990   Apuntes de campo: Cinco mitos huancabambinos. *Perú
Indígena* 12(28):95–109.

Quispe M., U.

1969   *La herranza en Choque Huarcaya y Huancasancos, Ayacucho*. Lima:
Instituto Indigenista Peruano.

Rasnake, R. N.

1988   *Domination and Cultural Resistance: Authority and Power among an
Andean People*. Durham: Duke University Press.

Reichel-Dolmatoff, G.

1971   *Amazonian Cosmos: The Sexual and Religious Symbolism of the
Tukano Indians*. Chicago: University of Chicago Press.

1974   Funerary Customs and Religious Symbolism among the Kogi.
In *Native South Americans: Ethnology of the Least Known
Continent*. P. J. Lyon, ed., pp. 289–301. Boston: Little, Brown.

Reid, M.

1985   *Peru: Paths to Poverty*. London: Latin American Bureau
(Research and Action).

Rodriguez Suy Suy, V. A.

1973   La medicina tradicional en la costa norte del Perú actual.
Boletín Chiquitayap 1 (Year 1, No. 1, part 5).

Roe, P. G.

1982   *The Cosmic Zygote: Cosmology in the Amazon Basin*. New
Brunswick, NJ: Rutgers University Press.

Rotondo, H.

1970   *Estudios sobre la familia en su relación con la salud*. Lima:
Universidad Nacional Mayor de San Marcos.

Rowe, J. H.

1967   Form and Meaning in Chavin Art. In *Peruvian Archaeology:*

Selected Readings. J. H. Rowe and D. Menzel, eds., pp. 72–103. Palo Alto, CA: Peak.

Schultes, R. E., and A. Hofmann
1973   *The Botany and Chemistry of Hallucinogens.* Springfield, IL: Charles C. Thomas.

Scott, J.
1985   *Weapons of the Weak: Everyday Form of Peasant Resistance.* New Haven: Yale University Press.
1990   *Domination and the Arts of Resistance: Hidden Transcripts.* New Haven: Yale University Press.

Seguín, C. A.
1970   Psiquiatría folklórica. In *Psiquiatría peruana.* O. Valdivia and A. Péndola, eds., vol. 1, pp. 301–39. Lima: Amauta.
1974   Introducción a la psiquiatría folklórica. *Acta Psiquiátrica y Psicológica de América Latina* 20:305–42.
1977   Estado actual y perspectivas de la psiquiatría folklórica. In *Psiquiatría peruana.* S. Peña, O. Valdivia, and J. Alva, eds., vol. 4, pp. 100–105. Lima: Villanueva.
1979   *Psiquiatría folklórica.* Lima: Ediciones Ermar.

Sharon, D.
1972   Eduardo the Healer. *Natural History* 81(9):32–47.
1976a   A Peruvian Curandero's Séance: Power and Balance. In *The Realm of the Extra-Human: Agents and Audiences* (9th International Congress of Anthropological and Ethnological Sciences, Chicago). A. Bharati, ed., pp. 371–81. The Hague: Mouton.
1976b   Becoming a Curandero in Peru. In *Enculturation in Latin America: An Anthology.* J. Wilbert, ed., 213–36. Los Angeles: UCLA Latin American Center Publications.
1976c   Distribution of the Mesa in Latin America. *Journal of Latin American Lore* 2(1):71–95.
1978   *Wizard of the Four Winds: A Shaman's Story.* New York: Free Press.
1982   San Pedro-Kaktus—Botanik, Chemie und ritueller Gebrauch in den mittleren Anden. In *Rausch und Realität: Drogen im Kulturvergleich*, Band 2:785–800. Herausgegeben von Gisela Völger und Karin von Welck. Hamburg: Rowohlt.

Sharon, D., and C. B. Donnan
1977   The Magic Cactus: Ethnoarchaeological Continuity in Peru. *Archaeology* 30:374–81.

Silverblatt, I.
1978   Andean Women in Inca Society. *Feminist Studies* 4:37–61.
1983   The Evolution of Witchcraft and the Meaning of Healing in Colonial Andean Society. *Culture, Medicine and Psychiatry* 7:413–27.
1987   *Moon, Sun, and Witches: Gender Ideologies and Class in Inca and Colonial Peru.* Princeton: Princeton University Press.

Singer, M.
1989   The Coming of Age of Critical Medical Anthropology. *Social Science and Medicine* 28(11):1193–1203.
1990   Reinventing Medical Anthropology: Toward a Critical Realignment. *Social Science and Medicine* 30(2):179–87.

Skillman, R. D.
1990   Huachumero. *San Diego Museum of Man Ethnic Technology Notes*, No. 22.
Sontag, S.
1977   *Illness as Metaphor*. New York: Vintage Books.
Soto, H. de
1986   *El otro sendero: La revolución informal*. Bogotá: Editorial Printer Colombiana Ltda., for the Instituto Libertad y Democracia (Lima).
1989   *The Other Path: The Invisible Revolution in the Third World*. New York: Harper and Row/Perennial Library.
Spalding, K.
1984   *Huarochirí: An Andean Society under Inca and Spanish Rule*. Stanford: Stanford University Press.
Starn, O.
1991   Missing the Revolution: Anthropologists and the War in Peru. *Cultural Anthropology* 6(1):63–91.
Stevens, E. P.
1973   *Marianismo*: The Other Side of *Machismo*. In *Female and Male in Latin America*. A. Pescatello, ed., pp. 89–101. Pittsburgh: University of Pittsburgh Press.
Tambiah, S. J.
1981   A Performative Approach to Ritual. *Proceedings of the British Academy* 65(1979):113–69.
Taussig, M.
1980a   Folk Healing and the Structure of Conquest in Southwest Colombia. *Journal of Latin American Lore* 6:217–78.
1980b   *The Devil and Commodity Fetishism in South America*. Chapel Hill: University of North Carolina Press.
1987   *Shamanism, Colonialism and the Wild Man: A Study in Terror and Healing*. Chicago: University of Chicago Press.
Tello, J.
1961   *Chavín: cultura matríz de la civilización andina*. Primera parte. T. Mejía Xesspe, ed. Lima: Universidad Nacional Mayor de San Marcos.
Trotter, R., and J. A. Chavira
1981   *Curanderismo: Mexican American Folk Healing*. Athens, GA: University of Georgia Press.
Turner, V.
1969   *The Ritual Process: Structure and Anti-Structure*. Chicago: Aldine.
Urton, Gary
1992   Communalism and Differentiation in an Andean Community. In *Andean Cosmologies through Time: Persistence and Emergence*. R. Dover, K. Seibold, and J. McDowell, eds., pp. 229–60. Bloomington: Indiana University Press.
Valdizán, H., and H. Maldonado
1922   *La medicina popular peruana*. 3 vols. Lima: Imprenta Torres Aguirre.
Vallée, L.
1982   El discurso mítico de Santa Cruz Pachacuti Yamqui. *Allpanchis Phuturinqa* 18:103–26.

Vásquez Guerrero, R.

1988a   La participación de clases sociales en el curanderismo.
         Bachelor's thesis. Trujillo: Universidad Nacional de Trujillo.
1988b   Las causas sociales en el curanderismo y causas que motivan
         su asisténcia. *2° Congreso Internacional de Medicinas Tradicionales*,
         pp. 287–90 (Lima).

Villoldo, A., and E. Jendresen

1990   *The Four Winds: A Shaman's Odyssey into the Amazon.* San
         Francisco: Harper and Row.

Villoldo, A., and S. Krippner

1986   *Healing States.* New York: Simon and Schuster.

Yarrow, J.

1972   Enfoque del curanderismo en el departamento de
         Lambayeque, Perú. *39th International Congress of Americanists,
         Proceedings* 6:241–48. Lima.

Index

on "Staff God" at Chavín de
Huántar, 185

Johnson, Mark, 246–47, 280n.2
Joralemon, Donald
   analysis of social impact of curandero
      practice, 189–90
   study of José Paz, 5–6
   on symbolic logic underlying mesa
      and ritual, 167–68
   tinku concept of competitive union
      and social analyses of, 272
Jugar, use of term, 279n.5

Kogi (northern Andes of Colombia),
   175–76

Labor, capitalism and migratory, 260–61
Lakoff, George, 246–47, 280n.2
Lathrap, Donald, 184, 185
Lewis, I. M., 269, 281n.5
Liberation, metaphors of, 249
License, official for herbalists, 161
Lock, Margaret, 189–90
López, Rodrigo
   as assistant team with Nilo Plasencia,
      125
   description of as curandero, 88–100

Machismo, 261, 265
Magic, as form of resistance, 264
Mal aire, 278n.2
Mal del hígado, 279n.4
Mal de los riñones, 278–79n.4
Macera, Javier, 274n.3
Marianismo, 281n.3
Marriage
   economic and social oppression of
      women, 263–64
   Nilo Plasencia's interactions with
      patients, 231
   spousal infidelity and patients,
      208–9
Martin, Emily, 247, 280n.2
Mass, performance of by Porfirio
   Vidarte, 69
Medical anthropology
   metaphorical analyses, 247
   recent critiques of, 189–90
Medicine, modern. *See* Biomedicine
Merino, Jorge

description of as curandero, 147–57
patients of, 234–37
relationships with patients compared
   to Eduardo Calderón, 233–34
Mesas
   cosmology and, 177–80
   cultural ideology and symbolism of,
      5–6
   descriptions of individual curanderos
   —Helmer Aguilar, 106–10
   —Eduardo Calderón, 19–24
   —Víctor Flores, 116–22
   —Masias Guerrero, 52–59
   —Rodrigo López, 93–100
   —Jorge Merino, 150–57
   —Ruperto Navarro, 41–47
   —Víctor Neyra, 29–35
   —José Paz, 139–46
   —Nilo Plasencia, 127–31
   —Roberto Rojas, 78–87
   —Porfirio Vidarte, 65–72
   descriptions of power objects on, 7–8
   metaphors in relation to symbolism
      of, 251–53
   metaphysics and interpretation of
      dualism, 168–73
   ritual use of as characteristic of
      curanderos, 4
   Spanish folk medicine and possibility
      of use, 277n.3
   structural continuity of, 186–87
   tripartite division of artifacts, 7, 8
Mescaline, physiology and symbolism of
   experiences, 167–68
Metaphors
   of illness, 246–49, 280–81
   in patients' speech, 249–50
   in relation to mesa symbolism and
      healing acts, 251–53
   in ritual discourse, 250–51
   social and economic context of daño,
      253–56
Metaphysics
   Christian moralism and native
      dialectics, 173–77
   cosmology and mesa, 177–80
   interpretation of mesa dualism,
      168–73
   pre-Inca antecedents of
      contemporary cosmology, 182–85
   shared world view of curanderos